Advance Praise for *Born to Be Wild*

"Yes, it's incisive, engaging and beautifully written. Yes, it's well grounded in the science and provides practical, clear and thoughtful advice. But what I found most outstanding, at an emotional level, is that this book brought me back to myself as a teenager, reliving a state of mind I had almost forgotten— and it gave me a clearer notion of what was actually going on inside my brain."

—Harold Alan Pincus, MD, professor and vice chair of
the department of psychiatry, Columbia University

"Why is age twenty-six the new eighteen? Why do adults make the best decisions using the least information? This fascinating and illuminating book will help you understand and influence your teenager, and yourself."

—Wendy Mogel, PhD, bestselling author of *The Blessing of a Skinned Knee*

"In this extremely accessible volume, Dr. Shatkin makes sense of humorous, irrational, curious or dangerous adolescent behaviors. Based on a more accurate understanding of how teenagers think and feel, parents and other adults who interact with teens are provided with more effective approaches to deal with adolescent risk taking."

—Gregory K. Fritz, MD, president, American Academy of Child and
Adolescent Psychiatry

"Refreshingly honest, empathic, and written with a clarity that can help parents, educators, and health professionals accept and understand why risk taking is often part of teen behavior."

—Robie H. Harris, author of *It's Perfectly Normal: Changing Bodies,
Growing Up, Sex and Sexual Health*

"This book by one of America's leading child psychiatrists is a must-read for anyone working with or raising adolescents. It demystifies this too-often baffling period of life and, most important, shares what we can all do as parents, teachers, and society at large to help turn our adolescents away from unsafe risks and toward a safe and healthy future."

—Dave Levin, cofounder, KIPP

"Skillfully integrating the latest scientific findings with expert clinical acumen, Dr. Shatkin has done a masterful job of capturing the complexities and contradictions that define the teenage years. Anyone who has teens, knows teens, works with teens, or even was a teen needs to read this book!"

—John Piacentini, PhD, ABPP, professor of psychiatry and
biobehavioral sciences, UCLA

"Take what you know about your teenager and risk taking and chuck it out the window. (Carefully, because you're an adult.) While giving you research-based tools to curbing the truly dangerous activities teenagers engage in, *Born to Be Wild* is also a joyous celebration of teenagers and their sometimes inexplicable impulsiveness. *Born to Be Wild* is smart, funny, and deeply comforting."
—Judith Newman, author of *To Siri With Love: A Mother, Her Autistic Son, and the Kindness of Machines*

"*Born to Be Wild* is for everyone who wants to develop the tools to connect better with adolescents—parents, teachers, policy makers, and, in my case, writer-performers."
—Ilana Glazer, comedian and cocreator and star of *Broad City*

"This book is brilliantly written, incredibly informative, and presented in a comfortable down-to-earth manner. It is definitely going to be my new go-to referral reading for parents, educators, and therapists who will better understand why kids do the darndest things."
—Dr. Laura Schlessinger, marriage and family therapist, SiriusXM Radio host

"Jess Shatkin's book is a must-read. . . . With colorful personal stories, he weaves a brilliant, highly readable, and scientifically grounded analysis of the paradox of adolescence. Without a doubt, parents, teachers, policy makers, and anyone who wants to better understand themselves, their children, or the younger generation will benefit from reading this book."
—Kathleen M. Pike PhD, professor of psychology and director of the Global Mental Health Program at Columbia University Medical Center

"Crafted with medical and scientific tough-mindedness, empathy, and compassion by one of the world's experts in adolescent emotional and behavioral development . . . *Born to Be Wild* should be required reading for anyone who has or plans to have a child."
—James J. Hudziak, MD, professor of psychiatry, medicine, pediatrics and communication sciences, University of Vermont College of Medicine and Medical Center

BORN
TO BE
WILD

Why Teens Take Risks, and
How We Can Help Keep Them Safe

JESS P. SHATKIN, MD, MPH

A TarcherPerigee Book

tarcherperigee

An imprint of Penguin Random House LLC
375 Hudson Street
New York, New York 10014

Most TarcherPerigee books are available at special quantity discounts for
bulk purchase for sales promotions, premiums, fund-raising, and educational needs.
Special books or book excerpts also can be created to fit specific needs.
For details, write: SpecialMarkets@penguinrandomhouse.com.

LIBRARY OF CONGRESS CATALOGING-IN-PUBLICATION DATA
Names: Shatkin, Jess P., author.
Title: Born to be wild: why teens and tweens take risks, and how we can help
keep them safe / Jess P. Shatkin, MD, MPH.
Description: New York, NY: TarcherPerigee, [2017] | Includes bibliographical
references and index.
Identifiers: LCCN 2017016376 | ISBN 9780143129790
Subjects: LCSH: Risk-taking (Psychology) in adolescence. | Adolescence. |
Adolescent psychology.
Classification: LCC RJ506.R57 S53 2017 | DDC 616.89/140835—dc23
LC record available at https://lccn.loc.gov/2017016376

Printed in the United States of America
1   3   5   7   9   10   8   6   4   2

Book design by Elke Sigal

For Huey

CONTENTS

*To be normal during the adolescent period
is by itself abnormal.*

—ANNA FREUD

I COME FROM A SUBURBAN TOWN ten miles north of San Francisco across the Golden Gate Bridge, where tract homes abound and just about every fifth house is identical. The layout of those houses pretty much describes my friends and me when we were teens. We wanted so badly to blend in with the crowd and be accepted, yet we also longed to be different from our peers and stand apart as individuals. Years later I saw a comic somewhere that depicted a boy complaining to his mother that he only wanted to be different, just like everyone else. My teenage desire to be the same yet different from my peers is a universal sentiment among adolescents.

Like far too many kids, I was often standing directly in the path of danger throughout my childhood. I first held a joint in my hand when I was seven years old. By my eighth year, I occasionally stole cigarettes from the grocery store. I got drunk for the first time when I was eleven. Two years later I was apprehended by the police for smoking marijuana, and I tried cocaine the summer before my fourteenth birthday. Because I was most often a well-behaved kid at home, my shenanigans fell largely under the radar. By midsemester of my first year of high school, however, I was playing on the freshman football team, rehearsing two evenings each week with a rock band, and failing my English class. Ultimately, after years of watching and waiting for me to grow up on my own, my parents took matters into their own hands. Two weeks before the end of the football season, they made me quit the team, which was unbelievably humiliating. They also made me quit the band, and they made sure that I was home immediately after school every afternoon until my grades turned around. I was resistant and angry with my parents for a few months, and there were lots of arguments. But by midwinter, I was earning B's, and by spring, I was earning A's.

Doing well in school empowered me, and I will be forever thankful to my parents for hauling my fourteen-year-old ass out of harm's way. The more I learned and excelled in school, the less I cared about popularity, and the more I saw my world opening up, not closing down. Not all kids are this lucky.

One morning back in fifth grade, when we were ten years old, my friends and I arrived at school to learn that our buddy, Huey, had gotten into an accident on a friend's minibike the day before. He was motoring down a dirt hill, hit a bump, and flipped over. He wasn't wearing a motorcycle helmet, and he was now on a respirator in a coma. For days we wondered about Huey, asked questions, and wrote cards and letters to him and his family. Finally, we learned that Huey wasn't waking up from his coma and would be disconnected from life support.

Risk-taking behavior begins to increase at around age ten or eleven, just about the age Huey was when he died. As puberty sets in, the intensity of risk taking ramps up even further, typically reaching a peak between thirteen and nineteen. Still, even young adults take lots of risks. Perhaps it was my siblings', my friends', and my own behavior growing up, coupled with the memory of Huey's death—I'm not certain—but I've been driven to understand why kids take risks for as long as I can remember. It's an interest that eventually led me to become a physician, then a child, adolescent, and adult psychiatrist.

Not all risk taking is bad, of course. How many times have you told a child, "You'll never know if you don't try"? But I'm not talking about running for student government or trying out for the track team. This book is about the kind of behavior that endangers our kids every day; that deprives them of a college education, satisfying relationships, and a good job; and that sometimes even injures and kills them. I'm talking here about drugs and alcohol, driving under the influence, criminal behavior, unprotected sex, cigarette smoking, and riding a motorcycle without a helmet. In the pages ahead, we will explore why our tweens, teens, and young adults are so vulnerable to these problems.

This book is intended to challenge many of our prevailing ideas about why kids take risks. Supported by cutting-edge research, interviews with well-established scientists, clinical vignettes, and personal experiences, we will discover that adolescents already know that many of their behaviors place them in grave danger. We will find, in fact, that tweens, teens, and young adults even believe they're more vulnerable to bad things happening to them than they actually are, which brings us to the first goal of this book: to convince you that no matter how much we tell kids they're at risk, it won't affect their behavior. We need other strategies.

Leaning heavily on physiological and psychological research, we will go on to explore the new science of the adolescent brain, bringing us to the second goal of this book: to make it clear that humans have been genetically selected and engineered for risk-taking behavior, particularly in adolescence, and that everything from our brains to our hormones to our peer relationships works to encourage and maintain the risk-taking behavior.

Finally, this book will help us all make better sense of our kids, heralding the third goal: to demonstrate that much of what we do to address adolescent risk-taking behavior is misguided because we haven't adequately understood why young people take risks in the first place. Once that understanding is established, you will be well primed to take advantage of the many suggested remedies to address risk that are provided in the final three chapters of the book.

By their mid to late teen years, our children are as tall as we are, they have hair on their bodies like we do, and their voices sound like ours. They can have deep and insightful conversations on almost any topic. So we've assumed that they can cope with their emotions and make decisions just like us, and this has been our downfall when it comes to helping them manage risky behavior. Because we've misunderstood adolescent development, behavior, and decision making, we've been going about addressing risk in all the wrong ways. It's precisely because our adolescents can be so bright, capable, and logical when we speak with them that we've assumed their brains are like ours and they think just like us. And we've been dead wrong.

The brain is the most protected organ in the body, so it's been tough to study until recently. As neuroscience has advanced over the past fifteen years, propelled in great measure by magnetic resonance imaging (MRI), which uses a strong magnet, radio waves, and advanced computer technology to give us extraordinarily precise images of the brain and its activities, we've learned that the adolescent brain is less similar to the adult brain than we had previously thought. MRI and other neuroimaging tools have given us a window into the developing brain and shown us that significant changes and neuronal rewiring continue onward well into our twenties, instead of being completed by age sixteen or eighteen as had been previously assumed.

The brain has a central role in this book, but it's not the only star of the show. In my more than two decades as a physician, I've come to believe that the primary achievements of a successful adolescence and transition into adulthood are the development of self-efficacy and emotional self-regulation. In other words, adolescents need to learn that they are capable of succeeding at what they set out to do, believing that they can make changes, and they need to learn how to manage their emotions.

Establishing self-efficacy and emotional self-regulation takes patience, guidance, and empathy from parents, teachers, and other role models. It requires that adolescents learn from personal and vicarious experience and have lots of practice with decision making. So you might think of this book as more of an ensemble piece, where not only the adolescent brain, but also evolution, hormones, peers, sleep, physical activity, good nutrition, the science of decision making, parents, teachers, schools, and society at large all share the stage.

Like many of us, I was taught to believe that adolescents take risks because they believe they're invincible. Nothing could be further from the truth. *Born to Be Wild* is about setting things straight.

BORN
TO BE
WILD

CHAPTER 1

Not Invincible

(or, What Adolescents *Really* Think About Risk)

> *I would that there were no age between ten and three-and-twenty,*
> *or that youth would sleep out the rest; for there is nothing in the*
> *between but getting wenches with child, wronging the ancientry,*
> *stealing, fighting.*
>
> —SHAKESPEARE, *The Winter's Tale*

NOW AND AGAIN YOUR WORLD gets turned upside down. These moments don't come all that often, but when they do, you remember them, down to the last detail.

Every August my wife and kids go away for a few weeks to a lake bungalow in upstate New York. During those weeks, I take the train up on Friday afternoons to be with the family and then return to the city on Sunday nights. Although I miss my family when they're away, I admit that I revel in the opportunity to catch up on my work.

So it was that I found myself going to the same Japanese restaurant on Second Avenue in New York City near my office three nights running in August 2010. That summer I was working on the development of a resilience program for high school students aimed at reducing high-risk behavior, and those three nights I plowed through a series of articles that I'd been collecting for months, in addition to a whole lot of sushi.

Physicians are becoming increasingly isolated, working away in our silos, unaware of what others are thinking, exploring, and learning. Every field is susceptible to this problem because knowledge is now growing at an exponential rate, and it's become simply impossible to keep up. Buckminster Fuller, the architect, theorist, and inventor of the geodesic dome, wrote about what he called the Knowledge Doubling Curve in his 1981 book, *Critical Path*. He suggested that the growth of human knowledge had been pretty slow up until the Renaissance but that by 1900 our knowledge was doubling about every one hundred years. By World War II, Fuller's calculations suggested that knowledge was doubling every twenty-five years. And although not all fields move at the same pace, on average we now believe that human knowledge is doubling about every thirteen months. With this much new information floating around, we often feel like spinning tops amidst a hurricane of ideas, powerless to master it all, much less put it to good use. For a physician, undoubtedly the most disconcerting aspect of this knowledge explosion is the fact that we sometimes don't know what we don't know. So as I sat eating my sushi and reading my stacks of articles those three nights in August, I really began to question for the first time some of my most deeply held assumptions about adolescence.

Risk Happens

At what age did you enter adolescence? When did you become an adult? These used to be pretty easy questions to answer. Most of us born before 1980 would probably say that our adolescence began at around thirteen years of age and that we became adults at around eighteen. This age range reflects the thinking in most industrialized societies, where adulthood is typically defined by law and generally begins at age eighteen.

But this well-worn definition is not internally consistent, at least within the United States, where we can be drafted into the armed services or stand trial as an adult at eighteen (depending upon the crime, in some states even children as young as thirteen can be tried as adults) but can't legally purchase or drink liquor until twenty-one. By contrast, traditional and tribal societies often define the start of adulthood as the age at which adolescent boys and girls achieve various milestones or rites of passage, such as when a boy kills his first big game or a girl gives birth to her first child. In some of these societies adolescence may last only two or three years.

When adolescence starts and ends matters because adolescents often think, feel, and behave differently from children and adults, which can result in risky behavior. The word "adolescence" comes from the Latin *adolescere*—literally, "to grow up." By most standards employed today, such as the age at which our youth first achieve financial independence or start their careers or get married, growing up takes longer than it used to. Whether we call them preteens, teens, kids, emerging adults, or young adults, the transitional period of life starting just prior to the onset of puberty and lasting until about twenty-six years of age is marked by enormous physical, emotional, and cognitive growth, and is the focal point of this book.

If you think back to your own adolescence, I'm willing to bet that you took some risks that you're probably not very proud of. Maybe it was small stuff, like driving over the speed limit or staying out past curfew. Maybe it was something bigger, like drunk driving or having unprotected sex. If you're a parent, I know you worry that your kids may do the same or even worse. Perhaps they have already. Whatever you and your kids have done, it's well recognized that risky behavior increases once we hit puberty. The data couldn't be any clearer.

According to an annual national survey of youth behaviors, over 80 percent of high school students rarely or never wear a bicycle helmet.

Just about one-third rarely or never wear a motorcycle helmet. Almost half acknowledge texting or e-mailing while driving. Meanwhile, one in four gets into at least one physical fight each year, and one in five reports being bullied on school property. As the father of a teenage girl, here's one that really frightens me: Over one in ten female high school students report that they have been forced to have sexual intercourse. Forty-three percent of high school students didn't use a condom the last time they had sex. Equally concerning is the fact that one in four adolescent girls becomes infected with a sexually transmitted disease, and three in ten teenage girls become pregnant, including 51 percent of Latina teens. But it's not only accidents and bad behavior that get our adolescents into trouble.

The prevalence of mental illness skyrockets during the teen and early adult years. Major depressive disorder affects one in six adolescents by the time they reach eighteen, and anxiety disorders affect up to one-third of adolescents aged thirteen to eighteen. Disruptive behavior disorders, substance use disorders, attention-deficit/hyperactivity disorder (ADHD), schizophrenia, bipolar disorder, autism spectrum disorders, and eating disorders affect smaller but significant numbers of adolescents and young adults, resulting in enormous suffering and lost productivity. A full 50 percent of all lifetime mental illness sets in by age fourteen, and 75 percent begins by age twenty-four. At the root of many of these diagnoses and troubles are traumatic childhood experiences, such as being abused, witnessing abuse, or being raised with a severely mentally ill and disruptive household member. Over half of all children in the United States are exposed to this level of trauma, which greatly increases the likelihood of later-onset risk-taking behavior, substance abuse, mental illness, smoking, sexually transmitted disease, and obesity, all leading causes of death among adults.

Nearly a half million people die each year in the United States because of tobacco, making it the greatest cause of preventable death, far more deadly than obesity, alcohol, or motor vehicle accidents. Tobacco costs our society billions of dollars each year in health care and lost work time. Regular tobacco use virtually always starts during the teen years because nicotine is perhaps the most habit-forming substance available to kids—it's far more addictive than even heroin, alcohol, or crack cocaine. One in three people who try tobacco becomes addicted. Given this huge risk, you would think that we would be more effective at stopping teens from using tobacco, yet one in six high school students is a regular smoker.

More than one in five high school students have binge drunk (defined as having five or more alcoholic beverages within two hours) in the past fourteen days. Even worse, one in ten high school students admits to driving under the influence of alcohol in the past thirty days, and more than one in five have ridden with a friend who has been drinking.

Over 90 percent of new marijuana initiates have tried either or both tobacco and alcohol before they happen upon marijuana. We call this the "gateway" phenomenon, meaning that adolescents pass through alcohol and tobacco on their way to the use of illicit drugs. So if we could more effectively stop kids from using tobacco and alcohol, we could also limit

> One in ten high school students admits to driving under the influence of alcohol in the past thirty days.

their exposure to illicit drugs. As it is now, one-third of high school freshmen have tried marijuana, and by senior year that proportion jumps to nearly half. With all of these threats and risks staring them in the face daily, it's no wonder that one-third of high school kids report feeling sad or hopeless each year, nearly one in five reports seriously considering a suicide attempt, one in seven has made a suicide plan, and one in twelve has attempted suicide.

Lesbian, gay, and bisexual (LGB) adolescents are at even greater risk of depression and drug abuse than their heterosexual peers. Two in five

LGB adolescents report seriously considering suicide (twice the rate of heterosexual adolescents), while nearly one in three has made an attempt within the past year (four times the rate of heterosexual students). LGB high school students are up to five times more likely to use illicit drugs than heterosexual students. In addition, LGB teens are nearly twice as likely to be bullied and more than twice as likely to be subjected to interpersonal violence than heterosexual teens. Emerging but as yet limited data on transgender adolescents similarly suggests a high rate of psychiatric difficulties and suicidal thoughts and behavior.

Lest you think this might be a problem just in the West, guess again. Worldwide, adolescent death and disability are largely a result of our kids' unbridled emotions, cognitions, and behaviors, just like in the West. It's because of how our adolescents feel, think, and behave, in other words, that they get hurt and die, not because of their vulnerability to the things that kill adults like cancer and heart attacks. In developing countries, the percentages of deaths due to accidents, homicide, and suicide would be even higher were it not for the vast amount of teen and young adult mortality accounted for by HIV/AIDS, other infectious diseases, and maternal deaths due to early childbirth. As it stands currently, road injury, suicide, and interpersonal violence are three of the top five causes of death, and depression, alcohol use, and anxiety disorders are three of the top five causes of disability among teens in the developing world.

The risks to adolescents are real, as are their repercussions. We've all seen some of our friends die in car accidents or by overdose or from AIDS. A friend of mine became pregnant in the ninth grade and simply disappeared from school, altering her life course forever. Becoming a parent, in fact, is the leading cause of high school dropout among teenage girls. To make matters worse, children of teen mothers struggle more with language and communication skills, social skills, and learning and school achievement than children of older mothers.

As a child and adolescent psychiatrist, I already knew a lot of what I just told you. What I didn't know at the time was how to help keep our kids safe. But the bigger problem is that I thought I did.

The Myth of Adolescent Invincibility

Leo Kanner wrote a highly influential scientific paper in 1943 describing eleven children whose ailment differed "markedly and uniquely from anything reported so far." These days, the Centers for Disease Control and Prevention (CDC) tells us that one in sixty-eight children is born with this disorder, which we now call autism. Although we currently understand many of the factors that contribute to the clinical impairments observed among children with autism spectrum disorders, in the not too distant past, the list of potential causes read like a free-for-all of unfounded and unstudied hypotheses. Just like the now debunked vaccine theory sounded almost reasonable at first glance when it was put forth in 1998, so too did the concept of "refrigerator mothers," who Kanner described as downright cold and entirely divorced from the emotional lives of their children, "just happening to defrost enough to produce a child." Today, fortunately, no modern physician believes that autism is anything other than a neurological disorder.

In the same way that refrigerator mothers were the supposed cause of autism, once upon a time we believed in the myth of adolescent invincibility. In the late 1960s, just as the refrigerator theory was making its ascent, noted psychologist David Elkind wrote about what he called the normal egocentrism of adolescents. We would probably all agree that adolescents are more than a bit self-absorbed, be it with their looks, opinions, ideals, you name it. Adolescents are seeking to define themselves and establish their independence, and this is part of what Elkind was talking about. But he went further. Elkind suggested that adolescents construct and then react to an "imaginary audience," which is watching them at least as much as they watch themselves. This too sounds sensible because we all know that in actual social situations no one could possibly pay as much attention to an adolescent as he pays to himself. The complement, that which completes the egocentrism equation in adolescence, is what Elkind called the "personal fable," or the idea that the adolescent feels himself to be unique and special, experiencing the world in a way that others simply cannot understand. This mental construction, Elkind suggested, may be the result of the adolescent's belief in his own importance to his family, friends, and imaginary audience. Haven't all parents heard their adolescents say or perhaps shout something like, "You have no idea how I feel!" No, how could parents *possibly* understand how their teens feel, having gone through adolescence themselves not so long ago?

Elkind's theory sounds right. It feels right. And it even gets better. Because adolescents live under what they perceive to be the sometimes admiring and at other times admonishing gaze of an imaginary audience, and because they believe their own personal fable of unique superiority, they must, Elkind reasoned, believe themselves to be invincible.

Everything Right Is Wrong Again

I entered my training in child, adolescent, and adult psychiatry in 1996, and in the past twenty-plus years much has been learned about how adolescents make decisions, how their brains work, and why they take risks. Remember that knowledge is adding up exponentially these days, so by the time I sat down for sushi in August 2010, many of the seemingly intuitive beliefs I held about adolescence were thrown into question by the new research I was reading. I had been taught that adolescents believe they're invincible, and that's why they take risks. Why else would a teenager drive drunk or have unprotected sex? This is our commonly accepted wisdom, just as it was when I was in medical school and residency—I had learned from some of the best medical minds of the twentieth century that adolescents think they're invulnerable. It follows then that the best way to deter adolescents from risky behavior is to teach them again and again that they are at high risk and are, in fact, extremely vulnerable.

There was only one small fly in the ointment of this thinking. It hadn't been tested, and the new research shows that thoughts of invincibility simply cannot account for adolescent risk taking. The early investigators in the field of adolescent mental health didn't survey large numbers of kids in research studies. They most often worked as clinicians, astutely observing individuals and theorizing about why adolescents behave as they do. But decades later, when we actually started asking kids questions about their behavior, we found something we didn't expect. Adolescents believe they're highly vulnerable. In most cases, in fact, they think they're more vulnerable, sometimes far more vulnerable, than they actually are to every possible bad outcome imaginable, from low-probability events like earthquakes and hurricanes to higher-probability occurrences such as accidents and pregnancy. High school students typically believe, for example, that the risk of sexually transmitted infections (like chlamydia, gonorrhea, AIDS, and syphilis) for sexually active peers is *six times and sixty thousand times* the actual risk.

The enormity of the seismic shift in perspective suggested by this data cannot be overstated. Adolescents do not think they're invincible! Whether we ask them about how likely they are to get pregnant, get sick from excessive alcohol use, or be a passenger in a drug-related driving accident, teens think they are much more vulnerable to bad outcomes than they actually are. But wait—it even goes beyond that. Adolescents

> Adolescents do not think they're invincible!

don't just think they're not invincible. They actually think there's a pretty good chance that they will die as adolescents. Although the expected mortality rate of people aged fourteen to eighteen in the United States was 0.08 percent in 1997, a large, nationally representative study of nearly 3,500 people aged fourteen to eighteen that year found that 18.6 percent believed they would die within the coming year. This is more than two hundred times their actual risk of dying.

I work with lots of adolescents who are at high risk of terrible things happening to them because of the decisions they make every day. *Should I drink and drive? Should I have sex with this person or that? Should I try cocaine or heroin? Should I ride a motorcycle without a helmet?* This revelation was simply too much for me. So I did what any parent would do. I decided to test out some of these novel ideas on my own children.

Kids Say the Darnedest Things

"Sweetheart," I said, "I want to ask you a few questions that may seem odd, but it's sort of an experiment. You game?" Parker, my then thirteen-year-old daughter, nodded in agreement. "Now, these questions are 'what if?' and only hypothetical, got it? I mean, I'm not suggesting you should be doing these things. I just want to see what you think about these situations. Okay?" Again she nodded, now encouraging me with her hands to get on with it. (Even from a young age, Parker did not suffer fools.)

"Let's say," I began, "you were to have unprotected sexual intercourse with a boy who you don't know." Now, let me take a moment to acknowledge how strange a question this is to ask your thirteen-year-old child. But my daughter, Parker, knows that I'm a psychiatrist, and she knows what a psychiatrist does and the kinds of challenges I often have with my patients and their families. More to the point, she knows that I specialize in child development and work with children, adolescents, young adults, and their families every day to diagnose and treat the mental illnesses, learning disabilities, and emotional and behavioral struggles they face. So even though my question to her was not necessarily the stuff of dinner table conversations for most families, it wasn't too far afield from some of the things she'd heard me speak of before. I went on. "What are the chances that you would get pregnant?"

Parker thought about my question for a few seconds and then said something that left me slack jawed. "Ninety percent," she confidently reported. I recovered, then asked another question. "Now, let's say that you have no idea whether or not this guy has ever had sex before. You have no idea about his past, and who he has or hasn't been with. You have no idea about his sexual orientation and whether or not he has HIV. What are the chances that you would catch HIV from having sexual intercourse with him just once?" Again, she thought for a few seconds and then said with just as much confidence, "Seventy-five percent." Wow! Again, I was really surprised. I asked her how confident she was in her answers. She said she was "pretty confident." I asked why she gave me these answers, and she said she's heard a lot about the risk of pregnancy and HIV at home and at school and that grown-ups and teachers wouldn't spend so much time talking about it if it weren't a real concern. Over the next few weeks, I asked these questions of some of my teenage patients and received similarly inflated responses.

What I didn't do was tell Parker or my patients that the risk of pregnancy from one-time, unprotected sexual intercourse averages 5 percent, or one in twenty. That breaks down to about 3 percent most of the month and approximately 25 percent during the forty-eight hours around the time of ovulation. The risk is even lower among girls twelve to fourteen years of age because young girls don't generally ovulate each month during the first two years of reaching sexual maturity. I also didn't tell her that the risk of contracting HIV from an HIV-positive person through unprotected vaginal intercourse is estimated to be between one in 1,250 (if the male sexual partner is HIV-positive) and one in 2,500 (if the female sexual partner is HIV-positive), or between 0.04 percent and 0.08 percent. Again, that's catching HIV from a person who is actually HIV-positive. The risk is certainly much, much lower for having sex with your average

Joe, whose HIV status isn't known. I certainly didn't want to dissuade Parker or my patients from these elevated risk assessments at the time because I figured, as most adults do, that a high level of fear would keep them safe and convince them not to have sex at a young age.

Each semester, I teach about two hundred undergraduate students in a lecture course on psychopathology at New York University. I was certain that the college students I instruct, at eighteen to twenty-two years old, would be more savvy than thirteen-year-old Parker and my teenage patients, so I was excited to test my hypothesis when fall classes started in 2010.

On the second day of classes, I announced an experiment. What are the chances, I asked the audience, that a female college student would get pregnant if she were to have unprotected sexual intercourse once with a male college student? The students' responses were just like those of Parker and my patients. For both pregnancy and HIV transmission, the estimates were astronomical, somewhere between 60 and 90 percent. I've asked these questions of my undergrads at NYU pretty much every semester since, and the students never disappoint me.

If teens think that they're in more danger than they really are, if they think that there is an absolutely enormous possibility of bad things happening from engaging in behavior that, albeit risky, only rarely results in a negative outcome, how could any ideas they have about invincibility account for their behavior? Invincibility simply does not jibe with an estimated 90 percent likelihood of pregnancy from unprotected intercourse or 90 percent probability of getting HIV from vaginal intercourse when you don't even know if your partner has HIV. I started to realize that I had happened upon more than just a cool party trick here—no matter how much we scare kids with data about bad things happening, we won't change their behavior. If adolescents really believe these numbers, why do they still take risks?

Lake Wobegon

In 1974, Garrison Keillor began a live radio variety show called *A Prairie Home Companion*, featuring a vastly popular monologue about the fictional small rural town of Lake Wobegon in central Minnesota where "all the women are strong, all the men are good looking, and all the children are above average." If you know anyone with a child, you will recognize the sentiment well. We all know parents, perhaps even ourselves, who insist that their children are gifted, even though they're not so good at math or geography or perhaps any subject in particular. Maybe they're gifted in athletics or social skills or some other area. Perhaps, but we know that statistically it's impossible that everyone is above average, don't we?

At what age will you die? If you're married, will you get a divorce? If you're a college student, how likely is it that you will have a good job one day? If you're a college professor, is your work above average? To these and many other questions, most of us overestimate our abilities. In the United States, on average men die at age seventy-six, and women die at eighty-one. Between 40 and 50 percent of all marriages end in divorce, and the divorce rate for second marriages is even higher. College students typically believe they are more likely than their peers to live past eighty and have a good job, and a whopping 94 percent of college professors believe their work is above average. How did your answers measure up?

Among psychologists, the Lake Wobegon Effect, as it's sometimes called, is known as self-assessment bias. Based upon your answers to the above questions, in all likelihood you just discovered that you too are vulnerable to this form of bias. During both our adolescent and our adult years, we tend to think we're quite a bit better than average and more competent than we actually are. Researchers don't know why we're so self-centered in our assessments, but it's generally thought to occur because we lack the necessary knowledge to judge ourselves accurately; and even when we have the facts, we often neglect that information due to self-preserving egocentrism.

A similar but distinct form of impartiality, known as optimistic bias, relates to our thoughts about the risks we face. As with self-assessment bias, both adolescents and adults may demonstrate some degree of optimistic bias, believing that although the risks are real, they in particular are somewhat less vulnerable than others their own age. We often believe that we do something special or take additional precautions that others don't know or think to do when engaging in risky behavior, which makes us unique and less likely to be harmed. This belief that others don't know or think to safeguard themselves as we do is called pluralistic ignorance and is thought to account for optimistic bias. An adolescent might believe that he can drive safely when he's drunk, for example, because he takes extra care to keep himself alert, such as rolling down the windows and turning on the air conditioner, even if it's cold outside. He imagines that his strategies for staying alert on the road while inebriated are unique, but he is ignorant of the fact that others have the same thoughts and do the same sorts of things in a naive attempt to protect themselves from harm.

Optimistic bias runs counter to what I've just told you about how adolescents overestimate their risks regarding just about every bad outcome. And here we have arrived at a contradiction: On the one hand, adolescents typically believe that most of the risks they face are far greater than they actually are; and on the other hand, they may think that they in particular have unique ways of minimizing those risks. The degree of optimistic bias depends on the particular risk we're talking about and how we ask our questions, but adolescents are not alone. Adults show just as much if not more optimistic bias as adolescents in many studies. Unlike adolescents, however, adults' estimates of bad outcomes from risky behaviors, such as the likelihood of pregnancy from unprotected sex, are more grounded in reality. If optimistic bias were powerful enough to explain risk-taking behavior, then we would expect adults to take more risks than adolescents because they're just as optimistic but estimate the probability of bad things happening to be lower than adolescents do. So, even though optimistic bias is real, the effect is not strong enough to account for why kids take risks that adults typically do not take.

When I ask my adolescent patients or college students about the risk of contracting HIV from unprotected sex, their answers are always enormously inflated. But if I ask one of these patients or college students what his particular risk is, it will vary depending upon his life experience—does he know people who are affected by HIV? Is he sexually active, and if so, with whom? What are his cultural mores around sex? What have people told him about HIV? What does he think of people infected with HIV? And so forth. An individual's risk estimates are determined by many different beliefs and experiences, so some adolescents will have optimistic bias and think that their own personal risk is lowered somewhat, while others will have little optimistic bias and continue to think that their personal risks are huge. The effects are not consistent, so we have to know which adolescent we're dealing with. One college student told me that the risk of pregnancy from unprotected sex was 90 percent for most people but 100 percent for him because he has "bad luck."

Adolescents receive lots of messages and have many different ideas about risk, and they're not mutually exclusive. Like us, adolescents are filled with contradictory and sometimes directly opposing beliefs, and inflated risk estimates may run hand in hand with optimistic bias. An adolescent may overestimate the actual risk of pregnancy from unprotected sex, believe that she's less likely to get pregnant from having unprotected sex than her peers are (demonstrating optimistic bias), and still know that she's at greater risk for pregnancy than her sexually active peers who are using birth control. This conglomeration of beliefs is actually fairly commonplace among adolescents and makes our job of helping them to stay safe even more complicated.

Risk and Resilience

As I hand out the final exam to my two hundred anxious psychopathology students each term, I tell them a story. My father is a doctor, and from the age of five, I dreamed of being a physician just like him. In high school I was even a member of the Future Doctors of America, a group that had meetings at a local hospital where successful physicians would tell us all about their careers. It was very inspiring. But by the time I had finished my first year of college at the University of California at Berkeley, I was becoming pretty discouraged about a career in medicine. First, it was the required premed classes—they were brutal, enormous in size (my chemistry and biology classes each had over 1,200 students), and often poorly taught by teachers who made it clear that they would much rather be doing their research. And second, it was the premed students themselves—many seemed so highly competitive, unkind, and disengaged from their peers that you wouldn't ever want any of these folks treating sick people. These students went through college with blinders on, seeing only the science course directly in front of them in their manic quest for A's. If that's what being a doctor is, I reasoned, I want no part of it. I became so disenchanted with the premedical classes and students that my second year of college I got a D in organic chemistry, as if in lame protest. If I could get a D in organic chemistry and still become a doctor, I tell my psychopathology students, then no matter how you're feeling right now about this final exam, just take a deep breath and do your best. That's called resilience.

We're all going to run into some bumps in the road now and again. That's unavoidable. It's how we handle those bumps that determines whether we stay on the road, maybe even grow from the experience, or get entirely derailed. As it happens, I retook organic chemistry the following year and successfully finished the premed courses, but I majored in history because I simply enjoyed the liberal arts classes more. I stressed a good deal and for many months over changing my major from biology to history. My premed adviser told me that I'd never get into medical school with a D in organic chemistry and a major in history, and he strongly urged me to consider another career. As you can imagine, by the time I graduated from college, I didn't feel too enthusiastic about a life in medicine, having been discouraged at just about every turn.

On a lark and along with a good friend, I had enrolled in a public health class in my sophomore year. I learned about the importance of health promotion and disease prevention on a population level, and one class led to another. By the time I graduated college, HIV had solidly hit ground, and it was all over the newspapers and evening news daily. I had a friend who became infected and later died, and I suddenly cared a ton about public health. I spent the next seven years working in reproductive and HIV education and occupational safety and health, in addition to earning my master's degree in public health.

When I finally enrolled in medical school, I was nearly twenty-nine. Older than the average medical student, to be sure, but I was also more resilient. By twenty-nine, like many of us, I'd taken some lumps and stayed afloat. Granted, I didn't grow up in abject poverty, but all the same, I'd worked my way through college and graduate school and paid for my entire education on my own; I'd traveled all over the United States in my eleven-year-old VW Rabbit; I'd had a number of romantic relationships, some of which didn't end so nicely; I'd traveled to Mexico and Central America repeatedly, suffered through three intestinal parasitic infections, and learned to speak pretty good Spanish; and I'd improved my fitness by maintaining a regular exercise routine. I was scared out of my head like everyone else when I did eventually start medical school, but I knew I had the internal resources to make a good go of it.

For the next nine years throughout medical school, residency, and fellowship, I learned what makes people sick and how to help them get well. Physicians focus on identifying the cause of an individual's problem and lessening or eradicating it. Public health is different. Public health focuses on preventing populations of people from getting ill in the first place, standing traditional doctor-patient treatment on its head. The two fields together make for a powerful one-two punch. Instead of only treating individuals for cancer, we also work to prevent a population's exposure to known carcinogens like fossil fuel emissions and cigarette smoke. Instead of only treating individuals for cholera and typhoid, we also bring in fresh water and install sewage treatment plants. And instead of only treating people for infectious diseases, we also design and provide vaccines.

Smallpox is extremely deadly, killing up to 30 percent of those infected. During the twentieth century alone, it's believed to be responsible for the deaths of between 300 million and 500 million people. Survivors are often plagued with severe scars, blindness, and limb deformities. By the late 1700s, it was known that milkmaids infected with cowpox, a related illness, didn't catch smallpox. But it took until 1796 for Edward Jenner to expose his gardener's son, James Phipps, to cowpox, and some weeks later to smallpox, thereby demonstrating the benefits of inoculation. James didn't get infected with smallpox because the cowpox exposure protected him. The smallpox vaccine was the first ever invented; the word "vaccine" is, in fact, derived from *Variolae vaccinae*, or "smallpox of the cow." The last known case of smallpox was diagnosed in Somalia in 1977, and by 1979 the World Health Organization declared the illness eradicated. That's a public health success story.

If we could vaccinate every adolescent against risk, we would. But we can't, so we have to come up with other ways to help our adolescents stay safe. We can do a lot as parents, teachers, and policy makers to lessen the risks our kids face, and this book will dive deeply into those areas. At the same time, we need to enhance our adolescents' resilience in the face of ever-present temptation and risks so that they can ride out those ubiquitous bumps in the road ahead.

Many factors contribute to resilience. Academic intelligence, supportive families, and higher socioeconomic status, three of these elements, we cannot teach, but we can support the development and enhancement of these and many other factors. For example, we know that prosocial children and adolescents, those who make friends more easily, are more resilient because they naturally develop supportive networks. Identifying the very shy kids and helping them to engage effectively with peers, even teaching them social skills, will enhance their strengths and self-confidence in the face of risks they will surely face as adolescents. Communication skills, like being able to express yourself effectively and being a good reader, are also protective, and we can do more to identify those kids at risk and help them improve their language abilities. Studies have shown that characteristics like being good at managing emotions and staying calm under pressure, having good impulse control, showing empathy toward others, having a sense of purpose in life, being determined and persistent, and believing that you can accomplish what you set out to do (e.g., self-efficacy) result in higher levels of resilience among adolescents.

In the same way that we can prevent cholera with clean water or vaccinate against smallpox, we can give people the skills they need to ward off anxiety and depression, lessen the impact of mental illness and emotional distress, and cut the frequency of substance abuse. We've known since the 1990s that emotional and behavioral difficulties are the leading cause of disability worldwide. These problems include depression, alcohol use, self-inflicted injuries, bipolar disorder, schizophrenia, and motor vehicle accidents. We can lessen that enormous burden of illness and injury by enhancing resilience among our adolescents, since it is during those years that the vast majority of these disorders first show up.

But we must not assume that our adolescents think they're invincible, because they don't. Instead, we need to understand the real reasons they take risks. We need to provide them and their parents and teachers with concrete actions that they can take to reduce their risks. And we need to teach self-efficacy and emotional self-control, give them lots and lots and lots of practice with these skills, and show them how to moderate the specific factors that put them at risk in the first place.

The Adolescent Paradox

Adolescents are stronger than they will ever be again in their lives. Their immune response is at its peak. They tolerate extremes of heat and cold better than those older and younger. They heal from physical injury more quickly. But their likelihood of getting sick increases greatly and their death rates rise enormously during the teen years, particularly for males. Whereas the mortality rate of girls triples between the ages of twelve and nineteen, for boys that rate increases *more than six times* during these same years. Beginning at age twelve, in fact, the death rate in boys increases at a rate of more than 30 percent per year, while the rate for females increases nearly 20 percent per year. And death rates continue to grow still higher as our teens reach their early twenties. This paradox of having greater physical ability yet greater vulnerability occurs because of the behaviors, emotions, and patterns of thinking in which adolescents and young adults engage.

There is no disputing that adolescents take outlandish risks. In the United States, accidents, suicide, and homicide are responsible for over 85 percent of the deaths among those aged fifteen to twenty-four. Suicide is the second leading cause and alone accounts for 20 percent of deaths in this age range, more than cancer, heart disease, congenital anomalies, stroke, flu and pneumonia, HIV, and chronic respiratory disease combined.

And what about crime? After the age of thirty, people rarely commit serious crimes. Violent crimes are predominantly committed by young people, and adults who violate the law were almost always teens who violated the law. As our population of young people grows, like after a baby boom, so does the amount of crime.

As a public health educator, then medical student and resident in psychiatry, I was taught that adolescents engage in high-risk behavior because they believe they're invincible. Why else would they get into so many motor vehicle accidents, have so many unwanted pregnancies and sexually transmitted infections, and use alcohol, drugs, and cigarettes? Invincibility sure seems like a highly plausible theory. But as we now know, invincibility just doesn't hold up under scrutiny.

Despite our efforts at educating youth about the risks they face, explaining to them time and again that they are, in fact, vulnerable, we've seen minimal to no change in the rates of binge drinking and drunk driving, condom use, obesity, bicycle and motorcycle helmet use, bullying, and so forth among teens over the past two decades. In fact, we've seen an increase in suicide and marijuana use; and although cigarette use is down slightly—likely due to the price of cigarettes, which has increased at twice the rate of inflation—e-cigarette use has more than quadrupled in the past four years.

What other factors besides invincibility might be at play? Maybe adolescents are irrational and lack good decision-making capacity or they seek strong emotions and new sensations. Maybe at times. But we now know that the causes of risky behavior go far beyond that. Adolescents are engineered for risk-taking behavior, and everything from their brains to

> Adolescents are engineered for risk-taking behavior.

their hormones to their peer relationships works to encourage and maintain a high-risk approach to just about everything.

Shakespeare had it right. Teens and young adults get into a whole lot of mischief and engage in some pretty risky behaviors. Curiously, they even think that the chance of getting hurt from these behaviors is *higher* than it really is. So why would they put themselves in harm's way by taking dangerous risks like having unprotected sex if they believe that the chances of "getting wenches with child" or HIV transmission are so high? They clearly don't think they're invincible, as repeated experiments have shown. Something else must be going on.

This book is about that something else. What lies within the pages that follow will challenge everything you think you know about why tweens, teens, and young adults make decisions every day that result in pregnancy, addiction, accidental injury, and death. The factors that matter are hidden deep within our brains and evolutionary history and are strongly influenced by our peer relationships and life experiences. The science is there, and this book is your escort. Once you understand what influences adolescents to make risky decisions, you will know why much of what we do to try to protect kids isn't working. You'll also have a much better idea of what we should be doing to help keep them safe.

CHAPTER 2

Achtung, Baby!

(or, What Doesn't Keep Our Kids Safe)

Thou know'st the o'er-eager vehemence of youth
How quick in temper, and in judgment weak

—HOMER, *The Iliad*

I COULDN'T WAIT TO GET ON the plane. I was sixteen and had never flown. My heart was pumping wildly, when my dad gently grabbed my arm seconds before I walked down the Jetway. "Don't show off," he said quietly.

The following day I was in Germany with Thomas, my foreign exchange partner, and a group of his friends hanging out during lunch by a small workshop at the edge of the school grounds. I was exhausted. I'd stayed awake for most of the twenty hours of travel, having not been able to sleep on the flight from San Francisco through New York and on to Frankfurt, where I was now spending the summer as an international student. I felt anxious in my new surroundings. Spring's hold on Frankfurt possessed an equally strong grip on my hay fever, and I had hardly slept the first night at my host family's apartment.

Around the side of the workshop was a steel ladder hanging down from an electrical tower. It rested loosely and stopped about five feet short of the ground. A number of the German boys grabbed on to the ladder and tried to climb it but failed. One of them dared me, the new American, to have a go at it. I hesitated. The ladder looked jerry-rigged. Maybe I would get into trouble if I climbed it. But I spit on my hands all the same, grabbed the ladder, hoisted myself up, and began to climb.

As I aggressively marched up the ladder, it swung a few inches from side to side. I looked down at the boys below me. I felt proud. I was strong and courageous. I had done something that the others couldn't.

Back home in my Northern California suburb, I was considered a decent athlete, desired on the team but not generally selected first or second for a pickup game of basketball, baseball, or football. I was a good friend, a nice guy, but not one of the jocks, the most popular boys in school. In Frankfurt, nobody knew that I had been the third-string running back on my freshman high school football team. Here I could remake myself.

Ascending the ladder, I looked around at the schoolyard below. I was now higher than most of the two-story buildings on the campus. With the boys egging me on, I decided to go all the way and reached the top of the thirty-foot tower. It was only then that I realized just how loose and rickety the ladder was, held in place by a single rusty bolt with live electrical wires within my reach. My mood changed immediately. I now felt angry at the boy who had dared me to climb, imagining that he probably knew just how dangerous it was. Most potently, I heard my father's parting words, "Don't show off." I had thought my dad was a big jerk for saying that to me as I marched off, self-satisfied, just thirty-six hours earlier in San Francisco. I was glad he couldn't see me now.

When you think about how adolescents and young adults die, it's no surprise that the big killers are not cancer and heart disease. These illnesses do affect our youth, of course, but thankfully are rare. Rather, when adolescents' and young adults' lives are cut short, it's almost always due to accidents, homicide, or suicide. These occur because of how young people think, feel, and behave. I was lucky not to have fallen or been electrocuted on that tower in Germany, but it wouldn't have been terribly surprising if I had gotten hurt. I was doing just what adolescents do—accepting a dare, taking a risk, and putting my life in jeopardy.

As it turned out, I didn't learn too much about the dangers of risk taking from climbing that tower. About two weeks later on a class trip to nearby Strasbourg, France, my friends and I celebrated climbing a castle tower with a cold beer. I have an old photo from that trip in which I'm holding two bottles of beer to my mouth, one with each hand, as I sit upon a stone parapet about fifty feet above the ground and drink from both bottles at once. I'm undeniably mugging for the camera, but I'm also doing the sort of careless thing that sixteen-year-olds do—it looks risky, and it was. And the really pitiful thing is that all I wanted to do was impress my male friends and a cute German girl we'd just met.

Soon after returning to California in the late summer, my high jinks continued. Whether it was swimming drunk or driving drunk, I foolishly continued to take occasional risks. They didn't happen all that often, but any single one of them could have resulted in tragedy.

"My Goal Is 100 Percent Not to Get Hurt"

Scott Pohl was an all-American kid. He played starting center on his high school football team in Howell, Michigan, and stood six feet, one inch tall and weighed 240 pounds. His senior year, Scott was named first team All-State by the *Detroit Free Press* and *Detroit News*. He was given honorable mention All-State by the Associated Press. Scott was the Howell High School Highlanders' homecoming king. He loved the outdoors, fishing, and hunting.

Scott was a genuinely nice person. His father, Karl, told me that when Scott would see someone sitting alone in the cafeteria, without friends, he would often sit with that kid. Scott told his father that he liked to brighten up others' days. "He wasn't just friends with the athletes," Karl said. "Everyone pretty much loved Scott."

Scott had offers to play college football, but instead he took a union welding job about forty-five minutes from home. In March 2012, he bought a 745cc Honda Shadow motorcycle for the commute. He received his motorcycle license a month later, in April. That same month Michigan governor Rick Snyder signed a bill repealing the state's mandatory helmet law. On May 23, Karl saw his son riding his motorcycle without a helmet. Karl texted him an hour later to express his grave concern, and Scott replied.

SCOTT: I understand where you're coming from. I'm always going to be more of a risk taker than you ever were. That's where I get a thrill out of life. You may call it stupid but I call it living. I hope you can understand that.

KARL: I just wish you were of the same mindset you were when you first got your cycle . . . talking about head injuries etc.

SCOTT: I didn't lose that mindset. I sure as hell don't want a head injury. Priority #1 is not to go down to begin with. I wear my helmet all the time except for the short distance I just went on. I was just giving it a try. I say a prayer every time I get on my bike too. I ask to be protected. It makes me feel safer so I hope you can relax a little more. My goal is 100 percent not to get hurt . . . Love you Dad!

KARL: I was relaxed when you told me you wouldn't ride your bike without a helmet . . . I'm not sure what changed . . . I love you too . . . I just wish you would wear your helmet all the time.

One month later to the day, Scott was killed after colliding with a Ford Explorer driven by an eighteen-year-old woman with her fourteen-year-old brother in the front passenger seat. Scott was twenty-five years old.

His helmet was safely stowed away in the right saddlebag of his motor-cycle, not on his head.

"Why," I asked Karl, "would Scott not wear his helmet?"

"He felt like this was living life," Karl replied. "Scott wasn't a worrier. I'm a worst-case-scenario guy, and he was just the opposite. I'm, like, this could happen and that could happen, but Scott was not going to worry like that. He knew it was risky to ride without a helmet. He'd had some close calls on the road before, and he knew I didn't like him riding without a helmet. In fact, I can almost bet you that he left the house that day with his helmet on because he didn't want to stress me out."

From Scott's texts and Karl's words, there is absolutely no question that Scott understood the risks of riding a motorcycle without a helmet. He even said a prayer every time he got on his motorbike. Trying to con-vince Scott or anyone else that they are at great risk when riding without a helmet proves to be a futile exercise. As you now know, adolescents al-ready commonly believe they are in greater danger than they actually are. Unfortunately, most of our youth risk prevention programs still focus on the wrong thing—trying to convince adolescents that they are at risk. Nearly 3,000 years after the death of Homer, we still don't do a good job of protecting adolescents from themselves.

I D.A.R.E. You

Teens experiment. Nearly half of all graduating high school students have tried marijuana. Approximately 25 percent of twelfth-grade stu-dents have used an illicit drug in the past thirty days, along with 16 percent of tenth graders and 8 percent of eighth graders. One-third of high school students drank alcohol within the past thirty days, and nearly 25 percent of twelfth graders binge drank (defined as drinking five or more alcoholic beverages within two hours) in the past two weeks.

So let's say you wanted to build a program to halt adolescent drug and alcohol use. What would you do? In 1983, the Los Angeles Police Department was convinced that it had the answer.

Drug Abuse Resistance Education (D.A.R.E.) is typically taught by uniformed police officers. In its original iteration, the sessions were held once weekly over the course of an academic semester. Students in the fifth through ninth grades were taught about the physical, emotional, social, and legal risks and the effects of alcohol, tobacco, marijuana, and other drugs on their developing brains and bodies. Students contrasted the normal beliefs of peers in the classroom with the national data about teen use of alcohol, tobacco, and other drugs. Later versions of the program also focused on prosocial behaviors and activities unrelated to alcohol and drugs in an effort to bolster the students' self-esteem and resistance to peer pressure.

Presidents love D.A.R.E. Presidents Reagan, Bush, Clinton, G. W. Bush, and Obama have each declared one day in April to be National D.A.R.E. Day. As of 2013, D.A.R.E. was taught in all fifty states, in 75 percent of U.S. school districts, and in more than fifty countries internationally. Over 200 million kids worldwide have been educated by D.A.R.E., about 114 million in the United States alone. In fact, D.A.R.E. is the most widely promulgated school-based risk prevention program in the country. Who hasn't seen a *D.A.R.E. to Keep Kids Off Drugs* bumper sticker on a police car or suburban automobile? D.A.R.E. seems like such a good idea. The program aims to stop kids from using drugs before they start. Who could disagree with that?

There's only one problem—D.A.R.E. doesn't work.

By the mid-1990s, studies were finding that D.A.R.E. was ineffective, yet it continued to be promoted by presidents and governments. To be clear, D.A.R.E. officers had taught a series of different programs over the years, but none of them fared particularly well. Over a dozen well-designed studies found that D.A.R.E. was ineffective at meeting its primary objective—that is, to deter kids from using drugs. While there is some evidence to suggest that certain versions of D.A.R.E. did increase students' knowledge about drugs and social skills and promote positive relations between kids and police officers, the fact remains that for more than twenty-five years the students who went through D.A.R.E. were no less likely to use drugs and alcohol than those who didn't go through D.A.R.E. Even more concerning, some research found that kids who went through D.A.R.E. were actually *more likely* to try cigarettes, drugs, and alcohol.

It's hard to know why D.A.R.E. hasn't by and large shown benefit. Yet we do know that overwhelming kids with antidrug information and frightening them about the outcomes of drug abuse clearly doesn't work. It seems that when you're twelve years old and a police officer sternly tells you that smoking marijuana will ruin your life, you believe it. But a few years later, or, as in the case of many patients I've seen, somewhere between fourteen and seventeen years of age, when some of your friends are smoking marijuana and still attend school and make pretty good grades and haven't become heroin addicts, you start to think that the cops back in middle school were off their rockers.

Thankfully, prevention scientists are now working closely with D.A.R.E. America, the nonprofit group that manages the program, and in 2009, they landed upon a different approach that works better. The new program, "keepin' it REAL," has moved away from fact-based lectures and now focuses on engaging exercises that teach kids decision-making skills and gives them practice in refusing drugs. So far, some results are encouraging.

D.A.R.E. Devils

D.A.R.E. isn't the only good-sounding teen risk prevention program that failed to meet its objectives. Youth between the ages of ten and seventeen commit half of all serious crimes in the United States, and just about every adult criminal was once upon a time a juvenile offender. In the 1970s, a group of felons imprisoned for life thought they would try to help solve the problem of juvenile delinquency by being pitilessly honest with adolescents about what it means to lead a life of crime. Enter Scared Straight. The kids were brought to Rahway State Prison in New Jersey for a few hours, where they got a firsthand view of life behind bars. The convicts were brutal in their graphic descriptions of prison life, including stories of rape and murder. They sometimes shouted at, berated, terrified, and intimidated the adolescent participants, all in a genuine effort to deter them from a criminal future.

Shortly thereafter, Scared Straight programs became all the rage and were widespread throughout the country. I recall watching the documentary *Scared Straight!* when it aired in 1979 about some of the kids who went to Rahway. The program won two Emmy Awards and an Oscar for best documentary feature. Peter Falk, the well-known star of *Columbo*, television's hit show about a seemingly discombobulated but shrewd homicide detective, narrated *Scared Straight!* and told us that 80–90 percent of the juvenile offenders who had visited the prison were reformed by the experience. I was impressed, as evidenced by the fact that I clearly remember to this day sitting in our family room and watching it on our new color RCA. It sure didn't make a life of crime seem sexy or exciting to me.

But nearly three decades of research have shown that Scared Straight doesn't work either. In a review of studies in eight states spanning twenty-five years, it was found that the odds of engaging in criminal behavior were actually *increased* by nearly two to one for those adolescents who attended a Scared Straight program. Whether the Scared Straight intervention was led by kindhearted criminals or those who were harsh, intimidating, and unforgiving made no difference. The fact is that Scared Straight generally makes things worse.

Anthony Petrosino, PhD, was a doctoral student at Rutgers University in New Jersey in the mid-1990s, studying criminal justice, where he was supervised by James Finckenauer, PhD, author of the book *Scared Straight! and the Panacea Phenomenon*, the first well-known critique of the program. In 2004, it was Petrosino and his colleagues who published what has become the seminal article in our understanding of the ineffectiveness of Scared Straight and similar juvenile crime prevention programs. When I asked Dr. Petrosino why Scared Straight didn't work, he explained that his team's review "wasn't organized to figure out the critical mechanisms here," as is common with program evaluation studies. But he did suggest that peer contagion might be important. Perhaps ironically, we generally separate disruptive and emotionally disturbed youth from the mainstream and put them together in a group, where they might find like-minded peers who support and reinforce the antisocial behavior, thereby making them more likely to offend in the future.

In his book, James Finckenauer suggests another factor of importance in the failure of Scared Straight. He notes that any deterrent effect resulting from Scared Straight and similar programs would be due to a credible threat that the inmates present to the adolescents. Even though the inmates in these interventions portray themselves as defeated, powerless, and not to be idealized or emulated, they yell and frighten the kids, who likely perceive them as very powerful and intimidating, which undermines their credibility as a deterrent.

So we know beyond the shadow of a doubt that Scared Straight, like the first twenty-five years of D.A.R.E., is not a good investment and, in fact, often makes things worse. In 2011, even the U.S. Department of Justice proclaimed, "The fact that [Scared Straight] programs are still being touted as effective, despite stark evidence to the contrary, is troubling." Remarkably, to this day, Scared Straight programs remain ubiquitous throughout the country. But surely, after wholeheartedly endorsing such faulty programs for years, don't we now have effective ways of decreasing bad behavior among our youth?

Less than Zero

Chris was a fifteen-year-old boy who lived in a comfortable Los Angeles suburb with his parents and sister. They were a loving family. He attended a well-regarded public school, where he was a good student. I began seeing Chris when I was a child and adolescent psychiatry fellow at UCLA in the late 1990s. He was admitted to our inpatient adolescent psychiatry unit after a suicide attempt. He had never before experienced depression or expressed suicidal thoughts. It all happened very abruptly, the day he brought a knife to school.

Chris had spent spring break traveling in Asia with his family. As a souvenir his parents bought him a decorative knife. The first day back at school he revealed the knife to a friend right outside of his locker. Chris wasn't threatening his friend. He wasn't planning to use the knife to harm himself or anyone else. He was doing the kind of thing that kids do all the time—he was showing his friend a new toy, and it was thrilling. Unfortunately, a teacher happened to be walking by at that moment, demanded the knife, and reported the incident to the administration. Because the school had a zero tolerance policy, Chris, a boy with no history of behavioral problems, was expelled from school. That afternoon he tried to kill himself.

"Zero tolerance" was a phrase first popularized in the 1980s by the Reagan administration in its "war on drugs." In 1989, Congress passed the Drug-Free Schools and Communities Act Amendments, which prohibited the unlawful use, possession, and distribution of drugs and alcohol by students and employees on school grounds and college campuses. Schools were required to establish disciplinary sanctions for any violations or they would risk losing federal aid. Five years later, Congress passed the Gun-Free Schools Act of 1994, which required states to pass laws that would expel from school any child found in possession of a gun. These laws were the catalyst for widening the scope of zero tolerance policies beyond alcohol, drugs, and guns to a wide range of offenses, including harassment, hate speech, fighting, and dress code infractions. In the late 1990s, students were being suspended and expelled from schools all over the country for things like bringing an asthma inhaler or aspirin to school, insubordination, and possession of a kitchen knife in a lunch box for cutting an apple. Many offenses read like a *Saturday Night Live* skit: a seventeen-year-old expelled for using a rubber band to shoot a paper clip at a classmate; a twelve-year-old expelled for a scuffle with classmates who called him fat; a five-year-old expelled for picking up a razor blade on the floor of the school bus and bringing it to his teacher.

Twenty years of zero tolerance has resulted in zero gain. In fact, as you probably now suspect, zero tolerance not only doesn't work, it often makes things worse. In 2008, a task force of the American Psychological Association reviewed the data. They found that schools are no safer, discipline is no more effective or consistent, and schools with more suspension and expulsion have less satisfactory learning environments, even when controlling for socioeconomic status. More concerning, the study found that students who have been suspended are more likely to be disruptive and disciplined again and that suspended and expelled students are more likely still to drop out and fail to graduate high school on time. To boot, the task force found that increased reliance on severe punishments and consequences results in more referrals to the juvenile justice system for transgressions that were once managed in school, which costs both parents and society gobs more money.

By providing a "one strike and you're out" approach to school misbehavior, it has generally been supposed that zero tolerance will result in color-blind discipline in schools. Unfortunately, here too the data prove that zero tolerance policies have not succeeded. Black, Latino, and Native American students are still overrepresented among those who are suspended and expelled from school. Between 1973 and 2006, school suspensions grew by 250 percent for both blacks and Latinos and nearly

300 percent for Native Americans but only 50 percent for whites. Black students are now over three times more likely to be suspended than white students, even though there is no evidence to suggest that black kids are more disruptive or violent than white kids. The American Psychological Association's task force suggests that black and Latino students are more severely disciplined for less serious infractions and more subjective reasons.

Chris was a good kid who got caught in a bad system. All things considered, he was lucky. His parents were attentive to his moods, got him the necessary psychiatric care, and made sure he stayed in treatment until he was well. But too many of our kids don't have the support they need, and once they're suspended or expelled, the future is bleak. They get labeled as a "bad kid." They're commonly seen as "troubled" and have difficulty transferring into a high-performing school, even when they have top-notch academic skills. Perhaps most concerning, their self-confidence and self-esteem suffer, which can lead to anxiety, depression, and social withdrawal, all of which increase the likelihood that they will further engage in risky behavior.

Drive Time

I remember exactly three things from my driver's education class in high school. First, I remember that the classroom portion of the course started at 7:30 a.m., an hour before the regular school start time, and that my friends and I often dozed off in class. Second, I remember that we used driving simulators (which we jokingly called "stimulators") some afternoons and tried to outdo one another as we purposefully ran into signposts, buildings, and occasionally, and shamefully, pedestrians. Third, I remember that we had the heavenly opportunity to drive.

My very first outing behind the wheel remains crystal clear to me. I drove a few miles in my hometown alongside my instructor, while three peers jokingly held on for dear life in the backseat. I drove well, and it was pure bliss. I have loved to drive ever since. Soon after I passed my driver's test, on my sixteenth birthday, I began taking the car out regularly after school. One of my favorite excursions was packing my beloved Dalmatian into our family's mid-1970s VW Beetle, rolling back the sunroof, and driving out to the beach, where I could let my dog run free and chase her into the waves. Teenage paradise.

Since 1949, the recommended driver's education curriculum in the United States has remained thirty hours of in-class teaching and six hours of in-vehicle practice. The goal of driver's education is to teach safe driving skills to students and reduce crashes, and the vast majority of us (86 percent, according to one national survey) think that driver's education is "very important" for training safe drivers. Unfortunately, however, driver's education doesn't achieve its stated goal. Numerous studies show that driver's education classes do not reduce the frequency of automobile accidents among young drivers. In fact, the data point in the opposite direction: By offering driver's education classes in school, adolescents are more likely to get their driver's license at a younger age, which actually increases the proportion of teens involved in motor vehicle accidents.

As D.A.R.E., Scared Straight, zero tolerance policies, driver's education, and the tragic story of Scott Pohl clearly demonstrate, kids don't smoke weed, engage in delinquent behavior, or take ridiculous risks like riding a motorcycle without a helmet because they don't know these things are bad for them. We've told them and told them and told them that drunk driving is dangerous, that stealing can land you in juvenile hall, and that bringing weapons to school can get you expelled. I too knew that the ladder on that electrical tower in Germany was loose and unsafe to climb. But I climbed it all the same.

My dad told me not to show off while I was in Germany, to be careful, to pay attention—*achtung!* Stay safe in this new place you're going, with this new thing you're doing. Be wary of peer pressure. Scott Pohl's dad tried to do the same when he told his son to wear a motorcycle helmet. We both heard the words, but neither of us listened and took heed. Only one of us was lucky.

As I've pored over countless research studies during the writing of this book, I've been disheartened time and again by the lack of data for so many of the adolescent health promotion and risk reduction programs that our society continues to support. Since 1995, the Centers for Disease Control and Prevention has endorsed National Health Education Standards, which articulate what students should know and be able to do to improve their health by grades two, five, eight, and twelve. The standards are thoughtful and well articulated. However, there is little to suggest that these standards and the programs that they have prompted have done much to benefit our adolescents: Obesity has quadrupled among adolescents in the past thirty years; fewer than one-third of high school students get the federally recommended one hour of exercise per day, and only one-half attend a physical education class regularly at school; adolescents are sleeping less than ever before; accidents, suicide, and homicide still account for the vast majority of adolescent deaths; drug and alcohol use remain unacceptably high; and there has been little change in overall tobacco use in years. Even in the area of sexual health education, the data are only equivocal—some programs have been shown to increase condom use and reduce pregnancy, while others have not. We're just not hitting the mark when it comes to preventing risk among adolescents.

After Midnight

As a parent of teens myself, I worry about that late-night call. As our kids age, we all feel a certain degree of helplessness when it comes to the risks our children face and how we can best help them navigate a safe adolescence. It's really tough because so many things change irrevocably during these years—it's not only their physical appearance, it's also the increase in responsibility, academic demands, and negative life events that pile up over time. They now look at the world and see it for what it really is. They realize that life isn't so safe, that there are lots of unknowns, and that people really do die and are cruel to one another. There's more friction between expected and actual life events—they were always told they were a great basketball player, but somehow they don't make the team. We tell them to get the rest they need, but how can they get to bed when our schools pile on more and more homework, they feel they must excel in extracurricular activities if they want to get into "a good college," and schools start early in the morning, putting them out of sync with their natural circadian rhythm? They engage in new and highly intimate relationships with peers, which influence them in myriad ways. They use caffeine and sometimes drugs, cigarettes, and alcohol, which further influence their behavior. And they do it all with less parental oversight than ever before in their young lives.

Prior to puberty, kids spend more time with parents and other adults than alone with peers, but after puberty the tables turn. In a typical week, high school students spend two to three times as much time with peers as with parents and other adults. Just when they need it most, we let up on our supervision. But it's not simply the amount of time we spend with our kids that matters. It's also the kind of time and the style of parenting we employ. Worse still, we fail to teach our kids how to think properly about risk. We mistakenly support prevention programs that don't work, and we neglect to adequately emphasize skills that will enhance their resilience. There's a lot we're not doing right to keep our kids safe.

In order to identify which strategies *will* work to prevent risky behavior, we must first understand something about the more than three pounds of neurons that sit encased in bone atop our shoulders and the yin and yang between our thoughts, emotions, and behaviors. In chapter 3, we will discover the wonders of the neural network and what's happening in the brain as it transitions from child to adult.

CHAPTER 3

From Railways
to Neural Pathways

(or, What You Need to Know About
the Adolescent Brain)

The young are heated by Nature as drunken men by wine.

—ARISTOTLE

ON SEPTEMBER 13, 1848, PHINEAS Gage, a twenty-five-year-old construction foreman, was working just south of the town of Cavendish on the Rutland and Burlington Railroad in Vermont. Gage was directing a group of workers who were using explosives to clear rocks from the railroad's pathway. While he was packing down a gunpowder charge with an iron rod, an unintended detonation occurred. The explosion propelled the thirteen-pound, three-foot, seven-inch solid iron tamping rod through Gage's left cheek and into his head. Amazingly, Phineas Gage quickly regained consciousness, suffered an intervening coma, and then went on to live twelve unlikely years after the accident.

Once his wound healed, Gage's personality was changed. No longer polite and responsible, he became hasty and reckless. His doctor, John Harlow, wrote that "the equilibrium or balance, so to speak, between his intellectual faculties and animal propensities, seems to have been destroyed." Friends of Gage said that he was "no longer Gage." This previously responsible and honest foreman became impulsive, often described as a womanizer, not to be trusted in polite company. In a manner of speaking, Phineas Gage became an adolescent.

The tale of Phineas Gage is generally accepted as the first well-documented neurological case study of a brain injury resulting in a major personality change. In many respects we have Phineas to thank for our discovery that different parts of the brain are responsible for different aspects of our functioning and personality. Now, thanks to advanced technology that allows us to scan the brain, such as functional magnetic resonance imaging (fMRI), diffusion tensor imaging (DTI), and positron emission tomography (PET), we no longer need to wait for people to get injured in order to study the mind. We can take a close look at the brain over time, observe how it changes from childhood into adulthood, and seek to determine how normal and atypical growth and development affect our emotions, thoughts, and behavior.

A Brain Owner's Guide

We were all nervous that first day. Spying on one another, trying hard to be brave, acting like it was an everyday thing to dismember a cadaver. Human dissection is only one of many rites of passage that thousands navigate annually in their first year of medical school. For most physicians, gross anatomy lab remains a strong and salient memory, and I suspect that most of us can still easily conjure up the olfactory burn from the heavy scent of formaldehyde that permeated the air. In a nearby lab were brains awaiting dissection. Brains don't preserve well in cadavers, so they're generally removed and stored elsewhere.

It was pretty arresting and hard not to utter an uncomfortable laugh the first time I stared at the sinks filled with brains floating in formaldehyde and water. The organ that most uniquely defines us, the sine qua non of human existence, just bobbing along like so many apples in a barrel, bumping into fifteen or twenty of its friends without so much as a hello. Yet this small, dense mass of nerves has been exquisitely organized and planned by evolution and remains to this day, by virtually all accounts, the most complex thing we've found in the universe.

As I stared at those brains in the lab sinks, I was looking mostly at the cortex, the outermost section that looks all wavy or noodle-like. Humans have the largest cortex, relative to total brain size, of all animals. Our cortex is *huge* by comparison, which is what makes us so imaginative, attentive, and capable of learning, organizing, and planning. A good deal of the power of our cortex lies within our conscious control. We can generally choose to concentrate, listen, remember, speak, kick, chew, and so forth. Below the cortex are the subcortical structures. While no other animal has a cortex as sophisticated as ours, all animals have many of these same subcortical structures, which are responsible for orchestrating basic physiological demands like hunger, body temperature, sleep, and reproduction.

Spanning both cortical and subcortical areas are a variety of structures, often referred to as the limbic system. The limbic system draws its name from the Latin word *limbus*, which means edge or boundary and is meant to describe a series of structures that border the cortical and subcortical areas of the brain. Some of the limbic structures, particularly those involved with reward and motivational drives like excitement and fear, are clustered in an area called the ventral striatum. By and large, the limbic structures are responsible for our feelings and emotions like joy, love, anxiety, embarrassment, anger, aggression, envy, and sadness.

The limbic system matures early in children, before the upper, foremost part of the brain, known as the prefrontal cortex. If we think of the limbic system as the emotional center of the brain, then the prefrontal cortex is the brain's CEO. The job of the limbic system is to produce emotions like love, envy, rage, irritation, happiness, and desire. It is these emotions that drive our behavior toward the things that matter for our survival, such as eating, procreating, and defending ourselves. The prefrontal cortex, on the other hand, guides our planning, organization, memory, attention, and decision making. More than any other part of the brain, it is the prefrontal cortex, the evolutionarily newest part of the brain, that makes us distinctly "human" and can act to inhibit impulsive and motivational drives. As we will see, the fact that higher prefrontal cortical areas develop more slowly than limbic emotional areas of the brain is no coincidence. Rather, humans are genetically engineered to prioritize emotions over logic in our adolescent and early adult years, which goes a long way toward explaining why we engage in such risky behavior at that age.

> Humans are genetically engineered to prioritize emotions over logic in our adolescent and early adult years.

The prefrontal cortex can be likened to Sir Arthur Conan Doyle's Sherlock Holmes, and the limbic system to his trusty sidekick, Dr. Watson. Watson (the limbic system) is often portrayed as impulsive and highly emotional, scanning the scene for possible rewards and threats that may help solve the crime. When Watson identifies a clue, he tells Holmes (the prefrontal cortex) because he cannot understand and organize all of these emotional stimuli on his own. Holmes, on the other hand, is measured, logical, and thoughtful. He takes his time to arrive at a conclusion. Watson needs Holmes the way the limbic system needs the prefrontal cortex.

Temporarily Closed for Construction

We are born with nearly all of the 100 billion neurons we will ever have. Throughout the first decade of life, our neurons (the gray matter of our brain) grow and grow in a relatively undifferentiated manner. The brain doesn't yet know what its ultimate purpose will be, so it keeps its options open—is this to be the brain of a baseball player, a mathematician, a painter, or a gardener? Sometime around puberty, the brain starts to differentiate. Perhaps the most profound changes in the adolescent brain involve the rewiring, reassembling, and upgrading of neural tissue. In order for us to get better at certain skills, those that we need the most, the brain must increase its connections between the areas that serve those functions. The correct parts of the brain must talk to one another quickly and efficiently, and memory functions must be well integrated so that we learn from our successes and mistakes. This process of building faster connections is accomplished by myelination, or the growth of fatty sheaths on neurons. Myelin acts like an insulator and makes these pathways between neurons like superhighways, boosting transmission speeds by up to one hundred times. Myelination also makes neurons more efficient so that they use less energy when sending messages, while reducing their recovery time between firings by up to thirty times. All told, the hundred-times increase in neuron transmission speed, coupled with the thirty-times decrease in recovery time, accelerates brain speed by up to three thousand times.

Myelination proceeds from the rear of the brain to the front, from areas close to the brain stem that attend to evolutionarily older and more primitive functions like vision and movement to newer frontal cortical areas that program more complicated functions like memory, planning, attention, organization, and decision making. But myelination comes at the cost of less brain plasticity or flexibility. That is, as the neurons become myelinated, they lose some of their ability to make new synapses and adapt to the changing environment. So if you haven't learned to ride a bicycle by thirteen or so, it only gets tougher. The brain follows a simple maxim: Use it or lose it.

We all know that it's easier to learn a second language as a child than as an adult. Children who learn two languages at home generally take a few months longer to begin speaking, but eventually they master both. Exposure to more than one language causes the language centers of the brain to propagate more than if we were exposed to only one language. For those who have learned two languages, learning a third is easier still. But for those of us who have learned only one language by the time adolescence begins, when the brain starts to reinforce those neural tracks that are frequently used and removes those utilized less often, learning a second language as an adult is more difficult. Thus, while the connections between frequently used brain areas strengthen in adolescence, as seen by the growth of white matter, or myelin, by about 1 percent per year, the total number of neurons, or the amount of gray matter, shrinks by about that same 1 percent per year concurrently, making the acquisition of new tasks more difficult.

The frontal lobes are one of the last areas to myelinate. This means that the bridge between the frontal lobes (or the brain's CEO) and the limbic system (or the emotional centers) doesn't fully link until we're older. With our current technology, it's a bit difficult to know when exactly this process is complete, but our best sense at this time is the mid-twenties. But remember that myelination comes at the cost of plasticity or brain flexibility. In order to build strong and fast connections between frequently used areas, the brain must prune some of its many branches (or dendrites) and connections (synapses) by cutting back on gray matter—the nerve cell bodies themselves. In the same way we might prune a rosebush by removing weaker branches so that the stronger ones can grow more effectively, so does maturation prune gray matter in the cortex of the adolescent brain.

The brain develops in stages, and structures mature at different rates. Motor nerve tracks, for example, which are responsible for physical movement and coordination, are well myelinated and networked by age fifteen to sixteen, which is why we begin to see some terrific athletic performances in this age range, and why I first lost a running race to my son when he was fourteen years old. The limbic structures, or the emotional brain system, which include most prominently the amygdala, nucleus accumbens, hippocampus, and anterior thalamus, develop early and are at peak functioning by mid-adolescence, which explains why adolescents feel their emotions so intensely. By contrast, the prefrontal parts of the brain, those associated with executive functions, such as planning, organizing, paying attention, problem solving, inhibiting automatic responses, regulating emotion, and employing past experience in new situations, grow more slowly and are not fully developed and networked with the emotional brain structures until at least the mid-twenties. It is precisely because the ventral striatal structures develop early in life that we see such a great outpouring of emotionally driven, reward-seeking behavior in adolescence, which logically leads to the high rates of risk-taking behavior, accidental injury and death, homicide, and suicide in this age range.

Beyond the sometimes frantic search for reward, adolescents also have more difficulty than adults understanding the emotions of others. Because the brain of an adolescent has yet to be fully myelinated, pruned, and streamlined in its function and because adolescents have only limited life experience, they activate more of their brain when trying to figure out the emotions of others, and this really slows them down. This skill is sometimes called "mentalizing," or theory of mind, a theoretical construct that indicates we can understand others' beliefs, desires, and intentions. Back to our Sherlock Holmes and Dr. Watson analogy, the limbic system (Dr. Watson) enters reward-seeking search mode long before the prefrontal cortex (Sherlock Holmes) is fully in command of the details of the case. To boot, Sherlock's experience is limited when he's young, and he doesn't yet understand everything as easily or quickly as he will with more time and a few more cases under his belt. It takes another ten years or so, until we are in our mid-twenties, for our higher-level cognitive structures and prefrontal cortex to take sovereignty over our early developing emotional brain.

Better than Expected

My son was five and my daughter was eight when they learned how babies are made. I was at work, and our kids cornered my poor wife. Elliot, our Chihuahua, was humping Parker's leg. Her brother, Julian, asked why. Alice explained that dogs hump when they're trying to make babies. She reminded the kids that the sperm comes from the man and fertilizes the egg in the woman. They had been told this story many times before, at their insistence, and it had satisfied their curiosity up to this point. However, now that our daughter was eight and our son was five, they wanted more detail. "But how exactly does the sperm get from the man into the woman?" they demanded. You know what followed, and for our kids, as for kids all over the world, the answer was a real spoiler alert. Regardless of whether you have this conversation at five or eight or ten years of age, when kids hear that a penis must be inserted into a vagina, well, it's just a bit too much information to take in right away. Parker was grossed out. Julian decided right then and there that he would never get married and have children. It was a very sensible statement, actually, because where's the fun in putting your penis into a vagina when you're five years old?

But our brains change with age, and our reward preferences follow. At five, Julian liked toy cars, kicking soccer balls, riding his bicycle, and listening to stories, and at eight, Parker liked school, gymnastics, arts and crafts, and reading. Sexual intercourse was a crazy concept. By puberty, however, it takes only the faintest whiff of perfume, the softest touch of a hand, or the slightest seductive smile to stir our loins. And therein lies the rub.

The desire for reward is of paramount importance when considering risk-taking behavior in adolescence. The nucleus accumbens, the key reward center within the ventral striatum (more broadly within the limbic system), is more responsive to dopamine during adolescence than at any other time of our life. Dopamine is an essential neurochemical that, among other things, helps us learn. The ventral striatum receives dopamine-rich transmissions from the ventral tegmental area when something is better than we expect it to be, what researchers call "reward prediction error."

We don't really know how an M&M is going to taste the first time we eat one, but with our parents excitedly egging us on, we place the object into our mouth and imagine it will probably be nice, predicting a good experience. But once we taste it, holy cow—it's a great experience! And that's the reward prediction error. The M&M is better than expected, and therefore something we must remember. For most children who try their first M&M, it's pretty amazing, and the dopamine starts flowing big-time. The dopamine isn't just a reward or a feel-good signal, as is often thought. Rather, dopamine's true purpose is to teach us that this M&M is really important—the taste of the M&M, and subsequent release of dopamine, signals that this little funny-shaped colored object matters.

Having once experienced the good taste of an M&M, our brains are now primed to associate M&M's with a squirt of dopamine. The next time the child is at the store and sees the M&M's on the shelves near the checkout stand, he anticipates the expected outcome of that sweet outside candy shell and delicious inner milk chocolate filling, and boom! He feels a burst of dopamine release. *Hey, this thing is really important!* the dopamine is telling his brain. Then, of course, he starts nagging his parents to buy him some M&M's. So dopamine hits us twice—the first time it strikes as we experience something we like; and second, forever going forward, we will now feel a pulse of dopamine release when we anticipate an experience that we believe we will like.

Dopamine's reinforcing effects rest upon its promise of future pleasure. Think about the people you've seen pulling slot machines for hours on end in Las Vegas—they appear robotic, and they're certainly not getting any apparent joy out of the activity. So it's not pleasure itself but rather dopamine's assurance that pleasure is on its way that is driving them to keep putting money in the slot machine.

Other limbic brain structures, such as the amygdala and hippo-campus, are also important for reward-based learning. The amygdala tells us how agreeable or disagreeable that M&M is, while the hippocampus stores the memories of the experience and many associated factors, like where we were when we had that good feeling and with whom we shared it. The basal ganglia, a group of structures near the ventral striatum, relies on dopamine to manage the coordination of motor movements that will help us get the M&M's from the package into our mouths, while the pre-frontal cortex helps us to plan and organize how we will obtain M&M's in the future.

As the primary neurochemical in our reward circuits, dopamine's main job is to focus our attention on what's potentially pleasurable, thereby helping us to learn about what really matters for our survival. Dopamine tells us what is salient. Without dopamine, we wouldn't learn which foods we like or that sex feels good. In other words, without do-pamine, we wouldn't eat and procreate and do the kinds of things we must do in order to propagate our species. One of the most significant distinctions between adolescents and adults is the amount of dopamine flowing in different parts of the brain.

Not surprisingly, more dopamine makes us more likely to take risks so that we might possibly experience more pleasure. As dopamine in-creases in our brains during adolescence, we often weigh the benefits as being more favorable than the costs of any given action. We become biased in favor of selecting the action with the highest potential for reward. We see the same thing when we give adults dopamine-enhancing medications or drugs. Parkinson's disease, for example, occurs as a result of too little dopamine in the brain's basal ganglia, which, again, coordinates motor movements. This is why people afflicted by Parkinson's have tremors and stiffness and other movement difficulties. When we give dopamine-enhancing medications to affected individuals, they not only move more easily because of the increased dopamine now hitting their basal ganglia, they also become more likely to take risks like gambling because of the increased dopamine now hitting their ventral striatum or reward center.

By contrast, dopamine activity in the prefrontal cortex (the CEO), which again is important for planning, organizing, remembering, paying attention, impulse control, regulating emotions, and making good decisions, is much more efficient and streamlined in adulthood. That's when, of course, we intellectualize, care more about the news, defer immediate pleasure in exchange for later rewards, and make better decisions about the careers and relationships we want to pursue and the subjects that interest us most. Intellectual pursuits become most rewarding when dopamine synaptic connections grow within our prefrontal cortex in large numbers, which begins to happen as we enter adolescence but becomes well integrated with our emotional brain only in adulthood.

Existentialism can be difficult to read. But Kafka, Sartre, and Camus are a whole lot more interesting when you're seventeen years old than when you're ten. Kids don't pay much attention to the news until their mid-teen years, at which point reading the paper or watching the news on TV is almost like a horror show to their impressionable minds. The world doesn't feel quite so safe, when you see that people are dying right and left of cancer, AIDS, Ebola, and murder. As dopamine projections increasingly connect (by building more synapses) within our prefrontal cortex, older teenagers appreciate the world in a whole new way, but seeing the world as it is also carries a great burden. And their advanced cognition, with all of its gifts, is also a major factor in the increases in anxiety and depression that we see in teens.

As every parent and teacher can tell you, adolescents seem to feel things more intensely than both children and adults. As previously noted, during adolescence, dopamine is more robust within our brain than at any other time of our lives. Never again will chocolate taste so good, a roller-coaster ride be so thrilling, or sex be quite so intriguing. By signaling the promise of pleasure, dopamine primes our brain to learn—and in adolescence, our learning forms memories more easily than it will later in life. This is perhaps the major reason that our memories of adolescence are so strong and our allegiances to the institutions of our youth, like high schools and colleges and sports teams, are so profound. Things

> In adolescence, our learning forms memories more easily than it will later in life.

will never feel this good again. Likewise, bad experiences may never again feel this bad. As adults, dopamine is shared better between our emotional centers and our prefrontal cortex, and these parts of the brain are much better connected, which allows the CEO to have a much larger impact on the emotional brain. All of which allows adults to take more time, act less impulsively, and be more thoughtful when making decisions that present an element of risk.

Twenty-Something

When did your adolescence end? Perhaps for some readers, that day has yet to come. But developmentally, at least, adolescence is generally considered to start with puberty and end when an individual has attained a stable and independent role in society. By this definition, adolescence is surely lengthening.

We are staying in school longer and starting both careers and long-term romantic relationships later and later, and not only in Western cultures. In 1950, around one-quarter of high school graduates in the United States enrolled in college, but only 7 percent of men and 5 percent of women attained a bachelor's degree; by 2009, 70 percent enrolled in college, and 30 percent of men and 29 percent of women graduated. The same is true in developing countries, where, for example, in India 59 percent of men and 39 percent of women enrolled in college in 2013, as compared to 39 percent of men and 20 percent of women in 1980, and Argentina, where 73 percent of men and 81 percent of women enrolled in 2013, as compared to 53 percent of men and 62 percent of women in 1980.

I was nearly twenty-nine when I started medical school, nearly thirty-three when I got married, and thirty-four at the birth of my first child. It turns out that I'm not such an outlier. The average age at which medical, law, and other students enter professional training is advancing. Whereas once upon a time, you started medical school right after college, at twenty-one or twenty-two, the average age upon entering medical school in the United States is now twenty-five. The more time adolescents spend in school, of course, the longer it takes them to achieve financial independence, which explains why it took me so long to get married. The average age at which men and women in the United States marry is currently twenty-nine and twenty-seven, respectively, up from twenty-six for men and twenty-three for women in 1990 and twenty-two for men and twenty for women in 1960. And in Taiwan, South Korea, Canada, Germany, England, and France, among many others, the age of first marriage is more than two years older than the U.S. age for both men and women. The average age at which women have their first child is also rising. In the United States that age hit 26.3 years in 2014, an increase of 3.6 years since 1980, when the average was 22.7 years. These changes are seen across the board in the United States and affect every ethnicity.

How long were you covered by your parents' health insurance? I dropped off at twenty-three, which was standard in the 1980s, after which time I paid for my own insurance or, on occasion between jobs or graduate programs, didn't have any. With the passage of the Affordable Care Act in 2010, however, federal legislation now allows parents to keep children on their health insurance until they are twenty-six. In many ways, twenty-six is the new eighteen. According to a recent Harris Interactive poll conducted for the *Wall Street Journal*, more than 40 percent of parents of children aged eighteen to thirty-five are still paying for their kids' cell phone service.

> In many ways, twenty-six is the new eighteen.

It's tempting to be critical of these "indulgent" parents, but allowing our adolescents to extend their adolescence into their mid-twenties may not be such a bad thing. It seems that the sooner we stop really stimulating and challenging our brains, the sooner our white matter sets in place. Although white matter increases the speed of brain signaling between commonly used areas and makes our brains more efficient so we can be successful adults, it also makes our brains less plastic or malleable, literally harder, and it becomes more difficult to learn new things. New research, in fact, suggests that higher education may make us better thinkers in part by improving the quality of the brain's white matter. It may be that by extending adolescence to allow for more education and experiential learning, we are giving our kids the gift of a lifetime of greater intellectual flexibility and potential.

So, for the adolescents who leave high school and immediately get full-time jobs in construction or work in a grocery store, their brains don't stay plastic as long as they do for those adolescents who go to college or travel the world. Starting a job and supporting yourself demands that you take on adult responsibilities, and this behavior makes us "grow up" faster. When I think back about how my parents behaved when they were in their forties, it seems very grown-up. My dad fought in World War II when he was eighteen. He had to grow up quickly. By contrast, I was in college at eighteen, taking classes, playing sports, and trying desperately to meet girls. When I was in my forties, I was a grown-up but distinctly different from how my father had been at that age—like him I was a doctor by then, but I was also looser, more lighthearted and spirited with my kids, and I played guitar two late nights each week in a rock band. Sure, our upbringings and times were different. He was born in 1924, most of his childhood was in the post-Depression era, and he and my mom had five kids. I was born in 1963, most of my childhood was in the 1970s, and Alice and I have two kids. But I'm willing to bet that part of what accounts for who my dad and I were in our forties also had to do with the additional years my brain was allowed to stay plastic and malleable during my adolescence. While I'm not going so far as to agree with Oprah that fifty is the new thirty, just imagine the advantages our twentysomethings might have if their brains stay plastic a bit longer.

Having a plastic brain for more years may also, however, increase our risk. The longer we are open to challenging ourselves, listening to and learning from others, and not settling down, the more our brains may remain vulnerable to the risks of adolescence, like drug abuse and unprotected sex. When you're a grown-up, you don't take as many chances.

So just as our ideas are shifting about how many years adolescence lasts, so is our understanding of neurobiology. Only two decades ago, it was assumed that most brain development occurred during childhood and was completed by around the time we turned eighteen. We now know that major growth and changes continue within the brain through our mid-twenties. Perhaps now society is starting to catch up with biology. Although our ancestors took on adult responsibilities earlier in life, it doesn't mean that they were necessarily ready for them.

Four Days in Verona

In a keynote address to the New York Academy of Sciences in 2004, Ron Dahl, professor of human development at the University of California at Berkeley, told a resonant tale of two adolescents who met at a party. At first glance, the boy was smitten by the girl's beauty, but she wasn't so interested in him. Still, with his continued flattery, she became inexplicably drawn to him. Two kisses and fewer than one hundred shared words later, they were in love. More than in love, they became obsessed with each other. Unfortunately, their families didn't get along well, and their parents forbade them to be together. But these two kids didn't let that stop them. They would do anything to be together, even if it meant abandoning their families forever.

In consultation with a local religious leader, the girl hatched a plan to take a special potion that would put her into a deathlike coma for nearly two days. The boy was to be told of the plan, of course, and then come and collect her body so that together they could run off into the sunset. But, alas, the boy didn't receive the message about the potion and, viewing her body at the gravesite, he killed himself in sorrow. The girl, who was only thirteen years old at the time and had known the boy only four days, awoke from the potion's spell to find him dead. Heartbroken, she too killed herself.

These kids sound mentally ill. If I told you they were my patients, you would be correct to suspect a diagnosis of psychosis, mood disorder, or both, which wouldn't be terribly surprising given the huge increases in mental illness that we see during the teen through young adult years. As noted in chapter 1, 50 percent of adults suffering chronic mental illness experience symptom onset by age fourteen and 75 percent experience symptoms by age twenty-four. Depression, anxiety, substance abuse, eating disorders, and psychosis all rise significantly during this time and lead to major increases in morbidity and contribute to the high rates of mortality seen in this age group.

I suspect you've caught on by now. The two kids are William Shakespeare's Romeo and Juliet, not psychiatric patients. They committed suicide because they simply couldn't imagine life without one another. And their emotionally charged and erratic behavior is just what we've come to expect from adolescents.

The Sleepy Brain

Given all of the brain reconstruction going on during adolescence, teens really need their sleep. It's during sleep that our bodies grow and we consolidate memory by strengthening the connections (or synapses) between neurons. Driven by an ever-increasing homework load and the need to start and end the day early to allow for busing and sports and other extracurricular activities, along with a dizzying array of video screens seemingly designed for endless distraction, sleep deprivation is, unfortunately, a major problem for today's teens.

"Sleep begets sleep," advised our pediatrician shortly after the birth of our daughter. Teaching your infant to sleep well is one of the first and, all too often, most challenging tasks for new parents. As the doctor told Alice and me, children who learn to sleep well tend to get sufficient sleep. In other words, the more they sleep, the more they sleep. Our daughter was not an easy sleeper those first two years, but we eventually got things under control. However, fifteen years later parents are no longer entirely in charge of their adolescent's sleep cycle.

According to the National Sleep Foundation's Sleep in America Poll of 2014, 75 percent of children in the United States have at least one electronic device in their bedroom, with a television being the most common (45 percent). Over one-third of these children leave the television on all night long, which is known to be especially disruptive to sleep because of the constant exposure to light and noise. With the mass proliferation of smartphones, tablets, computers, and video games, the median number of electronic devices in children's bedrooms has climbed to one for children six to eleven years of age, two for those aged twelve to fourteen, and three for those over fifteen. Because adolescents generally experience a major circadian shift in their sleep cycle beginning around puberty, the distraction of electronics in the room during the teen years is particularly damaging.

Adolescents' natural circadian rhythm forces them toward a delayed sleep phase, going to bed and awakening later. Any parent of a teen can tell you that the kids want to stay up late and sleep in until noon. For the average teenager, bedtime pushes later into the evening, total sleep time on weekdays decreases, and teens disproportionately complain of excessive daytime sleepiness. Given their tendency for a delayed sleep cycle, it's ironic that the older kids get, the earlier school starts.

One of my patients, Tony, is emblematic of a classic but all too common cautionary tale of the dangers of a delayed sleep phase. I met Tony during his winter vacation, just after being put on probation by his college. Leaving home for a university halfway across the country is a challenge for any adolescent, but it was a particular struggle for Tony. Although an extremely intelligent and kindhearted boy, he had always found intimate friendships a struggle, and, left to his own devices, he tended to isolate himself. He maintained a robust social life online, and he would stay up late into the evening gaming with friends and acquaintances. But in his classes and within his dormitory, he had virtually no friends. He began sleeping through his morning classes, playing on the computer late into the evening while avoiding his schoolwork. Eventually, his sleep cycle was so turned around that he was going to bed around five in the morning and sleeping until noon. Lots of things got in the way of Tony's studying and being an effective student, but his sleep cycle ultimately became a big contributor. He went back to school in spring, not heeding the recommendations from me and his academic adviser, and things only got worse. As he fell further and further behind in school, his anxiety mounted, and he just about entirely stopped sleeping for three weeks. By May, he was failing all of his courses, and the college placed him on academic suspension.

It's not really the television, computer, and smartphone that lie at the root of Tony's problems, of course, or the difficulties that so many of our adolescents have with maintaining a proper circadian rhythm. Tony struggles with anxiety and social skills, which are the real culprits in his case. But the contribution of devices and even electricity simply cannot be denied. Ever since we could keep the lights and radio on past dark, we've been extending our bedtimes later and later. Data from 1897 through 2009 demonstrate that not only has our children's bedtime been extended but doctors' recommendations have also followed suit, to the tune of 0.71 minutes per year. That may not seem like so much, but when you multiply 0.71 by those 112 years (1897 to 2009) you get 80, or one hour and twenty minutes. It turns out that a lot can happen in that time.

Most of us feel more on edge or anxious when we don't sleep well, and studies of sleep restriction bear out these observations and then some. Getting less sleep than usual can result in numerous neuropsychological difficulties, including trouble in making calculations and finding words, impaired verbal creativity, trouble with learning abstract concepts, inattention, and slowed reaction time. Teachers notice differences between well-rested and sleep-deprived pupils, even when they are "blinded" to the experimental condition. Teachers report more academic problems, restlessness, impulsivity, trouble with attention and focus, memory difficulties, and emotional reactivity among children who receive even one hour less sleep than usual.

Although early high school start times are correlated with lower grades and SAT scores, academic achievement is just the tip of the iceberg. Early-morning awakening among teens is also associated with an increase in automobile accidents. Moving the high school start time later by only one hour, from 7:30 a.m. to 8:30 a.m., resulted in a 16.5 percent reduction in motor vehicle accidents in a Kentucky county in a single year. Early school start times also mean more school absences and increased caffeine use. Most importantly, the broad range of cognitive skills involved in decision making are strongly affected by sleep restriction, leading to trouble with adapting to changing information, revising strategies based on new information, innovation, maintaining focus, insight, communication, memory, and risk assessment. Intuitively, we all know that even one night of poor sleep makes us irritable and less likely to make good decisions the following day. Experimentally, we now know that sleep calms the brain's threat perception center, housed within the amygdala (inside the limbic system, or emotional brain), allowing the prefrontal cortex to exert greater "top-down" control over our emotions when we're better rested. Strictly speaking, a good night's sleep reduces risky behavior among adolescents by allowing enhanced prefrontal control over emotional brain centers.

The Addicted Brain

The relationship between age and first drug or alcohol use is dramatic. To be clear, I'm not talking here about giving your child a sip of wine at the table with a family meal or religious ceremony; the data that follow refer to kids who experiment with illicit drugs and intoxicating amounts of alcohol. For these kids, the younger they are when they first try alcohol or drugs, the greater their subsequent risk of abuse and dependence, up to sixfold in some studies. Those with mental illness are also at greater risk, such that tweens and teens with depression, for example, are more than three times as likely to suffer from alcohol or drug dependence as those without depression.

The relative lack of connectivity between the frontal lobes and the emotional brain centers contributes to the addictive power of drugs and alcohol in our teen years. The high amounts of dopamine (think gas pedal) in the reward centers of the brain reinforce the behaviors that give pleasure, like using drugs. Meanwhile, the white matter connections between the prefrontal cortex and the emotional brain centers that can inhibit impulsivity (think brake) are not yet firmly in place, allowing emotions to rule the day.

Think back to the M&M's we discussed earlier. Presuming you like them, the first one is delicious. The second one is pretty good too. By the time you eat your tenth M&M, however, they don't taste quite so amazing. The M&M's haven't changed, so why are you still eating them? Remember that dopamine primes our reward system and gets us excited for what lies ahead. Dopamine tells us what's important for survival, what matters, what's salient. Dopamine doesn't keep flowing after we start eating M&M's or using drugs; other neurochemicals, like endorphins and opioids, take over when we're indulging in our tenth M&M, or continuing the "habit" of drug use. But drugs of abuse put more dopamine into our synapses than normal feel-good reinforcers, like eating an M&M or having a good conversation.

Things that cause our brains to release the most dopamine, like alcohol and drugs, rapidly become vital and move to the top of our priority list, and with all of that dopamine being released, we are driven to obtain the object of our desire. Your child might want an M&M when he sees them at the grocery checkout stand because the dopamine is firing. But when someone addicted to drugs or alcohol sees her desired object, or is in the neighborhood where she usually buys drugs, or is around people who use drugs, or senses other environmental or personal cues that remind her of drugs, the amount of dopamine firing in her brain leading her to engage in the drug-seeking and drug-using behavior is about five to ten times greater than your child is experiencing when his eyes fall upon those M&M's in the grocery store. Because of the huge dopamine surge that we experience with drugs, they become more important than food and sex and other things we need to survive, even when they don't give us that much pleasure any longer and are simply a habit. Driven by a dopamine surge, we will do whatever it takes to get our fix.

Johnny is a patient of mine who, like the vast majority of people struggling with addiction, started using drugs as an adolescent. He's now in his early thirties. I look forward to seeing him. He's fun to talk with, tells good stories, and loves his wife, child, and extended family. But he has a hard time holding a job and being the father he wants to be because he can't seem to beat his heroin habit. It started with OxyContin and then progressed to heroin, which is cheaper and easier to find. Johnny's underlying problem is severe anxiety. He began using marijuana and cocaine off and on in his early teens. He eventually turned to opioids because he found they settled his social anxiety and the frequent stomachaches and diarrhea. He tells me that he no longer really even gets high from the heroin. He just takes it to feel "normal." If I had a nickel for every time I've heard a story like Johnny's, I'd be a very rich man.

Neurochemicals like dopamine are released from one neuron and land on another to pass messages along, but they can't land just anywhere. They can exert their effects only when they hit specific receptors or landing pads designed to receive that particular neurochemical. In the case of substance abuse, there are two types of dopamine receptors that really matter, D1 and D2. Stimulating dopamine D1 receptors turns on neurons and gives us a feel-good signal, teaching us about positive outcomes, as in "pay attention—this thing really matters." By contrast, stimulating dopamine D2 receptors turns off neurons and gives us a feel-bad signal, teaching us about negative outcomes, as in "pay attention—stay away from this thing." Dopamine's job is always to get us to pay attention to the good and the bad so that we do what's necessary for survival.

People who regularly use drugs, such as cocaine, amphetamines, heroin, and alcohol, have been repeatedly shown to have smaller numbers of dopamine D2 receptors in key brain areas involved in addiction. Fewer D2 receptors in the brains of people who abuse drugs means that they are less likely to learn about the negative consequences of drugs. They will get the positive feelings, driven by the D1 receptor activation, with less negative feeling due to their smaller number of D2 receptors. Fewer D2 receptors also means that the brain is less able to exert inhibitory control via the prefrontal cortex, the brain's CEO. In other words, fewer D2 receptors leads to more compulsive behavior, like drug use and other forms of addiction like gambling and overeating, and less "willpower" to stop the behavior. To boot, recall that increases in dopamine are five to ten times greater with drugs of abuse than with natural reinforcers, such as food and sex, so if we use drugs regularly, we quickly "learn" that they are our top priority.

Long-term substance abuse makes it harder to get high, just like my patient Johnny reports. Regular use of drugs and alcohol keeps our brains awash in dopamine, to which the brain eventually adapts (via a feedback mechanism) by decreasing the number of dopamine receptors. With more dopamine in the neural synapses, we just don't need as many D1 and D2 receptors to react with the circulating dopamine. In other words, over time people addicted to drugs and alcohol become less responsive to the drug because their brains become tolerant of the effects. Because they now have fewer D1 receptors, they get less feel-good signal from the drug; and because they have fewer D2 receptors, they get less feel-bad signal. This leads to the need for larger and larger doses of the drug to induce euphoria, along with the withdrawal effects that occur when they are without the drug for extended periods of time.

When we attribute drug addiction to a lack of personal resolve, we do adolescents and ourselves a big disservice. We will only be able to help our kids grow safely into successful adults if we acknowledge the powerful biological influences of dopamine and neural connectivity on our adolescents' behavior.

Mark Twain is often credited with saying, "When I was a boy of fourteen, my father was so ignorant I could hardly stand to have the old man around. But when I got to be twenty-one, I was astonished at how much the old man had learned in seven years." Given our current understanding of the brain, Mark Twain was a pretty optimistic guy. He suggested that by twenty-one years of age he understood his father a whole lot better than he did at fourteen. Unquestionably, that's true. But were Twain alive today he would know that the parts of the brain most important for planning, attention, memory, organization, and employing past experience in new situations to make good decisions—those prefrontal areas—are not fully networked with the lower-level emotional brain structures by twenty-one; rather, it appears to take until we are at least twenty-five or twenty-six before the connections between the CEO and emotional brain centers are firmly established.

In one form or another, we've known this fact for years. Automobile insurance rates drop by about 60 percent at the age of twenty-five, when, statistically, young adults become much safer drivers. This drastic change in car insurance rates isn't magical. It corresponds to the prefrontal cortex being more completely online and having the ability to control the impulsive drives of the limbic system. The dopamine reward and learning system, and common maladaptive behaviors of adolescence, such as a decrease in sleep and an increase in the use of caffeine and other substances, contribute mightily to the impairments in judgment that we commonly see during adolescence and early adulthood.

Concentrating when you're anxious, or taking control of depressive thoughts when you're sad, is really hard to do. But it's even harder when you're an adolescent because you just don't have the same ability an adult has to grab hold of emotions and limit their impact. With everything you now know, the stage is set for a more complete evolutionary understanding of how our brains and biology are, in fact, designed to promote risk-taking behavior in adolescence and early adulthood. Hold on to your hat—rough weather ahead.

CHAPTER 4

It Turns Out That Youth Is Not Wasted on the Young

(or, Why Adolescence Is Crucial to Evolution)

You see us as you want to see us—in the simplest terms, in the most convenient definitions. But what we found out is that each one of us is a brain . . . and an athlete . . . and a basket case . . . a princess . . . and a criminal. Does that answer your question?

—THE BREAKFAST CLUB

WALTER MISCHEL WANTED TO UNDERSTAND willpower. He had observed that those who delay gratification and resist immediate temptation in favor of long-term goals usually achieve more both socially and economically. Smokers quit the habit so they might enjoy a long life, and commuters buy a Ford instead of a Porsche to save for a comfortable retirement. How and when do willpower and impulsivity get established, he wondered. Enter the marshmallow test.

In 1960, Dr. Mischel, a psychologist, designed the first experiment with thirty-two children aged three to five years. Eventually over five hundred preschool boys and girls were studied throughout the 1960s and early 1970s. The participants were selected from Stanford University's

Bing Nursery and were mostly children of faculty and graduate students. The experimental task was very simple. Children were placed in a room and presented with two options: Enjoy one marshmallow (or sometimes a cookie or pretzel) now, or wait about fifteen minutes and enjoy two. The children were then left alone with a single marshmallow and observed via one-way mirror until the experimenter returned to the room. Some kids ate the marshmallow right away. Others petted the marshmallow, treated it like a stuffed animal, or sang a tune to their marshmallow before succumbing and popping the treat into their mouth. But for those who were able to wait through what must have been an interminable fifteen minutes for the experimenter to return without eating the treat, the rewards have turned out to be remarkable.

Hundreds of the children involved in the original marshmallow experiments have been followed into adulthood. And just like Aesop's fable about the tortoise and the hare, those who showed patience and persistence won the day. The ability to delay gratification at three, four, and five years of age predicted a host of beneficial outcomes. In childhood, these kids had higher self-esteem and were less physically and verbally aggressive and less likely to bully others. In adolescence, they managed stress better, using both cognitive and emotional skills, and scored higher on SAT exams. By adulthood, they were better educated and had better coping skills, higher self-worth, and less drug abuse.

Mischel and colleagues proposed a "hot and cold" system to explain why willpower works or fails in the marshmallow task and in life. The "cold" system is cognitive in nature, calculating, thinking, and always reflecting on the pros and cons of each decision. The "hot" system, by contrast, is quick, impulsive, and reflexive. In the most simple of terms, we can think of the cold system as the angel looking over your shoulder, while the hot system is the devil. Willpower fails, according to Mischel, when the impulsive hot system overrides the cool and calculating cognitive processes. And willpower is persistent and pervasive. Studying nearly sixty of these children forty years later as adults revealed that these patterns not only persisted into middle age, but also correlated with brain imaging findings. Among those with high self-control, the prefrontal cortex, the brain's CEO, was more active, while in those with poor self-control, the ventral striatum, the brain's reward center, was more active. The marshmallow test gives us a glimpse into who among us is more likely to take risks, and it also suggests that we might benefit by putting more effort into helping kids learn to self-regulate and manage their impulsivity.

Engineered for Success

The adolescent's brain is designed to make him a successful adolescent. In contrast to the adult brain, which becomes more rigid with age as myelination proceeds and white matter is increasingly laid down, the adolescent brain is more flexible in all regards. With all of that undifferentiated gray matter, the adolescent brain has yet to solidify into the adult it will one day become; and so its capacity for learning, creating, problem solving, and even taking risks is greatly enhanced.

Remember that the adolescent brain is more "plastic," open to learning new things, and more flexible in its approach to problem solving. Our adolescents and emerging adults will do amazing things. Albert Einstein was twenty-six years old when he published a three-page article that described the relationship between energy and mass known as $E = mc^2$. John Lennon was twenty-three and Paul McCartney twenty-one when the Beatles invaded America. Steve Jobs was twenty-one when he founded Apple, and Mark Zuckerberg was twenty when he launched Facebook. Many, perhaps most, of our greatest innovations come from young minds. The adolescent brain has been fine-tuned by evolution and is no accident. It's not an incomplete or insufficient adult brain. The adult brain is the gold standard for adults, not for adolescents.

The development of the limbic system or emotional brain at a young age makes good evolutionary sense for our species. Thousands of years ago when humans lived a shorter life span, the need to reproduce early, fight others for territory, and explore new lands and sources of food was paramount. Only an animal driven by a strong emotional calling would take such risks, and adolescents are the best suited for that job. They are strong, have an excellent immune system, tolerate temperature extremes, and can run faster and handle pain better than at any other time of life. Certainly, many adolescent humans have died because they were driven by their emotions to take risks, and we owe a great debt to these risk takers for allowing our species to live on. Without someone willing to kill an elephant for food or find new territory, we would have gone extinct long ago.

Sensation seeking is universal among mammals. This is probably because, as discussed in chapter 3, a large amount of our cerebral resources are devoted to making certain behaviors highly pleasurable and reinforcing, like eating and procreating, so that we will engage in these behaviors frequently. Remember that dopamine is released into our reward center, the ventral striatum, when we try something new that we like and each time thereafter when we anticipate that behavior. Not surprisingly, this effect is generally more pronounced in males, who tend to engage in more risky behavior than females. And since females among our species tend to mate at a younger age than males, it's also no surprise that dopamine peaks in females around sixteen years of age, and later in males, around nineteen. Because the dopamine system of an adolescent is at its pinnacle and will never be this responsive again, novelty really rocks their world.

Adolescents are always on the lookout for excitement. They like what's new and different. My teenage kids are always discovering new recording artists and watching the latest YouTube videos. They dive right into the current fads without a thought, whether that's skateboarding, social networking, planking, parkour, or clothing styles, and embrace risk more readily. This may be explained, at least in part, by new research findings suggesting that adolescents tolerate ambiguity better than adults and children; that is, adolescents may be more comfortable taking risks when they lack complete information and are uncertain about the possible outcomes. Regardless, some of us certainly like novelty more than others. This trait, like willpower, is probably genetic to some degree. But think about some of the things that you did as an adolescent or college student. Would you really hook up with that person today? Drive that fast? Drink that much alcohol at a party? Jump off of that rope swing into the lake? Probably not.

The fact is that evolution hasn't yet caught up with society. While the genus *Homo*, or "humans," has been around for 2.5 million years, we've only been living within civilized societies for about fifty thousand of those years, or about 2 percent of that time. Since humans evolve slowly, over many thousands of years, our adolescents are living in a modern society with a caveman brain. Sound about right? Today, it doesn't enhance our adolescents' prospects of survival to take a risk like driving a hundred miles per hour dodging cars on the freeway to win a race, but a hundred thousand years ago it did serve them to risk running across the savanna dodging dangerous wild animals in search of clean water. Our species has been successful in no small part thanks to the fact that during our adolescence, when we are at our physical peak and our most fertile, we are also most likely to take risks. Sure, some of the risk takers will be eaten by lions or die of exposure, but enough will survive to mate and bear children. These successful risk takers then drive culture—not only by passing on their genes, but also by providing an example that their peers and children may follow. Memes, or ideas and behaviors passed on via nongenetic means, powerfully change society by influencing the actions of others, who learn by imitation. Social media, popular music, and just about every other adolescent fad provide the pathway by which memes affect both adolescents and society at large.

Fear Factor

I think her name was Nina. We were fourteen and biking home side by side along a frontage road in my hometown. We were both counselors-in-training at the YMCA summer day camp and had been flirting for days, cracking jokes and eyeing one another with keen interest while taking groups of seven-year-olds on hikes or teaching the kids to craft lanyards. I remember how cute she looked on her ten-speed. We smiled warmly at each other while approaching my turnoff, me knowing that the best part of my day was coming to an end. As we crossed the railroad tracks, I turned my Schwinn to the left and waved good-bye, just like the day before. Freeze frame.

The motorcycle came out of nowhere. I could swear I had just looked left over my shoulder to make sure that no cars were coming, but there was that big silver and black Harley-Davidson all the same. The action stopped for about one second—I can still see myself sitting on the rim of that motorcycle, feel the headlamp breaking against my thigh, hear the female passenger's scream. And then I'm flying across the road, landing hard on my back on the railroad tracks, and rolling over and over and over. I stood up immediately and couldn't keep my legs still. They bounced from one side to the other like an unhinged spring. I brought my hands to my head to steady my vision, but everything was spinning as I walked aimlessly across the road back toward Nina, lucky not to be struck by an oncoming car.

Although I was flirting and distracted, from the moment that motorcycle hit me, I remember every detail of the accident like it was yesterday. As I was struck, my brain released loads of norepinephrine, a neurotransmitter important for mobilizing the body for fight or flight. And I was surely flying. My brain and body had released so much norepinephrine that it spilled over, causing a great increase in my heart rate and blood pressure, widening my pupils, sending vast amounts of blood to my muscles, and causing my digestion to slow way down. (This was no time for a visit to the bathroom.) This burst of norepinephrine caused a permanently indelible "flashbulb memory" in my amygdala, the brain's threat detection center. Just like dopamine triggers a salience response (e.g., "this thing matters!") in the ventral striatum so that I'll learn to prioritize those things for survival, norepinephrine triggers a threat response in the neighboring amygdala so that I'll learn what to be fearful of and avoid. Flashbulb memories occur when we experience an event loaded with high emotion. Think about the day the Twin Towers fell or John Lennon was assassinated. You know just where you were and what you were doing—that's a flashbulb memory.

The really incredible thing is that I'm not even sure the girl's name was Nina. Not that she wasn't important to me at the time, but decades later I honestly can't be sure of her name. What I can be sure of is the fact that I've always looked twice over my shoulder ever since that accident when making a left-hand turn. Along with the abrasions to my left thigh, which resulted in scars to this day, I chipped my ankle, which remained swollen for nearly a year. That flashbulb event has had a permanent impact upon how I behave to this day and may have even saved my life during some subsequent left turn I made somewhere while piloting a bicycle, car, boat, or motorcycle. Today, it doesn't really matter what her name was. Recalling her name is of no value, compared to remembering to look twice over my left shoulder.

Fear has a special place in our lives. Housed within the subcortical amygdala, the brain's threat detection center develops early and is only loosely managed by the prefrontal cortex during adolescence, just like the ventral striatum's reward center. You know how you sometimes see something out of the corner of your eye that just freaks you out, like a spider on the toilet seat as you're about to sit down? That's your amygdala responding immediately to something picked up in your visual field and telling you that you're at risk. As you jump back and turn your gaze directly onto the object, a second passes, during which time your pre-frontal cortex takes over, analyzes the situation, and tells you that it's just a ball of lint. Ah, relax, you can sit down.

Being able to detect threat really matters. An animal can postpone rewards like sex and food and sleep for days, but it can't postpone a response to danger for even a second without placing itself at great risk. Children as young as three recognize snakes more easily on a computer screen than flowers. This negativity bias suggests that we are more attuned to threatening than pleasurable experiences, and my bike ride with Nina, or whatever her name was, is case in point. We need to remember those things that threaten us so that we can avoid them in the future. And not surprisingly, once adolescents are threatened by something, they have a much harder time unlearning that threat association than the rest of us. Studies of both mice and human adolescents show that once they learn something is a threat, they don't tend to forget it, even after they age into adulthood. By contrast, preadolescent and adult mice and humans have a much easier time forgetting or at least disregarding something that once threatened them in the past. Since our adolescents were evolutionarily the first-line explorers, and remain our first-line soldiers in the armed forces, this characteristic infers a great evolutionary advantage. Threatening experiences form memories that adolescents will hold on to for a long, long time. Remember—always look twice over your shoulder when turning left.

Adolescents are also more responsive to threat in laboratory experiments than children and adults are. Brain imaging confirms that the adolescent amygdala, or threat detection center, is more active when they are shown possibly dangerous cues like a fearful facial expression. It's remarkable that at the same time that adolescents are more reactive to threat, they are, paradoxically, drawn to the very things that frighten them. Do you still like horror movies, roller coasters, and popping wheelies or biking with no hands? Probably not so much, but I'll bet your adolescents do.

It's hard to know why adolescents are drawn to threats. Maybe they're driven so strongly by dopamine and the search for rewards that it overrides their fears at certain times. Alternatively, maybe they're trying to master their fears, practicing with threat, so that they will be successful adults. Some research, in fact, suggests that in the same way that adolescents are more driven by the potential promise of reward (via activation of the ventral striatum), they are also driven by stronger threat cues (via activation of the amygdala). This finding implies not that adolescents are fearless, but rather that they approach threat more readily because it's simply more exciting. In other words, they like the feeling of trying to overcome their fears. By seeing threat ambiguously, with features of both fear and reward, adolescents may be more drawn to trying new things.

Evolution is not perfect, however, and sometimes things go awry. The rates of anxiety and depression skyrocket during adolescence, possibly driven by the relative hyperactivity of the amygdala, which induces fear, and the relative passivity of the prefrontal cortex, which exerts emotional control. This same uncoupling of the subcortical and prefrontal structures is also observed among adults with depression, anxiety disorders, and post-traumatic stress disorder. To a lesser extent, we see the same thing when we don't get enough sleep; the prefrontal cortex just can't manage all of that emotional information as well, which leads us to feeling irritable, anxious, and sad.

You're Soaking in It

If you were an alien from a distant planet landing on Earth for the first time and happened to find yourself amidst a group of middle school students, your senses would go into hyperdrive. At a distance you'd notice the facial acne, dental braces, and fanciful hairstyles. As you came closer, you would be startled by the remarkably strong scent of body odor. Now near enough to hear the conversation, you might surmise that the words "like," "um," and "you know" were praise to some sort of a god, as they find themselves into every single utterance. No, my extraterrestrial visitor, this is no spiritual coming-of-age. It's called adolescence, and it's driven entirely by hormones.

As our children approach puberty, glands throughout the body begin to release various chemical messengers, or hormones, that travel to distant locations and exert their effects over the days, weeks, and months that follow. Ultimately, this cascade of triggering hormones leads to the production of the principal sex hormones. We're tempted to think that testosterone makes us aggressive, and estrogen makes us sensitive. But hormones aren't so black and white. Instead, research now shows that pubertal hormones induce a whole series of brain changes that tune adolescents into the social zeitgeist. By soaking our kids' brains in hormones, evolution hooks teens into the social order so that they will work to gain the respect of their peers and improve their status.

We all know that social success is where it's at for adolescents. Without at least some degree of peer admiration, they will lack the community support necessary to help them find food, identify a suitable mate, build a home, and raise children. Hormones are essential to this process. As we now understand it, testosterone's job isn't to make adolescents aggressive. Instead, testosterone is a social hormone that makes adolescents more concerned with *how they're perceived by others*. While it's true that boys the world over compete for social status through athletics and intimidation of other boys, culture frames this behavior as well. One way to achieve status in Tibetan Buddhist monasteries,

> Testosterone is a social hormone that makes adolescents more concerned with *how they're perceived by others*.

a colleague once shared with me, is by striving to be more kind and compassionate than the other boys. So testosterone isn't about aggression. It's about affiliation and social success. It may promote antisocial behavior when social status is enhanced by joining a gang of juvenile delinquents. Likewise, it may promote prosocial behavior when social status is enhanced by being kind and compassionate.

Hormones themselves don't change our behavior, but they do provide opportunities for us to learn how to be successful in our environment. If you skip lunch, for example, it's likely that you'll be pretty hungry by midafternoon. The blood levels of leptin, a hormone that tells your body it's satisfied with your food intake, drop if you don't eat; while the blood levels of grehlin, a hormone that tells your body it's hungry, increase if you don't eat. The combined effect of a high level of grehlin (which increases your appetite) and a low level of leptin (which makes your stomach feel empty) tells your brain that you'd better start looking around for food. Ghrelin and leptin don't make you eat, but the increase in hunger and decrease in fullness that you feel from skipping a meal sure makes it more likely that you will search out something to eat. In just the same way, pubertal hormones like testosterone and oxytocin make adolescents more likely to pay attention to certain types of information, like social status and peer bonding.

How happy are you when you find that you've been seated next to a mother and her crying baby on a plane? Not very, I'm guessing. Unless you've currently got babies at home yourself, you're likely to do everything possible to change your seat. Males and virgin females of many species tend to avoid newborns altogether and find all infant stimuli extremely aversive. Yet somehow we find our own babies, and all of their little burps and squeals, simply irresistible. Oxytocin is the powerful hormone responsible for the emotional reward we feel from being with our children and the lack of disgust with aspects of them that we would usually find distasteful, like poop.

Most of us know that oxytocin causes uterine contractions during childbirth and thereafter aids in milk letdown for nursing the newborn. Perhaps you've also heard oxytocin referred to as the "love hormone" because of its role in helping animals bond with one another. While it's no love potion, it's true that oxytocin enhances ventral striatal activity (or increases reward) and inhibits amygdala activity (or decreases threat) among parents in response to the cries of their infant, which makes us more empathic to our children and leads to a stronger attachment between parent and child. Oxytocin also fosters our trust in others. When parents advise their adolescents not to have sex, they aren't thinking of oxytocin; rather, they're worried that if their children have sex with someone, they will lose perspective and reorder their priorities in life. Well, it turns out that moms and dads understand a good deal about human nature because we now know that sexual activity does increase oxytocin in the brain, which encourages love and attraction to our partners and makes us more likely to invest in those relationships.

Look, I didn't want a Chihuahua. I grew up with Dalmatians, a big black Labrador, and a golden retriever. But when Alice and I moved our family to an apartment in New York City, we promised our kids a small dog. The idea of a Chihuahua never even crossed my mind, but from the moment I held our new puppy, Elliot, in my arms and he stared at me with those big brown eyes, I fell deeply and madly in love. Like humans, dogs use mutual visual gaze to connect and bond. Even though dogs have much smaller brains than humans, their visual system has become highly sophisticated over the past fifteen-thousand-plus years of domestication, exploiting a classically human characteristic to help them bond with us. Dogs' use of mutual visual gaze is, in fact, much more like that of humans' than that of their closest animal relative, the wolf. Gazing into Elliot's eyes increases both his and my level of circulating oxytocin, which helps us to establish and maintain our emotional bond. The relationship between humans and dogs is mutually beneficial—they warn and protect us from possible predators, we feed and shelter them, and together we share affection.

It makes good evolutionary sense that we would share a hormonal mechanism by which to create such an attachment. Similarly, it's evolutionarily advantageous for oxytocin to be at its peak during adolescence because this is the time of life when establishing and maintaining close bonds with peers most strongly supports survival. (By the way, our other most common mammalian pets, cats, have lived with us for only about five thousand years, which helps to explain why they are generally more aloof, maintain less direct eye contact, and feel less bonded to us than our canine cousins.)

The bonding effect of oxytocin is most evident during adolescence in helping us determine who is "in" and who is "out" of the peer group by alerting us to social signals. Similar to testosterone, which cues adolescents into the social order, oxytocin increases our empathy and trust for members of our peer group, but increases aggression and defensiveness toward members outside of our peer group. In other words, oxytocin's bonding effect fuels adolescent cliques and friendships—who's in and who's out.

Adolescents depend upon establishing solid peer relations for their current and future survival, much more so than do children and adults. By enhancing the rewarding effects of social cues and peer group interaction, testosterone and oxytocin focus adolescents' attention on the factor that will most help them to be successful adults—their relations with fellow adolescents. Life is a team sport, and those who succeed find effective ways to partner with peers. At the same time that testosterone and oxytocin are spiking and teaching adolescents to connect more effectively with one another, however, other hormones are making them feel more stressed out.

The hypothalamic-pituitary-adrenal (HPA) axis circulates greater amounts of naturally occurring steroid hormones, like cortisol, during adolescence than in childhood or adulthood. Cortisol is released when the body is under stress or when blood sugar supplies are low. Along with increases in adrenaline, stress hormones act on the amygdala, hippocampus, and frontal lobes, enhancing fear learning, memory, and the importance that adolescents place on their emotions. Like the elevated levels of testosterone and oxytocin, which aid in social connectivity, a heightened stress response during adolescence makes good evolutionary sense. Teens must be alerted to environmental threats in order to become successful adults. Good relationships with peers, aided by testosterone and oxytocin, thankfully, can buffer the stress response by lowering cortisol, which helps adolescents to manage their anxiety and boost their resilience.

Unfortunately, adolescents raised in poverty, in addition to those whose mothers are chronically depressed, show much higher, even toxic, levels of stress hormones that can result in memory impairment and reduce the prefrontal cortex's ability to calm the amygdala, the brain's threat detection center. Such chronic high levels of stress hormones also saddle these individuals with an increased risk for depression, obesity, cancer, and cardiovascular disease as they age.

Any parent can tell you that their adolescents have more difficulty maintaining their attention on a given task, like homework, in the presence of emotionally distracting stimulation, like a cell phone—even when the kids themselves find the distraction unwelcome. Although it's a thrill for all kids when they get their first cell phone, by about sixteen or seventeen years old they often start to lament the fact that they are now saddled with the constant awareness of their peers. They recognize the enormous burden in managing all of that social information available at their fingertips via Facebook, Instagram, and Snapchat, knowing who is doing what, where, when, and with whom. My daughter and son and scores of adolescent patients and college students have told me time and time again that they would be happy to grow up in a world without cell phones.

That's pretty levelheaded of them because, as you now know, pubertal hormones make teen and young adult brains super tuned into the emotional information in the environment, even if they don't yet understand it all, which, once again, makes perfect evolutionary sense. All mammals have an adolescence, during which time they experience heightened sensitivity to rewards and threats, greater interest in sensation-seeking behavior, and intensified emotional reactions to peers. These brain and behavioral changes are necessary to facilitate the exploratory behavior that will help them survive and procreate, but they can be really exhausting.

Hormones influence us in different ways depending upon the situation and context. If you're a good student who makes friends easily, testosterone and oxytocin will help you affiliate with like-minded peers. Together, you will find connection with and comfort from one another and are even likely to help stop each other from taking too many risks. If you're not so good at school or sports or trombone or some other skill that boosts your self-confidence and helps you connect with others, and if you're enough of a sensation seeker, these hormones will prime you for risk-taking behaviors—because adolescents will do whatever it takes to build meaningful connections with peers.

> Adolescents will do whatever it takes to build meaningful connections with peers.

Sensation seekers tend to find one another, and when you get a bunch of them in one place, the social environment they create favors risk taking. Remember those kids in high school who were always in trouble, regularly suspended from school, and getting high before class? In middle school they might have been cool, but by the last few years of high school, the blush was off of the rose. It was no longer cool to be failing classes and selling weed. You knew that few of these kids were headed for great futures, and so you backed away from them, even if you'd been friends for years. They themselves eventually became so disengaged from the mainstream crowd that they began to associate risk-taking behavior with positive affect and good emotions. Bad behavior was the only way for them to feel confident and admired by their ever-shrinking group of peers. Risky behavior was not just exciting. It was the most desirable thing possible. Just ask any teenager who the "stoners" or "pot-heads" are at their high school; who has been arrested for theft; or who has gotten pregnant. They will tell you that it's the kids who don't do well in school, who aren't good athletes, and who don't develop other skills that give them the self-confidence and peer admiration that will help them succeed in life.

Precocious Puberty

When my son was about seven years old, he faced a real dilemma. On the heels of losing a tooth and receiving a lovely note and a dollar from the tooth fairy, Julian was told by some kids at school that the whole tooth fairy thing was a hoax. He came home distressed. That night as he was going to bed, he looked up at me with tears in his eyes. "Dad," he said, starting to weep, "some of the kids say that the tooth fairy isn't real. I really need to know. Is the tooth fairy for real?" These are the moments that you're not prepared for as a parent. They come out of the blue, and neither my child psychiatry training nor my own childhood memories clearly pointed me in the right direction. By the seat of my pants, then.

"Julian," I asked back, "what kind of a world do you want to live in? One filled with magic and wonder and excitement? Or one where everything is clearly spelled out and nothing is left to the imagination?" Julian looked at me so earnestly. He really thought about my question. Then through big, flowing tears, he said, "I want to live in a world with magic and wonder, but I also want to know the real truth." Well, there you have it—the essential human dilemma, and out of the mouths of babes! "So what do we do, then?" I asked. And here's where my boy just hit it out of the park. "Dad," he implored, "how about you don't tell me yet, but we just wait until I'm sixteen. If I don't know by then, do you promise to tell me?" I made my promise and kissed my son a hundred times.

Julian's struggle is so familiar because we all wrestle with growing up. Maturation is filled with novelty and excitement, but it's also replete with challenges and risks. Adolescence is a time of transition, heralded by the whirlwind of pubertal hormones and subsequent changes in our bodies and minds. It's during transitions that we face our greatest risks, when we feel most unsteady on our feet and unsure of ourselves. Julian wanted to grow up and know the truth, but somehow he also knew that he was still seven years old and perhaps not quite ready for the whole story. Maintaining his belief in the tooth fairy allowed him to stay a child a bit longer, and even though he didn't know the "real truth," he felt safe within his innocence, with a parent agreeing to protect and shepherd him. Unfortunately, these days adolescence is hitting children earlier and earlier, limiting the number of years that they can rest within the safety of their childhood.

Children are reaching puberty at a younger age than in generations past. Puberty in girls starts with the development of breasts, progressing to armpit and pubic hair, facial acne, a growth spurt, and ultimately menstruation. In boys, puberty begins with enlargement of the testes and penis, progressing to armpit and pubic hair, facial acne, a deepening voice, and a growth spurt. Puberty generally lasts about two to four years and technically ends with sexual maturation. Girls usually experience puberty between about ten and fourteen years of age. Boys typically go through the process a few years later, between twelve and sixteen years of age. Very early puberty, or "precocious puberty," is ten times more common in girls than boys and is diagnosed when secondary sexual characteristics (like breast budding or armpit and pubic hair growth) occur before eight years of age or menarche (onset of the menstrual period) begins prior to age nine. Just twenty-five years ago, fewer than 5 percent of girls began puberty before eight; that percentage has now doubled. One recent multisite study within the United States found even higher rates—more than 10 percent of white girls had started growing breasts by age seven, along with nearly 25 percent of black girls and 15 percent of Hispanic girls. By age eight, these percentages had nearly doubled. This is a major shift in the timing of puberty.

Puberty starts when a neurochemical called kisspeptin stimulates a series of hormones that ultimately result in the release of estrogen and testosterone. Kisspeptin itself is stimulated by leptin, a hormone, as previously described, best known for letting us know when we've been satiated, or are satisfied with our food intake. Leptin is produced by fat cells. The more fat we have, the more leptin we produce. Virtually all developed countries currently face an obesity epidemic. In the United States, rates of obesity have doubled among children and quadrupled among adolescents in the past thirty years. In 2012, over one-third of children and adolescents were overweight or obese. Obesity is a major contributor to the early release of kisspeptin, which starts puberty. And yet, there's more.

Just as leptin stimulates kisspeptin and heralds puberty, so does melatonin inhibit kisspeptin and puberty. Melatonin, a hormone best known for making us sleepy, is released in the absence of light and blocked by the presence of light. Children growing up near the equator, where they are exposed to more sunlight throughout the year and consequently have lower levels of melatonin, reach puberty earlier than children in northern and southern climes where they are exposed to less sunlight. Another probable contributor to early puberty among children today, then, is the near constant exposure to light emitted by the many screens they view. The light emitted from a cell phone or computer screen or television is sufficiently powerful to block a large percentage of the melatonin our children produce, thereby disinhibiting kisspeptin, which is then free to start the puberty hormone cascade earlier than intended. And as if obesity and screen time were not enough, there are many other factors that are almost certain contributors to early puberty.

Endocrine-disrupting chemicals are man-made products that can mimic or block natural hormones, thereby altering the body's normal hormonal functioning. Many endocrine disrupters can act just like estrogens and contribute to early puberty. Pesticides (e.g., DDT), various chemicals found in plastics (e.g., phthalates, BPA), PCBs, and dioxins are but a few of the many products at fault. These chemicals are found in everything from plastic water bottles to dental sealants to baby bottles to food packaging to skin and hair care products. Our children absorb endocrine disrupters when they eat, drink, or apply products that have been stored within these containers. Additionally, psychosocial stressors, such as poverty, peer pressure, exposure to violence and bullying, and having a primary caregiver with a mood disorder, have also been suggested to act as endocrine disrupters. (Impoverished parents are more likely to give birth to premature babies, for example, which leads to higher blood levels of insulin within the infant, which itself can contribute to premature weight gain and increase the likelihood of earlier puberty.)

Regardless of what is causing the increase in early and precocious puberty, the problems for affected children are real. Research shows that girls who mature earlier are at increased risk of lower self-esteem and higher rates of depression. They are also more influenced by older and more deviant peers and have sex and abuse drugs and alcohol at younger ages. The problems don't stop with adolescents, however. Adult women who matured early also have higher rates of depression, a larger number of sexual partners, and lower academic achievement. In addition, they face a higher risk of breast, ovarian, and endometrial cancer as they age, given their additional years of hormone exposure, along with higher rates of obesity and high blood pressure.

At the end of the day, children who hit puberty early will spend more years with an active limbic system and an immature prefrontal cortex. They will struggle to understand and rein in their emotions for more years, extending their adolescence and placing them at risk for a longer period of time. But most importantly, they will be forced to reckon with the emotional instability of puberty and the subsequent risks of adolescence long before they're ready.

The Trade-off

Without a doubt, the same instincts and patterns of brain development that led our species to be so successful eons ago actually threaten many of our adolescents today. Our hormonally driven, fiery limbic system and immature prefrontal cortex make adolescents highly responsive to strong emotions and once upon a time drove them to explore new territories and fight wild beasts. Terrific. But by and large, we no longer need to fight animals. So why have these traits persisted? It's not just that evolution takes its time. It's that the same risky behaviors that threaten our adolescents also impart to them advantages for survival. We are part of an evolutionary process that cares little for the individual but greatly for the species. Evolution will, in other words, sacrifice thousands to save millions. Nature is replete with examples of such evolutionary trade-offs, like sickle-cell anemia and malaria.

Sickle-cell anemia results when a child inherits two affected genes, one from each parent. Although nearly one hundred thousand people in the United States suffer from sickle-cell anemia, another 3 million carry the sickle-cell trait (about one in twelve black Americans), meaning that they have only one inherited gene that produces sickle cells, from a single parent. Sickle-cell anemia causes the red blood cells to take the shape of a sickle, or crescent, limiting the amount of oxygen the cells can carry, causing the cells to cluster and stick together, and leading to early cell death. People affected by sickle-cell anemia suffer chronic pain, carry a high risk of infections and stroke, and have an average life expectancy of around forty years, about half the American average.

If sickle-cell anemia is so destructive, why does it remain today? Even carrying the trait causes some health problems for those affected. Well, it turns out that the sickle-cell gene confers a huge advantage upon those who carry it, which probably accounts for why it has stayed with us. Although those afflicted with the full-blown disease commonly die young, those with the sickle-cell trait have at least a partial resistance to the most severe form of malaria. The malarial parasite (*Plasmodium falciparum*) cannot remodel the red blood cells as required for its continued propagation within a sickle-cell hemoglobin. Resistance to the *Plasmodium falciparum* parasite is a big deal because even with all of our efforts at prevention, to this day malaria kills more children worldwide than any other infectious disease, five times more than HIV/AIDS.

Similarly, cystic fibrosis, an illness that primarily affects the lungs and pancreas and typically results in chronic infections and premature death, occurs when a child inherits two affected genes, one from each parent. As with sickle-cell anemia, we believe that cystic fibrosis remains in our gene pool because individuals with only one affected gene have enhanced resistance to a severe illness, in this case typhoid fever, which killed many of our ancestors. So even though sickle-cell anemia and cystic fibrosis result in much disability and often an early death, they have persisted throughout our species' evolutionary history because these genes also provide a survival advantage to those who carry them. In its typically detached and impersonal fashion, evolution seems to have determined that our species is better off if some of us suffer and die from sickle-cell anemia and cystic fibrosis than if more of us die from malaria and typhoid fever.

The serotonin gene has a similar story. The gene comes in two forms—long and short. Those who have one or two copies of the short gene transporter have more depressive symptoms, diagnosable depression, and suicidal behavior in response to stressful life events. Having the short version is also associated with less prefrontal cortical control over the amygdala, the brain's threat detection center. This leads to greater fear responses, an increased likelihood of post-traumatic stress disorder, and a less favorable response to antidepressant medications among adults with one or two copies of the short serotonin gene. So why in the world would the short serotonin gene survive the many thousands of years of human evolution?

First, two long serotonin genes make you more vulnerable to pulmonary hypertension, a relatively rare but often deadly illness. Second, and more importantly, animals with one short serotonin gene may have a reproductive advantage. It turns out that, at least among rhesus macaques, a close relative of humans, those with short serotonin genes leave the nest early. Although leaving home early may be risky, it also gives those who depart a head start in finding new food sources, nesting areas, and mates, thereby making them more likely to reproduce and pass on their genes. So here again, evolution appears to have made a trade-off— those who leave the nest early may be at greater risk of emotional disturbance and more likely to get physically hurt before they are mature enough to fully protect themselves, but they also have a greater probability of finding a mate and reproducing.

The Most Valuable Player

Even though we reach our physical prime during adolescence, it's only as adults, when our brains are fully mature, that we perform our best. Take baseball, for instance. The most important person on the team is the pitcher. Every play starts with the ball literally in his hands. He calculates the risk of which pitch to throw, and how fast, depending on which batter. Just like the rest of us, pitchers hit their physical peak during adolescence. A pitcher in his early twenties will throw a ball faster than a pitcher in his early thirties. The younger pitcher will also recuperate quicker between games and suffer fewer injuries. But the younger player isn't the one you want on the pitcher's mound during a major league game.

Jeremy Affeldt is a left-handed relief pitcher who played in four World Series and won three of them. The Kansas City Royals drafted him straight out of high school in 1997. He later played for the Colorado Rockies and the Cincinnati Reds, and then in 2009 he was traded to the San Francisco Giants, where he was a member of the World Series championship teams of 2010, 2012, and 2014. Jeremy told me that he threw his fastest when he was twenty-four, while playing in Cincinnati. "I would hit ninety-seven, ninety-eight, even ninety-nine miles per hour sometimes during that year," he told me. But Jeremy also told me that he pitched *his best* when he was twenty-nine and thirty. "Why," I asked, "did you pitch better when you were older?" "It's all a head game," he said. "Early in my career, I threw whatever pitch the catcher told me," but as the years went by, he explained, he learned more about the game, more about the batters, and more about what he was and wasn't capable of. He would trust in his experience and intuition. In other words, he learned to use not only his left arm in throwing a pitch, but also his understanding of how players think. "If I stare at the catcher before I throw the ball, for example, the batter doesn't know if I'm shaking off the catcher's pitch or if I'm just thinking. He doesn't know what's going on." Jeremy also told me that strikeouts shouldn't be a pitcher's primary goal. "I know everybody likes them," he said, "but they're overrated because you throw too many pitches to strike out all those batters and then you can't be available to pitch the next day."

Jeremy Affeldt speaks about baseball like an adult, not an adolescent. When he was a younger player, he spent most of his time on the bench, even though he could throw plenty fast. But with age, his planning, problem solving, focus, and patience grew much better, even if he threw a bit slower. This is precisely why the average age of baseball pitchers runs from a low of twenty-seven on the Houston Astros to a high of thirty-one on the Boston Red Sox. Although an adolescent can throw a ball with greater speed, the thirty-year-old pitcher can rely upon experience, use strategy better, anticipate what a batter is expecting, and ultimately deliver a more successful pitch. It is the older pitcher's ability to use the now well-myelinated frontal lobes of the brain to control his limbic emotional centers that makes him a better pitcher and the man you want on your team.

Similarly, National Football League quarterbacks, undoubtedly the most important player on the team, average twenty-seven years of age. Even in football, one of our most physically taxing sports, the team leader plays best when his brain has fully matured, despite being past his physical prime. Tom Brady, Joe Montana, Peyton Manning, John Elway, Roger Staubach, and many other quarterbacks had their best years when they were well into their thirties.

As adolescents, we can run fast, jump high, and fight hard. We are engineered to be physically resilient and are built for taking risks so that our species will survive. From an evolutionary perspective, the power of adolescence lies in its gutsiness, brawn, and willingness to take a chance. But whether we're talking about pitchers or quarterbacks, doctors or presidents, you don't want an adolescent in charge—because even though our strength, speed, and endurance diminish with age, our decision making vastly improves.

Adolescent risk-taking behavior is no accident. Our brains and bodies are primed for it by evolution. Adolescents are exquisitely designed to explore willingly where few adults would ever choose to roam. Thousands of years ago, many of our adolescent ancestors died when they wandered off of well-trodden trails chasing down an animal for food or searching for fresh water. They died eating poisonous plants that they mistakenly thought were edible. Such new experiences would have excited these early sensation seekers. For those who returned victorious with food for their families, there would be peer admiration. Like today's professional athletes, they would be highly regarded, favored as mates, and more likely to pass on their risk-taking genes. Every society admires courage and bravery.

Today our adolescents take many unnecessary risks, but the sensation seeking, hormonally charged social status seeking, and unbridled limbic system remain alive and well. More than two thousand years ago, Aristotle wrote that adolescents' "hot tempers and hopeful dispositions make them more courageous than older men are." Based upon what we know today, however, Aristotle would almost certainly amend those words by suggesting that adolescents feel great fear and do risky things anyway because of the potential for reward and peer admiration. We must understand that when our adolescents engage in risky behavior, they're responding to an ages-old instinct they're not aware of.

> When our adolescents engage in risky behavior, they're responding to an ages-old instinct they're not aware of.

Not long ago, I had another bedtime conversation with my now sixteen-year-old son. He was finishing his second year of high school and feeling frustrated and a bit overwhelmed by all of the academic and social pressures. "What," he asked me, "is the real point of all this homework and stressing us kids out?" The point, I told him, is to run into bumps and hurdles like geometry and global history and dating and auditioning for the school play and trying out for the basketball team and to emerge not always victorious, but alive. You won't get an A, make the team, or get the girl every time, but you will learn that you can take a hit and keep on slugging.

It's probably true, I agreed, that geometry proofs have little value for most kids later in life. Knowledge of geometry will probably make only a modest contribution to my son's spatial understanding and logic, and it's pretty unlikely that he will become a mathematician. But in geometry class you don't learn about just Euclid's theorems. By dealing with difficult subjects and, often, difficult teachers, collaborating with peers, and pushing yourself to do something that you thought was nearly impossible, you learn self-efficacy and emotional self-regulation—and that has all the value in the world. The adolescent years give our children the opportunity to enhance their willpower by learning to deal with meaningful challenges. And the benefits of willpower and discipline, as the marshmallow test has proven, are enormous for our kids' futures.

So it turns out that youth really isn't wasted on the young. They need that strength, speed, agility, immune system, peer awareness and bonding, and risk-taking behavior to become successful adults. It turns out, rather, that adolescence is just right for adolescents.

CHAPTER 5

Picked Last for Kickball

(or, The Real Skinny on Peer Pressure)

It takes a great deal of bravery to stand up to our enemies, but just as much to stand up to our friends.

—ALBUS DUMBLEDORE
(J. K. ROWLING, *Harry Potter and the Sorcerer's Stone*)

THERE ISN'T A SINGLE ONE among us who cannot remember that anxious feeling of standing in a lineup on the playground waiting to be picked for a kickball game during recess. Likewise, we all know the uneasy feeling of standing awkwardly in the high school gym waiting to be asked to dance. The strongest and most courageous among us don't wait—they insist on being the team captains who select the other kids, or they don't wait to be asked to dance but instead ask others to dance or just dance by themselves because they simply want to dance. But let's face it—most of us aren't that strong or courageous. We wait.

We wait and we wait and we worry. What others think of us affects just about everything we do throughout our entire lives, and although it dims somewhat, thankfully, with age and maturity, the impact of peer pressure and the importance that we place on peers' evaluation of us never entirely ceases. But its effect on us as adolescents is a whole other story. Not surprisingly, in the transition from preadolescence to adolescence, both boys and girls report a major increase in emotional distress.

Parents have lots of ideas and assumptions about why their kids experience more negative moods and intense emotions as they course through puberty. We witness these changes acutely as our kids reach middle school and throughout high school and their early twenties. Adolescents' heightened sensitivity to rewards and threats, greater interest in sensation-seeking behavior, and hormonally driven increased awareness of peers, as discussed in chapter 4, are real and have a major impact. Stressful events are also correlated with adolescence, but it's not clear which comes first—the increasingly stressful things that happen as we age, along with our ability to better understand their meaning, or the fact that we take on more stressful responsibilities as we get older. Likewise, a dysphoric mood may lead adolescents to have dysphoric experiences, or dysphoric experiences may cause a dysphoric mood. Similarly, studies have shown that sad and moody teens spend more time alone, but then again spending excessive time alone makes kids feel sad and moody. Although all of these factors undoubtedly contribute to the increase in emotion that we witness as our kids age, when we ask adolescents themselves about what changes during these years, they focus on one single thing.

According to adolescents, friends are the source of the greatest increase in negative emotion as both boys and girls age from "tweens" to teens. Although the combined effects of family, school, and extracurricular activities account for most preteen and teen anxiety, it is the stress of peer relationships that shows the greatest increase in intensity from preadolescence to adolescence, generally taking our kids by surprise, while family, school, and extracurricular stresses remain fairly constant or even decrease somewhat. As adolescents age and their brains grow, dopamine neurons begin to synapse within the frontal cortex in great numbers. It is during these years, then, that intellectual material becomes more engaging for teens, even pleasurable, and they start to appreciate the problems of the world, show much greater empathy for others, and think more broadly and less concretely. Nearly one hundred years before we knew about the importance of dopamine neurons, the limbic system, and the frontal cortex, however, behavioral observations had suggested that abstract thought lay at the heart of the increase in adolescent stress.

We Need the Eggs

Following upon the heels of Sigmund Freud's psychosexual theory of development and Erik Erikson's psychosocial theory of development, Swiss psychologist Jean Piaget (1896–1980) posited a cognitive model of development. According to Piaget, children mature through four stages in the growth of their ability to think, culminating in the "formal operational" phase, which for most adolescents occurs around the mid-teen years, at which point they can think in an abstract fashion. Thinking abstractly has great advantages. But in the words of Spider-Man's uncle Ben, "with great power comes great responsibility." Sure, our kids now know more. As adolescents, they can think more for themselves. Great. But because of our species' überstrong evolutionary drive to procreate during the adolescent years, they also care a whole lot more about what their peers think and how they interact. Consequently, adolescents get much more stressed by their friends.

In a 1989 study of more than four hundred fifth- through ninth-grade students who were signaled (by pager) to report on their thoughts, activities, and emotional states at random times throughout the day for one week, boys found friendships to be about three times more stressful as they grew into adolescents, while girls experienced nearly a doubling in stress caused by friendships. A closer look at this data shows that almost all of this increase in stress was due to feelings about individuals of the opposite sex. Hurt, disappointment, anguish, distress, worry, anger, guilt, jealousy, and frustration during these years are most commonly a result of situations involving a desired "other," be they real relationships or fantasized ones. Predictably, friends also provide the greatest increase in positive emotions during these years. So even though adolescents are often distressed by their friendships, by and large they continue to get enough "good" out of their peer relations to keep them intensely engaged with one another.

In the final moments of Woody Allen's movie masterpiece *Annie Hall*, he tells an old joke about a man who tells his psychiatrist about his brother, who thinks he's a chicken. When asked why he doesn't bring his brother in for treatment, the man says, "I would but I need the eggs." Allen's character then likens this joke to the trade-offs we so often make in relationships: "They're totally irrational and crazy and absurd, but I guess we keep going through it because most of us need the eggs."

Growing from children into adolescents over a relatively short period of just a few years, boys and girls make a similar trade-off, going from running away from each other on the playground for fear of cooties to being adolescents who "need the eggs"—seek out the good stuff—of intimate relationships. Their increased ability to think abstractly is essential in this transformation. But with all of the gifts and responsibilities of abstract thought also comes confusion, what psychologists call "cognitive distortions."

Thinking Errors

In the late 1950s, University of Pennsylvania psychiatrist Aaron Beck, MD, set up a series of studies of depressed adults designed to test the effectiveness of psychoanalysis as a primary treatment. Beck was trained as a psychoanalyst and was committed to the theoretical foundations of Freud's "talking cure." To his great surprise and disappointment, however, the experiments failed to validate the treatment. By the early '60s, Beck had penned two important articles on "thinking and depression," which ultimately led to the development of cognitive behavioral therapy (currently the premier evidence-based psychotherapeutic treatment for anxiety and depression in both adolescents and adults) and the design of the cognitive triangle, as shown in figure 5.1.

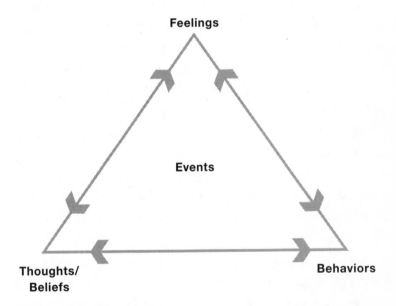

Figure 5.1: The Cognitive Triangle: The cognitive triangle displays events influencing our thoughts, feelings, and behaviors, and each of those, in turn, influencing the others.

At the center of the cognitive triangle sits an event. Something happens to start this process in motion and trigger the complex interplay between thoughts, feelings, and behaviors. In the case of a typical adolescent, imagine that event to be a male high school student, whom we will call

Alan, walking down the hallway and seeing a girl he likes, whom we will call Emily. As they approach one another, Alan tries to catch Emily's eye, but she doesn't appear to notice him. As they get closer, his gaze remains fixed on her, but she simply doesn't see him. He even says "hello," but she doesn't respond. After they pass, Alan begins to wonder—"Maybe Emily doesn't like me." "Did I say something to offend her?" "I knew I shouldn't have worn this shirt today!" These negative thoughts, or cognitions, then lead to various behaviors and feelings, as depicted by the double-headed arrows on the figure. Alan may subsequently decide to send Emily a friendly text in the hopes that she will respond, or perhaps he will circle around the next hallway and try to pass her again, hoping to catch her eye this time around. Alternatively, Alan may go to the cafeteria and eat a doughnut to make himself feel better and to soothe the pain of his desired object not having noticed him. In accord with the three points of the cognitive triangle, the event of Alan passing Emily in the hallway may result in him not only having certain *thoughts* and making some changes in his *behavior*, but also having *feelings* about this interaction. He may feel depressed, anxious, irritable, or angry about what has just happened. The simple act of passing Emily in the hallway has all sorts of implications for Alan's thoughts, behaviors, and feelings.

It's possible, of course, that Emily simply didn't see Alan. Maybe she was distracted by bad news from another friend, worried about an upcoming class assignment, bothered by a headache, or pleasantly preoccupied by something wonderful that had just happened. Since most adolescents act decently to their peers most of the time, the chances are pretty slight that Emily intentionally snubbed Alan, although that's always a possibility. Given, once again, adolescents' strong evolutionary need for connection to peers, however, Alan is very likely to interpret Emily's lack of acknowledgment in the hallway as a personal affront. This is the cognitive distortion, or thinking error.

Cognitive distortions are exaggerated and unreasonable thoughts that cause us to misperceive reality and then subsequently feel bad. Adults too, of course, are vulnerable to cognitive distortions and will sometimes feel bad because they think that someone has ignored them. But adults, by virtue of their age and experience, have had more practice in these matters and usually, though not always, have an easier time letting go of small potential insults. As a psychiatrist, I've heard parents tell their kids countless times, "Don't sweat it! Who cares what they think?" or simply, "Please, just let it go." Parents know that their kids sometimes misinterpret the world around them and need help identifying their thinking errors.

More than a dozen common cognitive distortions have been described to which we all, at least occasionally, fall prey. Here are a few classic examples:

- *Filtering*—magnifying the negative details from a situation while filtering out all of the positive aspects

- *All-or-nothing thinking*—viewing everything as "good" or "bad" in an overly dogmatic fashion; believing that you must be perfect or a failure, allowing for no middle ground

- *Overgeneralization*—coming to a conclusion about your capabilities based upon a single incident or piece of evidence; when something bad happens once, the expectation is that it will happen over and over again

- *Mind reading*—presuming to understand how others feel and to know why they act as they do; particularly believing that you know how others feel about you

- *Catastrophizing*—expecting disaster from every interaction or situation

- *Personalization*—thinking that everything people do or say is a reaction to you; constantly comparing yourself to others in an effort to determine who is more intelligent, better looking, and so forth

- *Blaming*—holding others responsible for the pain you feel, or blaming yourself for every problem

- *Shoulds*—having a list of restrictive rules about how you and others should act; becoming angered when others break these rules or feeling guilty if you violate them

Which cognitive distortions do you think might have gotten the best of Alan as he passed Emily in the hallway? I'd say that he's personalizing and possibly also overgeneralizing. Which cognitive distortions sometimes affect you and your kids?

Once adolescents begin to think abstractly, they are increasingly vulnerable to the impact of cognitive distortions, and that can lead to a lot of discomfort. They can imagine what their peers might be thinking, and they often imagine the worst. They simply can't help it, given their throbbing amygdala, the brain's threat detection center. Remember, the amygdala, as we discussed in chapter 4, is always on the lookout for threats and is not well controlled by the prefrontal cortex during adolescence. Unless they get a lot of practice identifying cognitive distortions and learn to challenge these thoughts in a very conscious way (as one would in psychotherapy), adolescents will frequently feel the confusion, irritability, anger, and sadness that distorted thinking can cause. And what do you suppose an adolescent might do to avoid or soothe the emotional pain of cognitive distortions? Perhaps, as in the case of Alan, he will simply write a text or eat a doughnut. But sometimes, to avoid such pain, our kids will go to much greater lengths and put themselves at significant risk.

The Heat of the Moment

Hazing isn't new. Reports of humiliating and ridiculing new members of clubs, fraternities and sororities, sports teams, gangs, and military units in the name of building solidarity and affiliation go back millennia. Unfortunately, as we all know, sometimes hazing results in dire consequences. Such was the case with Robert Champion.

Florida Agricultural and Mechanical University's Marching 100 is perhaps the most famous college marching band in the United States. Since 1946, the band has essentially written the book on technique and innovation. The band has played in four Super Bowls, at the Grammy Awards, in Coca-Cola and Welch's Grape Soda commercials, and for two presidential inaugurations. But on November 19, 2011, the Marching 100 became infamous for hazing when Robert Champion died after participating in the "rite of passage" called "Crossing Bus C."

Champion was with his bandmates in Orlando for the last football game of the season, the Florida Classic. He didn't have to go through with the hazing; Robert had started with the band as a clarinet player. He was so good that he was elevated to drum major, and the next year he was slated to become head drum major. That's like being the general of a nationally celebrated army platoon of 350 members. Crossing Bus C, the drummer's bus, was expected if you wanted the respect and loyalty of the senior percussionists, the largest and wildest group in the Marching 100. Robert Champion volunteered to be hazed.

The ritual began as it always did, in the "hot seat," wherein Robert sat in the front of the team bus, was covered with a blanket, and then was punched and beaten repeatedly with hands, drumsticks, and mallets. Next, he ran a gauntlet from the front to the back of the bus in total darkness, while being hit, slapped, and kicked. Some bandmates encouraged him forward, and some reportedly held him back to endure more punishment. The ritual ended when the inductee touched the back wall of the bus and was then fully initiated into the band, to great applause and cheering from his mates who had just pummeled him. In Robert's case, it was the last thing he did. Witnesses said that the bus rocked back and forth violently as Robert was repeatedly hit. After reaching the back wall, he collapsed and died shortly afterward due to hemorrhagic shock from soft tissue damage and blunt force trauma. In other words, he died from internal bleeding due to the severe beating.

Benjamin McNamee, one of Champion's bandmates, was convicted of felony hazing and manslaughter. He had no criminal record and was a leader in the Marching 100. At his sentencing, McNamee said, "I am utterly and completely embarrassed and ashamed to have played any part or role in any event which resulted in Robert's death. This is not the way I was raised, and this is certainly not how I saw my life's path unfolding . . . I would say that peer pressure killed Robert Champion."

Robert Champion himself expressed doubt about engaging in the ritual before it started. Keon Hollis, Robert's roommate, said that hazing went against everything Robert believed in and that he didn't want to participate but did so to earn the respect of his peers. What is it about the influence of our peers that makes us do risky things like "Crossing Bus C," even though we know better?

Once we hit around sixteen years of age, our "cold" cognition is quite good. That is, we can make clear and logical decisions about as well as adults can, when we're not pressured, tempted, or otherwise impassioned. Decisions made under cold cognition are generally around issues that are emotionally neutral, where we can assess the data without bias. Such decisions might include whether to order steak or fish at a restaurant, or whether to walk to school or take the bus. But when we are emotionally or physiologically aroused, as we are during "hot" cognitive states, when we're underslept or feeling horny or hungry or anxious, our decision making is more likely to falter and the probability of risk-taking behavior increases. This effect is not surprising to any parent who has been paying close attention to their child. Nor is the fact that peer influence can trigger hot cognition and promote risk-taking behavior.

A certain susceptibility to peer pressure and influence appears to be part of our genetic makeup. Remarkably, the peer effect is even seen in adolescent mice, who will self-administer ("drink") more alcohol in the presence of other adolescent mice (cage-mates), while the presence of peers among adult mice has no impact upon their alcohol intake. Being noticed by our peers seems to be a hardwired process conserved throughout evolution, at least among adolescents.

Just being around peers increases adolescents' interest in rewards. There are even data suggesting that female adolescents are more sensitive to dopamine signals in the ventral striatum (the brain's reward center) at key times in the monthly menstrual cycle when the female is most fertile, when estrogen is high and unopposed by progesterone. For example, women are more attracted to testosterone-enhanced male features, such as a low voice and chiseled face, during the roughly six days before and after ovulation than at other points in the month. Throughout these days, females also tend to dress more provocatively, subtly increase the pitch of their voice, experience skin changes that make their faces appear more symmetrical, emit an attractive scent, and flirt more. And, of course, males respond to female ovulation by emitting more testosterone and moving physically closer to these women, preparing for sexual behavior and engagement. The observation that females are more strongly driven by reward during this so-called late follicular phase of the menstrual cycle (when the egg has just been released by the ovaries and has its greatest chance of being fertilized) suggests that they are more likely

> Just being around peers increases adolescents' interest in rewards.

to take risks, such as engage in sex or drug use, midway into the menstrual cycle.

Greater sensitivity to dopamine within the brain's reward center (ventral striatum) causes rewards to influence our behavior more strongly. So it makes sense that ovulating females, who are primed for reward by being more sensitive to dopamine in the ventral striatum at that time of the menstrual cycle, may engage in more risky behaviors during the six days around ovulation. Flirting and kissing and smoking marijuana will all feel even better than they usually do.

Similarly, typical adolescents release higher than normal levels of circulating dopamine in the presence of peers. More dopamine leads to increases not only in reward sensitivity, but also in the probability that adolescents will impulsively select an immediate reward, even if it's smaller than a potentially larger reward down the road. In one study, college students were more likely to prefer a reward of $200 immediately rather than $1,000 in six months if their peers were watching, but not if they were alone. Accepting sham money in a study is benign; however, enhanced reward-seeking behavior can have serious consequences. If an adolescent believes that a peer is watching, even if it's a peer he doesn't know, he is more likely to do something that he thinks this peer will approve of, like jumping off of a bridge into a river, for the benefit of being seen as strong, capable, and audacious. The immediate reward of being viewed as in control and fearless, even given the risk of injury or death, far outweighs the potential later reward of definitely staying alive. (As with the imbibing mice, this is not true with adults, who are less influenced by the presence of peers.)

> If an adolescent believes that a peer is watching, even if it's a peer he doesn't know, he is more likely to do something that he thinks this peer will approve of.

Life in the Fast Lane

Adolescent drivers should scare you. Those aged fifteen to twenty-four constitute only 14 percent of the U.S. population, but they account for 30 percent of the total costs of injuries due to motor vehicle accidents each year. In this country, just about 1 million teen drivers were involved in motor vehicle accidents in 2013, resulting in nearly four hundred thousand injuries and nearly three thousand deaths. The risk of a fatal motor vehicle accident per mile driven is nearly three times greater for teen drivers aged sixteen to nineteen as compared to drivers aged twenty and older, and on average six teens die from motor vehicle injuries each day. In 2012, 23 percent of drivers aged fifteen to twenty who were involved in fatal motor vehicle accidents were under the influence of alcohol. But it's the impact of peers that has perhaps the greatest influence on adolescent drivers.

A number of studies of the peer effect conducted by Laurence Steinberg's team at Temple University observed adolescents and adults in driving simulators. When adolescents were alone in driving simulators, they tended to brake at yellow lights as quickly as adults. They were in a cold cognitive state, without any physiological or emotional arousal and without peers present. But when the investigators told adolescents that a peer was observing them from another room, they took statistically longer to brake at yellow lights and took three times the number of risks. Yet again, the presence of peers had no effect on adult drivers.

When you look at the brains of these adolescents and adults under an fMRI scanner while they're engaged in the driving simulator task, you see differences as well. There is greater activation among the adolescents' brains in the emotional/limbic brain centers and greater activation among the adults' brains in the prefrontal cortex. This suggests that adults are better able to recruit the frontal circuits, the brain's CEO, to suppress the reward system while they engage in deliberate decision making. In other words, the adults can use the prefrontal cortex, the CEO, to exert top-down control over the emotional/limbic brain centers. Not surprisingly, having teen passengers in the car while an adolescent is driving increases the risk of an accident by more than four times, and the relative risk of both motor vehicle accidents and fatalities increases linearly with the number of teen passengers in the car. As you're no doubt not surprised to hear, no such increase is noted with adult drivers.

At this point, you also won't be shocked to learn that more juvenile crimes than adult crimes are committed in the presence of peers. It's been suggested that the peer effect is driven by a few "bad seeds" who spur others toward risk. But remember that adolescents are more likely to engage in risk-taking behavior when they believe they're being observed by peers, even peers they don't know. So it must not simply be the influence of a few particularly wild and reckless peers who push other teens into making risky choices. As the brain imaging study of adolescents in the driving simulator shows, when teens believe their peers are watching them, the brain reward center (ventral striatum) becomes overactive, priming them for a possible dopamine-driven pleasurable experience that might be on the way. This effect drives adolescents to place more focus on the pros of risk taking than on the cons, resulting in a greater likelihood of harm.

Thankfully, the most important peer factor doesn't appear to be the risky behavior itself. "The best interpretation of our findings from the driving simulator studies," Dr. Steinberg told me, "is not that there's an increase in adolescent risk taking when peers are present; but rather that adolescents show an increase in reward processing in the presence of peers. So adolescents might be more motivated to do *particular* things in the presence of *particular peers.*" In other words, in the presence of positive or well-behaved peers, adolescents tend to behave in a positive manner; whereas in the presence of antisocial peers, they will behave in a more antisocial manner. The take-home point for us parents, of course, is that we must pay close attention to our tweens' and teens' friendships because they have an enormous influence our own children.

Sticks and Stones

What's the most painful experience you've ever had in your life?

If you're like most people, your mind just now probably went to thinking about a personal relationship or a time when you faced rejection. Perhaps it's a romantic breakup, or maybe instead it's failing a major exam or being fired from a job. The fact that a minority of people talk about physical pain, like a surgery or breaking their arm, when asked about the most painful things in their lives is just what Naomi Eisenberger noted when she was a graduate student at the University of California, Los Angeles. While working toward her doctorate degree in social psychology in the 1990s, she observed that the words we use to describe emotional experiences, words like "hurt" and "painful," are the same labels that we apply to physical injuries. We've all felt left out, dismissed by others, ignored in the hallway by somebody we like, picked last for kickball. Why does this hurt so much? And is this "hurt" in any way related to the physical pain we feel when we are injured?

To understand this better, Dr. Eisenberger put college students into an fMRI scanner and had them play a game called Cyberball. The experimental subjects were told that they were going to be playing this game with two other same-aged peers in adjoining MRI suites while their brains were being scanned. The students played the electronic ball toss game on a screen back and forth by activating catches and throws with switches they held in their hands. The twist was that each student was unknowingly playing against a computer, not a peer, and there were no fellow students in the adjoining suites. Cyberball started off very nicely with the student receiving and throwing an equal number of balls with each "peer." But within a few minutes, the game changed, and the student in the scanner began to be left out of the game by the two computer players. Dr. Eisenberger was now able to compare the images of the students' brains that the fMRI captured under the two conditions, being included and being excluded.

"What we found here was really interesting," Dr. Eisenberger told me. "The regions of the brain that process physical pain are the same ones that get activated when we experience social exclusion." The brain's insula and anterior cingulate cortex (ACC)—areas involved in the detection of perceived errors, or incongruence between what is expected and what is observed—are strongly activated in each case. The insula and ACC appear to function as something akin to the brain's alarm system, on the lookout for conflict and sensing when things are not as they appear. Pain and hunger, both evolutionarily very old or primitive signals that alert us when something is wrong, lead to activation of the insula and ACC. Dr. Eisenberger's important and novel discovery is that emotional pain has essentially piggybacked onto the brain's physical pain and survival system. To the brain, and therefore to us, emotional pain due to social exclusion feels just like physical pain, signaling that our very survival is on the line.

> To the brain, and therefore to us, emotional pain due to social exclusion feels just like physical pain.

When we think about Dr. Eisenberger's experiment from an evolutionary perspective, her conclusion makes a lot of sense. Humans cannot survive without one another—no mammal can. We need one another not only for reproduction, but also to gather food and water, protect ourselves, and raise a family. If being left out or socially excluded feels physically painful, then you can imagine that we would do an awful lot to avoid that terrible feeling. Any animal would go to great lengths to stay connected to its peers if its very survival depended upon it.

Imagine a nineteen-year-old college sophomore named Steve. Steve and his friends are planning on seeing Disney's *Fantasia* at the local movie theater near the campus on Friday night in one of those "let's go do something really silly and childlike" moments that are so common in college. Steve is excited about Friday night. Frankly, he couldn't care less about the movie, but he likes this group of friends a lot and is very happy to have been invited along. Friday afternoon rolls around, and now begins a flurry of texting. Somehow, tonight's plan of a sweet moment of hanging out with friends and seeing a kids' movie becomes all about everyone taking psychedelic mushrooms before the movie and "tripping" throughout the show. Steve is now in a pickle. He's never had any intention of taking mushrooms. He's actually a little scared of psychedelics and knows that his parents, who are working hard to pay for his education, wouldn't approve. But Steve is also experiencing extreme "FOMO"—fear of missing out. If Steve decides to skip the movie and "shrooms," he won't only feel the emotional pain of exclusion. His brain will also feel as if his very survival were at risk, like one of our evolutionary ancestors would have felt were he shut out of the cave on a cold night. It takes a very strong, self-assured, and assertive college student to walk away from FOMO.

Just like the college students, these findings hold true for younger teens as well. Using the Cyberball experimental paradigm, Dr. Eisenberger's team placed twelve- and thirteen-year-olds into fMRI scanners and observed the same thing. The neuroimaging data show extensive brain metabolic activity in the insula and ACC, the neural alarm system. Interestingly, among both the college students and the young teens, those with greater baseline sensitivity to physical pain report more distress in the experiment. That is, those who are more pain sensitive are also more emotionally sensitive.

Both the college students and the young teens who felt less distressed by the Cyberball experiment activated more of their prefrontal cortex (specifically, the right ventrolateral prefrontal cortex). This part of the brain has an important role in regulating the amount of emotional discomfort that people feel. As discussed in chapter 3, an adult's mature prefrontal cortex is able to override much of the intense emotion felt by the limbic system (of which the insula and ACC are a part), thereby compensating in some way for the bad feelings that people have when they are socially excluded. The prefrontal cortex is also what we activate when we fight back our cognitive distortions—it's the part of the brain that Alan would have to use to refute the cognitive distortion of "personalization" by telling himself that Emily was probably just distracted as she walked down the hallway and that she wasn't, in fact, purposefully snubbing him.

On average, college students activate the prefrontal cortex much more than young teens do during the Cyberball experiment. This means that the college students are better equipped to handle emotional distress and rethink cognitive distortions. As we age and gain experience, we all improve at managing negative thoughts because our prefrontal cortex matures and becomes increasingly networked to our emotional brain centers (due to the growth of myelin, which insulates the neurons and makes their transmissions more efficient), as explored in chapter 3. Since their prefrontal cortex isn't well linked to their emotional brain yet, especially during hot cognition, younger teens don't have the advantage of relying upon a mature prefrontal cortex for comfort and advice when they feel social exclusion.

In summary, then, evolution has mounted the social attachment system onto the brain's physical pain system. Because social bonding in mammals is vital for our survival and we will go to great lengths to avoid physical pain, this evolutionary adaptation is very practical. The more distress people feel, the more they tend to activate the insula and ACC, parts of the limbic system, or emotional brain, and the more they try to compensate with their prefrontal areas, the brain's CEO.

Dr. Eisenberger's study eloquently explains why teens can be so distraught by social exclusion, even something as simple as not being invited to a party or not having their photo tagged on someone's Facebook page. It also suggests another potent reason that kids might take risks: to avoid pain. Kids might, in fact, do all sorts of things to avoid social exclusion, which to their brain feels just like pain or severe hunger. They might smoke marijuana, drink alcohol, or have sex because the pain of rejection is just too great. This sensation of pain is so strong that acetaminophen (Tylenol) has been shown to make adolescents feel emotionally better when faced with peer exclusion and emotional distress. Furthermore, fMRI studies show that acetaminophen reduces the neural signals associated with physical pain in socially painful situations. These studies demonstrate that physical pain and feelings associated with social exclusion overlap in the brain.

There's also some genetic evidence for these findings. Humans have natural opioids, such as endorphins and enkephalins, that function like morphine and help ease our pain and discomfort. Those who carry the OPRM1 gene, a rare type of opioid gene, are more sensitive to physical pain and more vulnerable to addiction. Not surprisingly, carriers of this gene report greater distress when facing social rejection and demonstrate increased pain-related brain activity when socially excluded.

Similar to the pain studies, Dr. Eisenberger's team has subsequently shown that reading kindhearted personal messages stimulates some of the same brain receptors as holding something warm in your hand. In other words, physical warmth and emotional warmth systems also overlap in the brain. Likewise, providing support and kindness to others as they're going through a tough time, like experiencing a painful physical shock, has been shown to stimulate brain reward areas, suggesting a neural basis for altruism. And more recent studies by other research teams have shown that even witnessing social rejection in others is enough to activate the brain's physical pain system.

While it may be sticks and stones that break our bones, we feel the same pain, and perhaps even worse, when we're socially excluded. Taken together, these studies demonstrate that we are wired for social attachment, which is necessary for our survival. The older we get, the better able we are to employ our brain's prefrontal areas to make sense of all that we and others are feeling and, in turn, manage our behavior in a way that balances desire with safety. But when we hit puberty and our emotional brain, with all of its fear and anxiety and great desire for reward, is leveling pressure down upon us, driven all the more intensely by the presence of peers, we are likely to adjust our behavior so that we feel the most reward and the least pain.

What would the adolescents you know do to avoid the pain of social exclusion? The list is endless.

Breakfast at Gregory's

"I'm very happy with how much time my kids spend on screens," said no parent ever.

The average child between eight and ten years old currently spends five and one half hours a day on digital media, while adolescents average eight-plus hours per day, seven days a week. It seems that no matter how much media access we give our kids, they still desire more. Media use among kids aged eight to eighteen increased by 20 percent from 2004 to 2009 alone, and the median number of texts sent by kids fourteen to seventeen increased from sixty to one hundred per day from 2009 to 2011. Today's youth aged twelve to seventeen report using text messaging as their primary means of communication, even more than face-to-face socializing. Teens aged thirteen to seventeen average 3,364 texts each month. How much of your child's day is occupied by screen time?

Not long ago, two parents came to see me about their fourteen-year-old son, Gregory. Mom and Dad described Gregory as "a great kid" who had "lots of good friends" and was "a good student and athlete." My psychiatric evaluation of Gregory and his family revealed that all was progressing quite normally in his development. So why were these lovely parents taking such pains to come and see a psychiatrist? Well, on a handful of recent occasions Gregory had "blown his top" and threatened to kill himself, even going so far as to beg his parents to kill him. Curiously enough, each event occurred in the morning, at breakfast, before school, when Gregory's parents took away his cell phone.

Mornings can be difficult for families getting kids off to school, and Gregory's home was no exception. What with getting out of bed and getting dressed, preparing the backpack, having something to eat, and, most importantly from Gregory's perspective, catching up on all of the group text messages that had transpired between his friends between the time he'd gone to bed and woken up, mornings were definitely full. About two months before Gregory's parents came to see me, he had started "dating" his first girlfriend. His parents made air quotes around the word when they told me about his relationship with Andrea because by their estimation it was just occasional hand-holding and kissing, routine for some of the eighth graders in their school. Commonly, when kids have privileges like cell phones, however, the parents may subsequently remove those privileges when the kids don't do as they're told. In the case of Gregory, it was his repeated ("and repeated!") refusal to put the phone down and get ready for school that drove his parents to take away his phone on a few occasions.

The first time it went like this: "Gregory," said his mother, "give me your phone. You need to eat your breakfast and get ready for school." "He acted like he didn't hear me," his mother told me. "Gregory," said his father, "give your mother the phone and get ready for school." Gregory entered the bathroom with his phone and locked the door. His father, now knocking on the door, said, "Don't take the phone in the bathroom. You don't need it in there." No answer. "Give me the phone!" shouted Dad. Gregory: "I just need to text Andrea back for one second." Frustrated and feeling powerless, his parents acquiesced and gave him "two minutes" to finish texting. About five minutes later, and after much expressed irritation by his parents, Gregory emerged from the bathroom, at which point his mother, seizing an opportunity, snatched the phone from his hand. "Give me my phone back!" shouted Gregory. His parents refused. "Give me my phone back—I have to text Andrea!" "You've had plenty of time to text with Andrea," said Mom. "Now you have to get ready for school. You're going to see her in a half hour!"

"At this point," his parents told me, "he did a full-on Elmer Fudd, like the cartoon character, you know, when Bugs Bunny outwits him. We've never seen anything like it. He threw himself on the floor, literally pounding his fists and feet into the ground, shouting, 'I hate you! I'm going to kill myself! You don't understand anything! Fine, just kill me then!'" Mom and Dad were shocked. Where was the fun-loving, sensitive, smart, insightful boy they had raised for fourteen years? He'd become "insane" in their eyes, and, unfortunately, it wouldn't be the last time. This routine would be acted out at least three more times before they decided to bring Gregory to a psychiatrist. "Is he really suicidal?" they wanted to know.

The communication revolution has taken parents by surprise, and with it we have unwittingly allowed evolutionary pressure to run rampant in our kids' brains. Because our children are spending much of their waking time on digital devices, they're constantly being exposed to peer influences and messages via Facebook, Instagram, Snapchat, and other social networking platforms, incessantly being reminded that they're missing out on some social opportunity. As such, their survival system is continuously being taxed. Remember Naomi Eisenberger's research—that evolution has piggybacked the social attachment system onto the physical pain and survival system. In a sense, our kids' survival is now always on the line. So when they're on a smartphone and see that they've not been tagged in a Facebook photo or they are not invited to a social event, their very survival feels threatened and they feel real pain. Undoubtedly, their ready access to all manner of communication devices allows this pressure to bear down on them much more so than in the past.

One remarkable study simulated the effects of Instagram, a highly popular social media photo-sharing app, on adolescents' brains and behaviors. The teens, aged thirteen to eighteen, were observed in an fMRI as they viewed a broad variety of photos, some of which they had submitted themselves. Behaviorally, the teens were much more prone to endorse, or "like," photos that had more "likes," demonstrating once again the power of peer influence even when the peers are perfect strangers. Neurologically, the ventral striatum or brain reward center was particularly active when their own photos were "liked" by others and when viewing other teens' photos with many "likes." So as we would expect, the brain's dopamine-driven, feel-good areas are triggered by peer engagement and popularity. Finally, and perhaps most importantly, when the teens viewed risky photos (such as pictures of drinking and smoking) that had many "likes," their brains showed significantly less activation in areas responsible for cognitive control and response inhibition (including the dorsal anterior cingulate cortex, bilateral prefrontal cortex, and lateral parietal cortex). Although looking at Instagram photos online is not in and of itself a risky behavior, this study does suggest that even online peer influence is strong enough to disengage adolescents' prefrontal cortex, thereby limiting their ability to control impulses and increasing the likelihood of faulty decision making and risky behavior.

Every day that we allow unfettered access to media, we are inviting our children to be leveled with social evolutionary pressure and the toxicity of stress, which results in bad outcomes. Research clearly shows that kids who spend more time on screens report lower grades, get into trouble more frequently, and have lower levels of personal contentment, including more boredom, more frequent feelings of sadness, and less satisfaction with school.

"Gregory is not suicidal," I told his parents after completing my evaluation. Gregory was actually fighting for his survival by seeing what his friends' texts said and which photos he'd been tagged in. His communication with Andrea in particular felt to him like the most important thing in the world, like he had a gun to his head if he couldn't text with her. Getting ready for school doesn't compare with survival. How could it? I empathized with Gregory's parents. "I know how annoying and frightening this is for you," I said, "but just imagine what this stress feels like to him."

Monkey See, Human Do

Screen time doesn't only facilitate the peer effect, as it did with Gregory. It also enables powerful role modeling via media. Adolescents are bombarded by references to drugs and alcohol, far too many of which are framed in a positive fashion. Among films produced between 1960 and 1990, for example, characters smoked at a rate of three times the national average. Ninety-three percent of the two hundred most popular video rentals in 1996 and 1997 depicted alcohol use, and 22 percent depicted illicit drugs. More than one-quarter of these films depicted graphic portrayals of drug preparation and/or ingestion, yet few of these movies gave any indication as to the reason for drug use among the characters; and only half portrayed any short-term consequences of substance abuse, while only 12 percent depicted long-term consequences. Among the twenty-five top-grossing films each year between 1988 and 1997, over 75 percent of them contained tobacco use. Likewise, nearly 90 percent of the two hundred most popular movie rentals in 1996 and 1997 depicted tobacco use. You might think that this sort of media pandering had come to an end with our expanded knowledge of the ills of smoking, alcohol, and drug use. But even with federally mandated tobacco package warnings, smoking incidents in movies with a G, PG, or PG-13 rating increased an average of 34 percent per movie from 2010 to 2011. These films tend to portray smoking positively, and the characters who smoke as sexier and more romantic than other characters in the films. Not even our youngest children, the most vulnerable among us, get away unharmed. Among all G-rated animated feature films released between 1937 and 2000, 47 percent portrayed alcohol use and 43 percent portrayed tobacco use.

One fascinating study analyzed 279 of the most popular songs of 2005, according to *Billboard* magazine, and found that 33 percent contained explicit references to drug or alcohol use. This translates into thirty-five substance references per hour of listening to music. Given that in this study adolescents listened to an average of nearly two and a half hours of music per day, these typical teens were exposed to approximately eighty-five references to explicit substances daily in the songs they heard. The number of references varied by genre—about 9 percent of pop songs had lyrics relating to drugs or alcohol, 14 percent of rock songs, 20 percent of rhythm and blues and hip-hop songs, 36 percent of country songs, and 77 percent of rap songs. Only 4 percent of songs contained explicit anti-drug-use messages, and none portrayed refusal of substance use. The authors also found that the substance use depicted in popular music was generally motivated by a desire for peer acceptance and sex and usually had positive associations and consequences.

In their normative struggle to establish themselves as independent of their parents, adolescents commonly see entertainment figures as role models. Madison Avenue tastemakers have known this for years. They also know that adolescents are, as a result of their desire to assert their independence, highly vulnerable to media messaging, and so they dish it out in abundance. Remember that adolescents are spending eight-plus hours a day on digital media. That's at least fifty-seven hours of media per week, or over 33 percent of the time! Because kids often multitask their media use by, for example, watching TV at the same time as they are listening to music or playing video games, they are actually packing more than eleven hours of media exposure into those eight-plus hours each day. And that's a big opportunity for our kids to receive messages of all sorts about drugs, alcohol, and addiction.

We are raised or "trained" by our parents and other adults, but we succeed, or don't, in the world of our peers. Building effective social relations with peers is vital to our evolutionary success. It makes perfect sense, then, that throughout the animal kingdom, socially savvy monkeys and rats get the best nesting areas, more food and water, and establish relationships with more fit partners. Isn't it the same with us?

Studying dopamine's role in addiction is illustrative of the adolescent quest for social competence. Remember from chapter 3 that dopamine regulates the motivation of behaviors necessary for survival. It directs our attention to what is salient, thereby teaching us what we need to do in order to stay alive. Eating, having sex, and engaging with peers, among other behaviors, increase dopamine, which makes us feel good so that we will do more of these things. More importantly, just anticipating these behaviors increases dopamine so that we will do what is necessary to obtain food, find a mate, and get to know others. Having a robust dopamine response to social interaction promotes a human's chances of social success and, therefore, finding more fit mates. As was also discussed in chapter 3, we now know that drugs of abuse have a big impact on dopamine, which is crucial to their reinforcing and addictive effects.

Still, dopamine isn't enough to explain addiction. If someone who is not addicted takes drugs, he will experience an increase in dopamine in the brain that is equal to or even greater than that seen in the brain of an addicted individual, but most individuals who experiment with drugs do not become addicted. So what else matters?

The answer may lie within the brains of macaques. Research shows that socially dominant monkeys have higher dopamine D2 receptor levels. Remember from chapter 3 that having more D2 receptors means that these monkeys can learn from negative consequences more easily. The interesting thing is that higher D2 levels are not biologically predetermined. That is, monkeys raised in isolation and then put into a social grouping will form a hierarchy, and the monkeys who come out on top of that social order will develop more D2 receptors, even if they didn't start that way. Therefore, being socially successful triggers higher D2 receptor levels. Even more impressive is the fact that subordinate monkeys end up with fewer D2 receptors and more readily self-administer cocaine when given the opportunity, suggesting that low social status makes us more willing to use drugs to extinguish the pain of social failure.

The studies on dopamine and addiction matter in our effort to understand adolescents and the peer effect because they demonstrate that social success makes us more sensitive to dopamine by enhancing our quantity of dopamine D2 receptors. And the more socially successful we are, the less likely we are to use drugs and alcohol because we're getting enough reward from our regular reinforcers like good food, conversation, and school. College graduates, for example, smoke cigarettes at less than 50 percent the rate of those who don't go to college and are nearly 50 percent less likely to abuse illicit drugs. Consequently, we cannot overstate the importance of parents, teachers, and society at large in promoting strong, emotionally rewarding, and healthy peer relations among adolescents.

> The more socially successful we are, the less likely we are to use drugs and alcohol.

As we age through adolescence, peer relations become vital to our success and survival. We are engineered on many fronts for this change, but it's always unexpected by both parents and children to a certain degree. Parents talk about their adolescent children seeming like "aliens," and they often express great confusion and self-doubt about how to parent these "strangers." Just a year or two before, they more or less knew exactly how to raise their kids, but now they've been thrown a curveball. But if we remember that adolescents are now thinking abstractly (which brings lots of opportunity but carries a big burden), are driven by rewards especially when they believe their peers will notice, and feel the pain of social exclusion with an urgent and often frightening intensity, we will be better positioned to guide them through the morass of peer pressure. Our job is to help our kids achieve social success, which is protective against risk, while moderating the impact of their social failures, which may precipitate risky behavior. With this understanding, we are now positioned to explore how adolescents make decisions.

CHAPTER 6

One Lump or Two?

(or, How We Make Decisions)

Wisely and slow.
They stumble that run fast.

—SHAKESPEARE, *Romeo and Juliet*

EACH DAY IS FILLED WITH hundreds of decisions. Many of them we make with little awareness, while a smaller number require a lot of thought. Choosing what to eat for breakfast is most often a relatively easy decision. Others are a bit more complex, like which clothes we choose to wear. We want to be comfortable, yet fashionable, and appropriate for the venue. Some other decisions are pretty tough, particularly when it comes to the health and safety of our children. Do I push my daughter to break up with her boyfriend because I'm worried she might have sex? Do I allow my son to get his driver's license even though he's getting a D in his math class? As parents, we have time to mull over these questions. Meanwhile, our kids are making difficult split-second decisions with oftentimes enormous and long-lasting implications every day. Do I go to the party? Do I get drunk with my friends? Do I jump off of the bridge into the river because my friends are doing it? Do I get into the car even though we've been smoking weed? Do I push my girlfriend to have sex?

A big part of my job as a child and adolescent psychiatrist entails helping adolescents, parents, and teachers make healthy decisions. The adolescents I see in my clinical work, along with the two I have at home, face risky situations every day, just like the adolescents you know. How can we support their normal development and drive toward independence, while directing them toward safety? As parents we struggle with how to monitor and supervise our kids, helping them to negotiate the difficult transition from child to teenager to young adult. Which approaches will be effective? How can we maintain our empathy while being crystal clear about our expectations, and assertive in our responses to unacceptable risk taking? As teachers we are challenged with providing the best instruction, while managing adolescent emotions and classroom behavior. How do we instruct our youth in not only the necessary academic foundation they will need to excel in life, but also the essential prosocial behaviors that will be the cornerstone of their success and moderate their risk-taking behaviors?

I think the most frequent phrase my parents said to me throughout my adolescence was "use good judgment." They would say it at predictable times—when I was going out at night with friends; when I was having a sleepover with friends; when I was driving out to the beach with friends; and when I was going away for the weekend with friends. Basically, whenever I would be with friends and without adult supervision, they would advise me to be careful. There were times when it would frustrate and anger me, especially when I was a younger teen, as I recounted in chapter 2 when I left for Germany at age sixteen and my father told me not to show off. With the passing of years, however, I felt connected to my folks in a special way and even proud that they would tell me to "use good judgment." They were saying that they knew what adolescents do when they get into an unsupervised group and that they trusted me to do the right thing. They were, after all, still letting me be with my friends, most often taking the car. My parents were born in the 1920s and are children of the Great Depression; they're pretty serious people, and they wouldn't wink at me when they made these statements. But it was almost as if they were sharing an inside joke. "Hey, son," I interpreted them as saying, "we know what happens when groups of teens get together without adults around. We get that you want to be with them and hang out. Well, okay. But keep your head about you. Be your own man. You don't have to do everything they do." As you know from reading chapter 2, my adolescent behavior wasn't always sterling, but I've come to understand that my parents were certainly right about the importance of developing good judgment and decision making.

For well over a decade, I have directed psychiatry training programs, first at the University of Pittsburgh and since 2005 at New York University. During these years, I've taught hundreds, maybe thousands, of medical students and psychiatry, pediatrics, and neurology residents how to assess and treat children, adolescents, young adults, and their families, both psychologically and medically. I've also handpicked over one hundred residents for advanced training in child and adolescent psychiatry. Closely watching the outcomes of these selections, I've learned one key thing—hands down, the most important factor in a physician is good decision making. There is an awful lot we can teach in medicine, but instilling good judgment de novo into a thirty-year-old psychiatry resident is a herculean undertaking, one that may just be impossible. We can certainly improve any doctor's judgment with supervised practice, and we can teach medical decision-making algorithms, which help a great deal. But learning to use good judgment that will allow for making thoughtful and safe decisions involving the health of others begins at an early age and becomes well established long before they interview with me for a position in my training program.

Caution to the Wind

After graduating from college and spending a year volunteering as an HIV educator by day and waiting tables and bartending by night, I left Berkeley, California, for the University of North Carolina at Chapel Hill to earn my master's degree in public health. During the second year of my graduate program, I had the good fortune of taking a course with a true master. Godfrey Hochbaum was by this time nearing the end of his illustrious career. I remember him as very kind and playful, with a soft Austrian accent. He was not too tall and the tiniest bit portly, with sparse gray hair atop his head and a twinkle in his eye. I really enjoyed his class. He was an extremely personable man who took a genuine interest in his students, and perhaps with good reason: A core component of his instruction was the importance of individual perceptions and beliefs in maintaining good health. Godfrey enjoyed our youthful enthusiasm, and he encouraged us to think outside the box, challenging prevailing ideas and our own assumptions. Godfrey is best known for his conceptualization and research of the Health Belief Model, perhaps the first social-psychological model that attempted to explain why and how people make decisions that affect their health.

Godfrey's interest in decision making began while working with the U.S. Public Health Service in the 1950s to eradicate tuberculosis. He puzzled over why people wouldn't voluntarily get screened. Tuberculosis was a major threat to public health in the 1950s and '60s. It ravaged people and communities, but even back then, lifesaving treatments were available. The test was easy, free, and almost entirely painless. Screenings were available nearly everywhere in clinics and trucks parked in local communities. Currently, nearly one-third of the world's population carries tuberculosis, among whom nearly 10 million fall ill annually and 1.5 million die. So who in the world wouldn't want to be screened for tuberculosis?

Why adults wouldn't get screened for tuberculosis in the 1950s is akin to why adolescents still take up cigarette smoking in the new millennium. After all, we know that if you're going to become a smoker, it virtually always starts during the teen years. But who would do such a thing? There's surely not a teenager alive who doesn't know that cigarette smoking is unhealthy and can cause cancer, emphysema, and a host of other horrendous illnesses. Since 2009, the U.S. federal government has required that nine unique warnings be displayed in rotation on every tobacco package and advertisement, with statements like "Smoking Can Kill You" and "Cigarettes are Addictive," so you'd literally have to be living under a rock not to know that tobacco is just pure poison. Tobacco is the leading cause of preventable deaths each year in most countries. In the United States alone, tobacco is responsible for nearly 450,000 deaths and costs our economy almost $200 billion in medical expenses and lost productivity each year. So what teenager in his right mind would pick up cigarettes?

Godfrey Hochbaum wanted to understand why, even when the odds argue so clearly, overwhelmingly, and indisputably in favor of changing a behavior that affects health, like smoking or getting screened for tuberculosis, many people still seemingly throw caution to the wind and don't make the healthy choice. His basic conclusion was one of pros and cons. In other words, the likelihood of taking the recommended illness prevention action increases if the perceived benefits of the recommended behavior outweigh the perceived barriers to the behavior, provided you believe yourself to be susceptible to the disease in question and view the illness as a serious threat. In later years, the concept of self-efficacy, or the idea that you are capable of succeeding at what you set out to do, was added to the model to help explain individual variability in health behaviors.

The Health Belief Model and others that followed, such as the theory of planned behavior, are still widely used in public health program development. These models can help us understand and predict health-related behaviors so that we can develop better health promotion programs and protect adolescents from making bad decisions. By and large, these models focus on attitudes and beliefs in determining why people behave as they do. However, and unfortunately, beliefs and attitudes aren't the entire story when it comes to risky behaviors.

It's hard to know for certain what percentage of our decision making around health behaviors, like getting screened for tuberculosis or using condoms or applying sunscreen in summer, is accounted for by the various health belief models. Most research studies have estimated the variance to be about one-third. That is, many behaviors are not logical and do not rationally follow our beliefs about health in the way these models suggest; in fact, when it comes to health behaviors, only about one-third of our decision making can be accounted for by our health beliefs and intentions.

Let's face it, it's hard to imagine that choosing to swim while drunk or climbing an electrical tower in Germany on a dare, as I did, was a rational or logical choice. If you had asked me days before if either act was a good idea, when I wasn't inebriated or jet-lagged and trying to impress my peers, I would have certainly said no. So while our behavioral intentions are often well predicted by these models, two-thirds of the time our actual behavior is not. So what else matters?

The major problem with these models is their assumption that what we believe about our health and vulnerability to illness will cause us to change our behavior. But young people in particular aren't generally consumed by thoughts about health and illness. Furthermore, these models don't account for behaviors once they have become habits, like smoking or wearing a bicycle helmet. They also don't explicitly take into consideration environmental factors, such as having access to a gym for exercise, or choosing to engage in a behavior not because you think it's good for you, but because of how it makes you look, like exercising or changing your diet because you want to lose weight. Finally, these models fail to incorporate the impact of emotions and unconscious, irrational, and impulsive decision making, factors that often contribute mightily to adolescent risk-taking behavior.

Willing and Able

Remember the first time you had a drink at a party and knew you had to drive home in a few hours? Did you stop at one drink? Some people do, and some people don't. For those adolescents who intentionally take risks, like planning to drink excessively at a party while knowing full well that they must drive home later that evening, the Health Belief Model can be quite useful in helping us think about how to intervene. The model suggests that by enhancing adolescents' perception of the likelihood of an automobile accident while driving under the influence of alcohol, and the seriousness of how badly they could be hurt or hurt others, we can increase their perception of the benefits of calling a taxi, parent, or friend to drive them home. In this case, the Health Belief Model may work quite well. But most adolescents don't intend to drive drunk. In a moment of "cold" cognition, when there is no peer pressure and nobody they're trying to impress, most adolescents will tell you that it's a terrible idea to drive drunk. The problem is that most adolescents who drive drunk or take other risks never intend to do so, but they do so nonetheless.

I remember being on an unsuccessful date when I was around twenty-one. We were having dinner at a Middle Eastern restaurant in Berkeley. My date and I were only vaguely familiar with the cuisine. However, the waitress, who had a stunning smile and seemed to me sophisticated and charming, knew the menu well and was ready for us. We didn't really know what to order, but the waitress effortlessly guided us to hummus, baba ghanoush, dolma, tabbouleh, lamb kabobs, and "just the right wine." I ordered far too much food and wine for the two of us, simply, I now believe, because I had some sort of an unconscious crush on the waitress. Toward the end of the meal, my date finally called me on my misplaced attentions, which at first I earnestly denied, but later, upon reflection, I shamefully acknowledged. I didn't intend to hurt my date's feelings by flirting with the waitress, nor did I intend to spend so much money on dinner, but what can I say? I was captivated by her smile.

Well, it turns out drinking more than you intend (or perhaps ordering more Middle Eastern food than you can eat) can be easily manipulated with just a smile, and I suspect that, either consciously or unconsciously, my waitress knew this well. Research has shown that thirsty undergraduate students, averaging in their early twenties, will pour and drink more of an unfamiliar beverage when they are first subliminally presented with, or "primed" by, smiling faces. The same undergraduates are also willing to pay more for the beverage and report wanting to drink more. By contrast, being subliminally primed by frowns results in the opposite effect. Equally fascinating, all of this can happen entirely without our awareness or any change in our feelings whatsoever. But it's not only smiles and frowns that cause shifts in our usual behavior.

We all make some pretty rotten decisions when we're hungry, thirsty, in pain, tired, horny, or in any state of intense physical or emotional need. George Loewenstein, professor of economics and psychology at Carnegie Mellon University, has described a number of such examples, starting with the biblical story of Isaac and Rebekah's twin sons, Esau and Jacob. Jacob had long been envious of Esau, the firstborn, who was entitled to their father's full inheritance. Returning from the fields with a great hunger and feeling faint one day, Esau traded his inheritance to Jacob in exchange for a bowl of stew. Similarly, Stalin and other infamous dictators throughout the ages extracted false confessions from feared adversaries by keeping them awake and undernourished for days on end. To this day, police investigators will typically begin an interrogation with the easy questions, like simple demographics and details, in an effort to tire the suspect, saving the potentially damaging questions for when the suspect is tired and hungry, less able to concentrate, and more likely to make an error or grant a concession simply to end the questioning. Lawyers use the same tactic with witnesses in courtrooms, as do employers when bargaining new contracts with labor unions, always arriving at an agreement just before the midnight hour when the prior contract is set to expire.

Just as Esau's hunger swayed him to trade his birthright for a bowl of stew, so too are adolescents more likely to engage in unsafe sex when they're driven by intense sexual desire. It's clear that both physiological drive states, like thirst or hunger, and emotional drive states, like feeling angry or horny, influence decisions that adolescents might make when they're under stress in "hot" cognitive states. In these moments of intense passion, an adolescent's emotion may override his cognitive control or any plan he has made, leading to a greater likelihood of risk. Adolescents in hot cognition not only take more risks, they also experience shifts in their moral attitudes. For example, a sexually aroused adolescent may be more willing to lie to convince a potential partner to have sex. And because adolescents frequently don't get enough sleep or eat regular meals or have ways to satisfy their sexual drives, they often inadvertently end up in risky situations. Mixing highly caffeinated energy drinks along with alcohol, like the popular adolescent party drink Red Bull and vodka, for example, can result in the same sort of effect. A number of studies suggest that such combinations may lead to more drinking and worse decisions because the caffeine gives the drinkers more energy, thereby masking the alcohol's effect to some degree and causing them to feel more alert and less fatigued and intoxicated than they really are. Early school start times and lots of late-night homework, as we've already seen in chapter 3, result in less sleep, which also increases the likelihood of bad decision making in risky situations. Adolescents don't generally intend to get into trouble. But given their strong innate drives for food, sleep, sex, and social acceptance, and the desire to avoid pain, they will find themselves in lots of risky situations faced with tough decisions.

I've seen a lot of adolescent patients in my years of clinical practice who never intended or necessarily expected to engage in risky behavior but who ended up in trouble all the same. These adolescents lack experience and maturity and so they typically approach risky situations passively. However, you don't have to be one of my patients to run into this sort of trouble. Some adolescents are firm in their resolve not to get drunk or have sex, but most eventually become "willing" at some point. They're not planning on having sex, so they don't keep condoms readily available; or they don't plan on getting drunk, so they don't prearrange how they will drive home from the party. But if they are presented with the possibility of having sex or drinking too much, they find themselves in a jam. Do I have unprotected sex? Do I drive home drunk? For that multitude of adolescents who are willing and able to take risks, but who don't intend or expect to take risks, our approach to protecting them from themselves must be more intensive than any of the health belief models can muster.

What in the World Were You Thinking?!

If you're the parent of an adolescent, then you've probably uttered the above sentence countless times. And you can probably remember your own parents asking you the same rhetorical question when you were a teen or young adult. The thing is that our kids' answers are usually pretty awful. Is there even a good answer to "Why did you drive drunk or have sex without a condom?" From an adult's perspective, not really. Adolescents take some pretty big risks that don't seem to make a lot of sense at first glance, even to them. It's all the more shocking because you know that in a moment of cold cognition, your child would never have made that decision and taken that risk.

So far in this book, we've talked about a lot of the likely reasons that adolescents take risks. In chapter 3, we started with the concept of neurodevelopmental imbalance, or the idea that the emotional, or limbic, brain develops earlier than the prefrontal cortex, or the brain's CEO, which exerts top-down control, leaving the emotional brain free to run rampant in adolescents. We then talked about the rewarding effects of dopamine, which are more intense during adolescence than at any other point in our lives, driving our kids toward high-risk/high-reward behaviors like sex and drugs. In chapter 4, we posited that adolescents have been exquisitely engineered by evolution to take risks, and we reviewed some of the key hormones that drive adolescents to bond with one another. In chapter 5 we spoke at length about the peer effects. Additionally, we've made reference numerous times to various behavioral contributors to adolescent risk taking, like alcohol, drugs, caffeine, and lack of sleep. Each of these many factors contributes to why adolescents make the decisions they do and take risks, but that's not the whole story.

We discussed in chapter 5 how cognitive distortions, or thinking errors, can affect feelings and behavior among adolescents. But we haven't yet talked much about how adolescents' cognition or thinking contributes to decision making and risk taking. There's plenty of fertile ground here to explore. By the time kids reach puberty, it's not just neurodevelopmental imbalance, dopamine, hormones, evolution, and peer pressure that's driving them to take risks. Logic and critical analysis now become another factor to consider in how they behave.

Cartesian Dualism

Genesis 2:7 states, "Then the Lord God formed the man of dust from the ground and breathed into his nostrils the breath of life, and the man became a living creature." According to the Bible, humans are composed of a body ("dust") and a soul ("the breath of life"). Similarly, the ancient Greek philosophers Plato and Aristotle believed that the human mind or soul was separate from the physical body. In *The Symposium* (c. 370 B.C.E.), Plato writes that humans were created with four arms, four legs, and a single, two-faced head. Because the humans were strong and prideful and threatened to overtake the gods, Zeus literally split their bodies, forging male and female halves, who would live in misery that would last until, and only if, they could find their other half, their soul mate. Drawing from these stories of creation, all of which rely upon some sort of dualism, or separation of the mind or soul from the body, French philosopher, mathematician, and scientist René Descartes (1596–1650) famously stated, *Cogito ergo sum*, or "I think, therefore I am." Descartes' pithy phrase has become emblematic of the dualist perspective—the ability to think and even doubt our own existence is proof that we have a mind separate from our body. The mind and body are two unique, virtually opposing entities that cannot exist without the other.

Descartes may have really been onto something because when you think about it, we tend to split nearly everything in our world along two opposing dimensions. In my field of psychiatry, Sigmund Freud described the battle between the conscious and the unconscious mind. No matter what subject or culture you slice into, you cannot avoid the presence of Cartesian dualism—success/failure, weakness/strength, love/hate, yin/yang, risk/benefit, start/stop, pro/con, heaven/hell, plus/minus, hard/soft, male/female, straight/gay, clean/dirty, young/old, fire/water, fast/slow, good/evil . . . we can go on and on. Categorizing concepts in our minds as all or none has definite advantages in helping us make decisions. You might either love or hate chocolate ice cream, which makes your decision to choose chocolate or vanilla very simple. But speaking and thinking in such a dualist fashion can also sometimes be misleading, promoting an "all-or-nothing" cognitive distortion and causing a failure to appreciate the spectrum of choice that lies in between.

The formal study of decision making began with the field of modern economics in the eighteenth century. Early economists devised mathematical formulas to calculate probabilities of outcomes. They reasonably assumed that individuals typically try to maximize their "utility" or satisfaction when making a decision. Economists further deemed decisions to be "rational" when people considered all of the available information at their disposal and the costs and benefits of the possible options. The assumption was that people generally act rationally, and when they don't, it's because their emotions get in the way. And so we've arrived back at Cartesian dualism—most of us probably assume that we make important decisions based upon a logical weighing of the costs and benefits, pros and cons, pluses and minuses, yin and yang. But the thing is, we don't.

In the 1970s, psychologists Daniel Kahneman and Amos Tversky suggested that when people don't act rationally, it's not necessarily because their emotions, like joy or fear or anger, get in the way. While they recognized that intense emotions or affects can certainly influence our thinking and decision making, they believed that other factors were equally or more important. The cornerstone of Tversky and Kahneman's radical contribution was their suggestion that rationality often falls prey to our own laziness. Thinking through big decisions takes a lot of brainpower, and given all that our brains are called upon to do, Tversky and Kahneman suggested that we take mental shortcuts where we can, basing decisions upon simple rules of thumb, also known as heuristics. In essence, we simplify difficult questions by substituting easier ones and answering them instead. When I ask a depressed adolescent how he has been feeling since I saw him last week, for example, he's likely to answer by referring to his mood at the moment I'm asking the question, as opposed to pushing himself to think through how he's really been doing over the past seven days. It takes a lot of concentration and effort to think about your mood over the period of a week, so his brain takes a shortcut. He calls upon what's known as the "availability" heuristic and tells me about whichever mood most easily comes to mind at that moment, that which is most "available" to him. Since he can most easily identify his current mood, that's what he reports to me. Similarly, if I ask an adolescent if he's a risk taker, he's likely to respond based only upon recent events that come to mind without considering the totality of his behavior. We substitute even more when we're physically exhausted, emotionally worn out, or distracted, as adolescents often are.

Rules of thumb can be very helpful and save us a lot of time and mental effort when making decisions, especially considering how many decisions we have to make each day. However, rules of thumb can be too simplistic at times and cause us to make biased decisions in some circumstances. Some of the most common rules of thumb (aka heuristics) and the decision-making biases they can cause are listed in table 6.1.

Table 6.1. Heuristics and Biases

Heuristics, or rules of thumb, facilitate easier decision making but commonly result in biases, which may lead to thinking errors and poor decisions.

HEURISTIC	DECISION-MAKING BIAS
AFFECT	"Affects," or feelings, such as liking or dislike, guide decision making with little conscious thought or deliberation. (E.g., *I like Lisa, so I'll drink whatever she's offering me.*)
ANCHORING	Relying heavily on the first piece of information presented biases decision making by "anchoring" thoughts around a starting point. (E.g., *My father drinks at least two whiskeys every night, and he seems fine. So I'm sure that having a handful of beers on the weekend won't hurt me.*)
AVAILABILITY	The probability or likelihood of an event is overly influenced by how easily an example comes to mind or how "available" an example is to your memory. (E.g., *I know that car accidents kill more adolescents than any other single cause, but it hasn't happened to anyone I know, so it won't happen to me.*)
FRAMING	Impressions are biased by how data is presented or "framed." (E.g., *Since almost half [45 percent] of graduating high school students in the United States have tried marijuana and I haven't, I feel left out and like a loser; versus, since more than half [55 percent] of graduating high school students in the United States haven't tried marijuana and I haven't either, I'm like most people and don't feel like I'm missing out.*)
REPRESENTATIVENESS	Similar objects or experiences are organized together in the mind, such that one thing comes to "represent" another. (E.g., *My boyfriend is a good student and dresses well. He must not be a risk taker, and I am safe with him behind the wheel.*)
UNPACKING	Providing more specific descriptions, or "unpacking" the details of events, makes them seem more likely. (E.g., *My grandfather smoked cigarettes nearly his whole life and died a long and terrible death from emphysema and cancer, so there's no way I'm ever going near a cigarette.*)

In his bestselling book *Thinking, Fast and Slow,* Daniel Kahneman describes two types of thought processes important for decision making: fast System 1 (innate and automatic) thinking, and slow System 2 (effortful and conscious) thinking. (Perhaps you are thinking Cartesian dualism?) System 1, Kahneman suggests, is elusive and located "everywhere" throughout the brain. System 1 accounts for unconscious and automatic decisions that are largely based upon useful heuristics. System 2, he believes, is housed within the prefrontal cortex, the brain's CEO. System 2 accounts for conscious decision making and thought processes that we're aware of and actively engage in. System 2 learns from maturity and experience. The System 1/System 2 paradigm was designed to explain how it is that we can sometimes be so biased in our reasoning and decision making.

Kahneman, who won the 2002 Nobel Prize in economics, believes that adults' maturity and life experience shield them from many risky situations. "When you're an adult," he told me, "you have already made decisions for a lot of situations. You've been there. You've got experience, and you know if you are the kind of person who takes a risk in a certain situation or not." It's true that most of the risks I took as an adolescent I wouldn't take now. I'll bet it's the same for you too. Maybe it's because we recall the extraordinary fear we felt when we did those things or the bad feelings we had afterward; maybe it's because we don't like lying to the people who care about us; maybe it's because we don't feel the need to impress our peers as much these days; or maybe it's because we have friends who took similar risks and had even worse outcomes. Maybe it's also because as adults we have taken on responsibilities to others, like spouses and children and employers. Regardless, there's no doubt that acquired knowledge and life experience, System 2 in Kahneman's terms, play a role in every mature adult's risk-avoidant behavior.

So can we teach adolescents enough about decision making and risk taking so that they don't have to go through the pain and possible tragedy of experiencing bad outcomes themselves? In other words, can we hot-wire their System 2 and rapidly instill within them the necessary maturity and personal experience to help them minimize risk? Kahneman says no. "You can't substitute teaching for experience," he told me. "It's very clear to me that you cannot enhance adolescents' System 2 enough to help them manage risk like an adult." That is, Kahneman believes that it's our System 2, the brain's conscious deliberator and rational decision maker, which is built upon hard-earned experience and maturity, that helps us make good decisions and protects us from high-risk situations. When you think back to chapter 2 and our discussion of popular risk prevention programs like D.A.R.E., Scared Straight, and driver's education, it's absolutely clear that our efforts at teaching adolescents how to think about risk have generally had little impact upon their risk-taking behavior and have often made things worse. All of these failed interventions focus on enhancing adolescents' logical, conscious, experience-informed, frontal cortical System 2 decision making, and none of them is effective. Kahneman suggests that these interventions don't work because it's impossible to speed the development of an adolescent's System 2. I agree that we can't teach our adolescents a lifetime of experience. But what if System 2 isn't the only thing that can protect us from risk?

Adolescents, like adults, rarely make rational decisions involving risk based strictly upon anticipated health outcomes. However, "willing" teens in hot cognition often find themselves in risky situations, even if they weren't planning on it. And the impact of any one of these decisions can last a lifetime.

Brain growth, dopamine, hormones, evolution, and peer pressure are without a doubt enormously important in how adolescents make decisions and why they take risks. However, if these factors were all that mattered in how adolescents make decisions, then we may as well throw in the towel right now. We can't fight evolution or neurodevelopment or hormones. So our only strategy in helping keep our kids safe in this case would be intensive supervision; and parents, teachers, and society at large would have to become a virtual police force to keep our adolescents alive. Thankfully, we can do much better, and in chapter 7 you'll learn why.

CHAPTER 7

Getting to Gist

(or, How Mature Decision Makers Confront Risk)

In the beginner's mind there are many possibilities,
but in the expert's there are few.

—SHUNRYU SUZUKI

WHEN I MEET A NEW adolescent patient in the waiting room, I shake his hand. I feel for the tension in the handshake—how tight is the grip? Does his hand fit all of the way into mine, or does it make it only halfway? Is the palm dry or wet? I make eye contact and watch for the movement of his eyes—does he look at me straight, how long does he maintain focus, or does he look away? How is he dressed—like someone of his age, clean and neat, or is he disheveled in any way, emitting a particular scent, showing a certain style or flair? I say, "Hello, I'm Jess Shatkin," and I await his response. What is the timbre of his voice, the cadence of his speech? Does he refer to me as "Dr. Shatkin" or "Doctor" or "Jess" or not by name at all?

These are the very first seconds of my interaction with any patient, and they are remarkably revealing moments. We all experience first meetings, and with rare exception (e.g., those diagnosed with an autism spectrum disorder, or suffering significant brain damage or dementia),

the vast majority of us are experts at sizing up others and forming immediate opinions. We experience the greeting consciously, but we tend to
be less aware, often unconscious, of our feelings about the meeting,
which are arguably more important in determining how we behave
toward the person we've just met. (Think back to our discussion of the
cognitive triangle in chapter 5.)

As a psychiatrist, my goal in the first moments of meeting with a new
patient and family is to take in all of the data I can and to measure it
against what I expect, what is usual or typical for someone of this age and
culture. Most of us do this upon first meetings with others, but what
makes a psychiatrist different is that we are also at the same time exquisitely alert to our own feelings about the interaction, using our emotional
responses as a barometer of sorts. What did I feel when this adolescent
male gripped my hand so tightly during the handshake? If this guy is
trying to intimidate me with his handshake, what must it be like to be
him, or his mother, father, or sibling? How did his eye contact make me
feel during the handshake? Was it welcoming, kind, fearful, piercing, sus-
picious, or competitive? How did he position his body relative to mine?
Did he try to hold the door for me, as we left the waiting area and entered
the hall, or did he allow me to do so as I intended?

By the time we begin the hundred-foot or so walk from the clinic
waiting area to my office, I've already begun my clinical assessment. I'm
examining how the family members interact with one another. I'm observing the patient's level of activity, movements, and mood. I'm listening to the conversation, the form of speech, and the linearity and
content of thought as represented through the discussion.

No one can be alert to all of these micromoments all of the time, and
there is certainly a balance to be struck between engaging with people as
a fellow human being and observing their behaviors and our feelings and
interpreting any meaning. Hey, maybe this guy just has a tight grip. As
psychiatrists often quip, "sometimes a cigar is just a cigar." But let's make

no mistake—our behavior most often carries significant meaning, and our interactions with others, even in the first few moments, tell us a great deal about who we're dealing with.

With all of this activity going on, you would think that my mind is pretty busy when I'm meeting a new family. You might even imagine that I would be completely overwhelmed with all that I'm taking in and trying to process. But in my more than twenty years as a physician, I've somehow learned to make all of these observations and experience all of these feelings pretty much automatically. I'm not thinking that x number of symptoms means that the patient has obsessive-compulsive disorder or major depressive disorder. I will get to the point of reviewing all of the patient and family complaints and symptoms during my clinical evaluation as we sit together later in my office to make sure I don't miss anything. Right now, I'm just "being" with the patient and family and absorbing the most important information—who they are and how they relate. Back during my training and in my early years of medical practice, I often felt loaded down with rules—say this to a patient, don't say that to a patient, count out five symptoms for major depression, six symptoms for ADHD, and so on. It was overwhelming. These days, by contrast, I function clinically with almost the same level of expertise with which I choose my clothes each morning. And I thank my lucky stars too, because otherwise I could never appear welcoming, calm, and at ease, providing an environment in which patients will feel comfortable speaking with me, while at the same time getting a sense of who these people really are.

By the time we reach my office, having spent only three or four minutes with the family, I've usually got a pretty good idea about why they've chosen to see a psychiatrist. I am not clairvoyant. But I am a well-trained and experienced clinician who has learned to use his senses for a specific purpose, which allows me to make intuitive inferences with the data I have before me.

The Friendly Skies

Becoming a pilot for the U.S. Air Force is a dangerous business. Not only does the training take many years and cost a great deal of money, but each pilot is also operating a multimillion-dollar machine. In the 1970s, the air force wanted to understand the best way to teach their young pilots how to respond to emergencies. At the time, they were teaching emergency preparedness through an instructional, rule-based approach, but they could find no evidence that memorizing a bunch of rules in any way improved their pilots' performance in an emergency. The air force wanted to know how people become "experts" in emergency management so that they could invest their resources in the most efficient way possible. Two brothers, Stuart and Hubert Dreyfus, both professors at UC Berkeley, received a grant from the air force to figure out expertise.

The brothers Dreyfus, Stuart a mathematician and Hubert a philosopher, proposed a five-stage model to describe how adults acquire skills. The brothers knew little about flying, but they came up with a compelling pathway to expertise all the same. Their model has since been applied to numerous other areas of adult learning with high skill levels, such as driving an automobile, playing chess, learning a second language, and training as a physician or firefighter.

We might apply the Dreyfus brothers' pathway to how children and adolescents learn to improve their decision making when it comes to risk. They begin by learning rules as children (a stage the Dreyfus brothers call *novice*), totally reliant upon their parents and teachers to guide them. Such rules would include "cross the street only when the walk light is green" and "look both ways before you cross the street." Risky behavior at this age is largely due to unabated impulsivity.

Kids begin to recognize familiar situations in their tween and early teen years, establishing maxims to guide themselves (*advanced beginner*),

and are just starting to have enough autonomy to make independent behavioral decisions; these years mark the start of high-risk behavior.

Adolescents gain more experience with time. By the mid- to late
teens, as their brain further develops and dopamine, hormones, and peer
effects take hold, they become overwhelmed, filled with doubt, and emotionally taxed, placing them at great risk of making a bad decision in a
risky situation due to ambivalence and internal debate about the various
possible outcomes. At the same time, they also start identifying the relevant features of any given situation and have a clearer understanding of
themselves and the world, rendering decision making easier and better,
especially when they're not aroused or emotionally agitated in hot cognitive states (*competence*).

As adolescents learn more about themselves, grow in their independence, and choose a perspective and approach to how and who they want
to be in the world by their late teens and early to mid-twenties, risky decision making becomes easier, safer, and still more accurate (*proficiency*).

Finally, by early adulthood—the mid- to late twenties—the brain is
fully wired, hormones have settled, and individuals commit more fully
to themselves and various activities, interests, and other people; effective
routines are established, and risky decision making becomes intuitive. If
we are fortunate, by the age of thirty or so, we become excellent decision
makers when it comes to risk. At this point we achieve what the Dreyfus
brothers would consider *expertise*.

"The whole essence of expertise," Stuart Dreyfus told me, "is having
learned what works and what doesn't work. It's not trying to understand
why. It is, in a sense, letting your acquired instincts take over."

Stuart Dreyfus makes a good point. Think about driving your car.
Can you explain how it is that you know when and how much brake
pressure to apply as you head into a turn? Or when and how much accel-
eration to apply as you come out of the turn? Or exactly how much to

turn the wheel of the car as you move through the turn? Did anyone teach you these things in a classroom? Not really. An instructor surely taught you these concepts during your required thirty-hour driver's education class, but they didn't stick until you had done them repeatedly, on many different roads, in many different cars, and in many different seasons. You learned these things by practicing them over and over again, and you now do them instinctually, automatically. You're now probably so expert at driving that you can hold a conversation, take a sip from your coffee, or do both while making a turn. Only when a driving situation becomes particularly hairy does your conscious attention turn to your driving. When you mistakenly hit that turn too fast, or a car suddenly slows in front of you, then you become single focused. The noise of the radio disappears, the coffee cup gets put down or dropped, and your full attention returns to driving. You respond quickly and intuitively. You don't spend any time trying to figure out *why* you're in this position. You're completely focused on how to make it right.

In the same way that you now drive like an expert and cannot account for your every action behind the wheel, firefighters, critical care nurses, cardiologists, and others who make high-pressure decisions cannot easily explain how they know exactly what to do in a given high-risk situation. They just "know."

An Affair to Remember

Consider this hypothetical scenario: John and Nancy are both forty-five years old and reasonably happy people. They meet during a workshop at an out-of-town conference and immediately hit it off. Each is married and has children, but their spouses and families are not with them on this trip. Each finds the other very attractive and desirable, and they're now having a drink in the bar together after the day's events. Now consider a similar scenario: Michael and Susan are both eighteen years old and are also reasonably happy people. They attend different high schools but live in the same city. They meet at a house party, and they too immediately hit it off. Neither Michael's girlfriend nor Susan's boyfriend is at the party this evening. They too find one another very attractive and desirable and are now having a beer together on the porch.

Here's the first question: Which couple is more likely to have sex that evening?

If you're like the hundreds of people of whom I've asked this question over the past decade, then you almost certainly said Michael and Susan, the teenagers, are more likely to have sex. My personal and clinical experience also suggests that's the right answer.

But here's the question that really matters for our purposes: Which couple considers more information in making a decision about whether or not to have sex?

Virtually everyone I've asked about this scenario immediately says that John and Nancy, the middle-aged couple, would evaluate more pieces of information in making this decision, and you almost certainly did too. John and Nancy are older, they have experience, and they can weigh all of the information from a mature perspective. Of course that makes the most sense. It's what economists have been telling us for years—we weigh the pros and cons and arrive at a decision that maximizes our utility and gives us the greatest benefit. But it's wrong.

You see, middle-aged John and Nancy are what the Dreyfus brothers would call "expert" decision makers. As experts, they rely upon experience, pattern recognition, and acquired intuition, and they tend to make better decisions involving risk in high-pressure situations with *less information*, not more. John and Nancy have been there, one way or another, in the past. They know that as appealing as a sexual affair might seem at first blush, it almost always causes much more pain than gain. They've seen friends or family members go through similar experiences; maybe they even went through something similar themselves when they were younger. More often than not, our John and Nancy will finish their drink together in the bar and then excuse themselves to get on with their respective evenings. While it's true that experience matters, neither John nor Nancy is having an internal debate or actively weighing the pros and cons of whether or not to have sex with one another. Their experience and pattern recognition have become automatic and intuitive. If they actually get to the point of weighing the pros and cons, there's a good chance that they're headed toward an extramarital affair.

Michael and Susan, on the other hand, are busy as bees. Amidst all of the flirting and excitement of meeting someone new, their heads are each abuzz with a fast-paced internal dialogue: "Do I have sex with this person tonight? What would my boyfriend/girlfriend think if he/she found out? Do I have a condom? Do I even need a condom? I mean, he/she looks pretty responsible. Where could we go to hook up? Would I ever see him/her again? Would he/she like me tomorrow? Did I even take a shower this morning? Why am I so attracted to this person? Maybe I don't really like my boyfriend/girlfriend. OMG, wouldn't it be crazy if I ended up marrying this person?!" The risk/benefit analysis and weighing of pros and cons could go on all night long.

When Less Is More

During my medical internship at UCLA more than twenty years ago, I was once assigned the task of trying to stump an experienced neurologist visiting from another university hospital. I presented him with a patient who had what I believed to be a difficult diagnosis, one that the resident neurology team and I had determined only after the patient had already been hospitalized for three days and gone through repeated clinical evaluation and testing. As our visitor marched through his questions and observations of the patient, it took only about ten minutes before he came upon the right diagnosis. He smiled at me kindly, somewhat condescendingly as I remember it, and announced to the team, "Okay, let's get on to something more difficult." I was dumbfounded. Interns, residents, and physicians early in their career weigh more information and take a greater number of possibilities into account, which generally makes us very good at multiple-choice tests, but it doesn't make us good doctors. As an intern, I was an "advanced beginner" in the Dreyfus brothers' terminology. Only continued study, maturity, and experience would make my thinking about patients automatic and intuitive, turning me into an "expert."

Lee Goldman is a physician who helped to pioneer the application of statistical methods to clinical medicine. Along the way, he came up with four simple measures to help determine which patients presenting to a medical emergency room with chest pain are at risk of an actual heart attack. His four measures include looking at the electrocardiogram readout, measuring blood pressure, listening to the lungs for signs of fluid, and assessing the subjective quality of pain felt by the patient. His criteria have been validated in numerous studies and are much more effective than typical clinical care in decreasing mortality. Similarly, expert cardiologists have been found to evaluate fewer cardiac risk factors compared to primary care doctors and medical students when trying to determine the appropriate level of care for patients presenting to hospitals with heart troubles. When it comes to risky decisions, less is generally more.

> When it comes to risky decisions, less is generally more.

Gary Klein is a psychologist by training and a pioneer in the study of how people make decisions in real-life naturalistic settings, not in a lab. He began by studying fire chiefs, who are responsible for making rapid decisions on-site. In one of Klein's first studies, he tried to identify every decision point at which the chiefs deliberated between two or more choices, but he found that such deliberations occurred in only about one in nine decisions. "Most commonly," Klein reported, "the fire ground commanders claimed that they simply recognized the situation as an example of something they had encountered many times before and acted without conscious awareness of making choices at all." When alternatives were considered, it was in situations where the chiefs had limited experience and expertise, and this resulted in slower decision making. Klein later went on to study how critical care nurses, nuclear power plant operators, pilots, battle planners, and chess masters make high-stakes decisions and found the same thing—experts make rapid, high-risk decisions (like the decisions our adolescents face daily) using experience and intuition, not logical debate or by weighing the pros and cons.

Counterintuitively, our best decisions, particularly those with high stakes in high-pressure, risky situations, are generally made with less information. By knowing just what to look for and limiting the amount of information coming in, we make safer and more satisfying decisions. Unfortunately, however, not only do our adolescents lack experience, but our culture does little to help them limit the flow of incoming information.

About twenty years ago, Barry Schwartz, now professor emeritus at Swarthmore College and author of *The Paradox of Choice*, went to his local clothing store to buy some jeans. He gave the young salesperson his size and was presented with scores of options that he couldn't recall facing the last time he'd bought jeans—"Slim fit, easy fit, relaxed fit, baggy, or extra baggy? Stonewashed, acid-washed, or distressed? Button-fly or zipper-fly? Faded or regular?" He felt overwhelmed.

Walk into a grocery store. How many salad dressings do you find— twenty, thirty, fifty? Blue cheese or Italian is a much easier choice than selecting among scores of blue cheese and Italian dressings. Barry Schwartz told me, "The official dogma is that more choice is good and leads to greater freedom and personal welfare. It's a value deeply embedded into our culture." But Schwartz suggests that people suffer more anxiety and depression when they have too many choices, and research shows that evaluating more options when faced with a risky situation delays the decision and often results in a worse outcome.

More choice also leads to greater expectation in the outcome, which leads to less satisfaction with the results, even when the results are good. The inevitable outcome of too many choices is paralysis, regret that you didn't make another decision, escalation of expectations, and self-blame. When there are few options and you're disappointed, the world is responsible. When there are many options and you're disappointed, it's your own fault.

Whether we're training pilots, assessing chest pain in the emergency room, debating the pros and cons of a sexual affair, or even choosing a salad dressing, when we are faced with too many choices, we make worse decisions that are less satisfying. When it comes to risky behavior, mature "expert" decision makers home in on essential details, recognize patterns, and ignore irrelevant cues, making better decisions *with fewer pieces of information*.

Fuzzy Trace

Right about here, I hit a snag in my research: How do we reconcile the seeming contradiction that adults know much more than adolescents, have better and more streamlined mental processing, and have more advanced analytic thinking, but preferentially use less of that sophisticated processing power, not more, when making decisions in risky situations? So let's take a closer look.

One of the most important thinkers in child development in the past century was the Swiss psychologist Jean Piaget. I remarked in chapter 5 that at the core of Piaget's developmental schema was the growth of cognition and reasoning. He believed that adolescents eventually arrive at the ability to abstract and explain their thinking, at which time they are developmentally mature. Piaget's ideas run hand in hand with the development of Daniel Kahneman's System 1 and System 2, as we discussed in chapter 6, and other Cartesian dualist models of cognitive development; that is, when we're young, we function innately via fast System 1 (automatic thinking), and as we age, we become more conscious and aware of our own thought processes, acting more deliberately via slow System 2 (effortful thinking). This model also parallels the neurodevelopmental model we discussed in chapter 3: The emotional, or limbic, brain and primitive reward systems develop early, while the prefrontal cortex, or cognitive control system (the brain's CEO), develops later. However, experimental evidence has thrown us a curveball. We now know from studies of firefighters and pilots and critical care nurses and doctors and other high-risk professions that mature decision makers rarely stop to deliberate at a moment of high-stakes risk; rather, they act based upon an internalized sense of what to do without consciously considering all of the possibilities one by one. Clearly, being able to explain your thinking isn't the same thing as being able to act effectively at a moment of risk, but most of us tend to think it is.

"To most people, being rational means that we can solve logic problems," Valerie Reyna, professor of human development and psychology at Cornell University, told me. "So we think that more advanced cognition is abstract and allows for rational thought; this is just part of Western philosophy. But the development of logic simply doesn't come to grips with how adolescents make decisions around risk. In fact, they can be too logical."

To explain how it is that our logic and abstract thinking improve with age while our decision making in high-risk situations becomes less analytical, Valerie Reyna and her colleague Charles Brainerd developed "fuzzy-trace theory." The essential idea is that adults have a preference for "fuzzy processing," or relying upon the least precise mental representation needed to make a decision. Said another way, adults tend to base their decisions less upon precise details and more upon general meanings.

Fuzzy-trace theory posits the existence of two thought processes, labeled "verbatim" and "gist." Unlike traditional Cartesian dualist theories, however, fuzzy trace suggests that people of every age form both types of mental representations, verbatim and gist, simultaneously when faced with any problem or situation and that these representations lie on a continuum. Research, in fact, has shown that these mental representations are coded into memory at the same time but that they are independently stored and retrieved. Verbatim representations appear earlier in development and capture the literal and detailed surface form of problems and situations (e.g., exact words and precise numbers), whereas gist representations develop more slowly over time and capture the basic essence of problems and situations. In other words, verbatim mental representations are quantitative in nature, and gist representations are qualitative.

Most importantly, Valerie Reyna and Charles Brainerd's "gist" is more than just experience alone. The bottom-line gist of something is its essential "meaning," which is built upon not only our experience, but also our emotions, culture, education, identity, understanding of numbers and statistics, and worldview. Expert firefighters and pilots, as well as mature adults like John and Nancy, attain qualitative gist thinking based upon all of these factors, not just by fighting more fires, logging more flight hours, or having more dates. Experience matters, of course, but experience doesn't tell the whole story of gist. How we interpret our experiences, the emotions we feel, how well we truly understand proportions and percentages (like the fact that the risk of pregnancy from unprotected intercourse is 5 percent) and can apply this understanding in real-life situations, our cultural expectations, and our ethics and morals all combined account for gist as we truly experience it.

When it comes to risky decision making, adults almost always get to the gist immediately. Fuzzy-trace theory suggests that adult decision making around risky behaviors is qualitative and relies upon gist (e.g., experience, pattern recognition, emotions, culture, education, identity, statistics, and worldview) and not upon verbatim memory (e.g., specific cues, literal understanding, and the quantitative weighing of pros and cons). By so doing, fuzzy-trace theory accounts for the fact that experienced professionals like firefighters and pilots automatically follow their acquired intuition at high-risk decision points. They see the potential problems looming and won't put themselves in a risky situation to begin with, in the same way that the middle-aged John and Nancy just "know" to have only one drink together before they go their separate ways.

We're certainly inclined to think that adults would weigh the risks and benefits or pros and cons of any given situation more than adolescents would. We believe that the adults would take their time and be more thoughtful about risky decisions. It's how we tend to think of adults' decisions—well thought through, measured, and balanced. It's what Piaget told us, and what economic theory has taught us—with increasing age, we use conscious reasoning more and more in our decision making and pull back from automatic and unconscious reasoning. But in reality, the development of our thought processes is not so linear. In study after study, we find that even though we can reason through problems better with age, our decision making becomes actually more qualitative and gist based.

> Even though we can reason through problems better with age, our decision making becomes actually more qualitative and gist based.

Counter to what most people think, the more we debate a decision, like an adolescent does, the more likely we are to rationalize any given risky behavior, like having unprotected intercourse. Adults engage in simpler, but not simplistic, reasoning. They think about risk in absolute terms, as opposed to relative terms like adolescents do. If you think categorically or in absolute terms (e.g., "it only takes once to get hurt" or "no risk is better than some risk"), you're less likely to take a risk, and that's protective. By thinking about risk in a quantitative fashion or in relative terms (e.g., "less risk is better than more risk"), adolescents are more likely to weigh the pros and cons, and, ultimately, land upon and justify a bad decision.

A deceptively simple research study by psychologists Abigail Baird, Jonathan Fugelsang, and Craig Bennett in 2005 beautifully illustrates adolescents' tendency to evaluate risk in a quantitative manner. In the "What Were You Thinking?" experiment, adolescents and adults were asked questions about things that were clearly good for them, such as, "Is it a good idea to eat a salad?" And they were asked questions about things that were clearly bad for them, such as, "Is it a good idea to swim with sharks?" or "Is it a good idea to set your hair on fire?" or "Is it a good idea to drink a can of Drano?" Everyone agreed that the good ideas were good and the bad ideas were bad. Adolescents and adults took about the same amount of time responding to the "good idea" questions. Reliably, however, adolescents took a statistically significant greater amount of time to answer the "bad idea" questions, the ones involving risk.

When I asked my wife if it's a good idea to swim with sharks, she immediately said, "No way." No questions asked. Her answer was absolute and based upon a qualitative assessment of the situation—it's never a good idea to swim with sharks, and we all know this. But when I asked the same question of my then sixteen-year-old daughter, I received this response: "Well, it depends . . . do I have a harpoon? Am I in a cage? What kind of shark is it?" Her answer was based upon a quantitative assessment, a balancing of the perceived positives and negatives. I get the same responses when I ask these questions of my undergraduate college students.

It's never a good idea to set your hair on fire, we all agree, but adolescents think about these sorts of risky questions in more detail. They consider the risks and benefits. They wonder what the experience would be like, and they may even quickly consider a series of caveats—*Is there a fire extinguisher nearby? How long would I have to let my hair burn? All of my hair or just some strands?*

Equally fascinating is what we see happening in the brains of adults versus adolescents under fMRI when we ask these questions. Remember, the fMRI detects blood flow in the brain, which is an accurate measure of which parts of the brain are the most or least metabolically active during a task. The areas of the adult brain that get activated when doing this task, as seen by fMRI, are the same areas that get triggered when we're shown something that we perceive to be disgusting or scary, including the insular cortex and amygdala. Essentially, there is no consideration of the problem at all by the adults in this study. These experienced and confident decision makers don't debate. They act. Among adolescents, by contrast, the areas of the brain that are activated by this experiment are the same as when they're deliberating an actual decision, most notably the right dorsolateral prefrontal cortex. In other words, we can see that their brains appear to be truly debating the pros and cons, quantitatively mulling over the data to make their decisions, whereas adults are answering intuitively, without deliberation.

Developmental Reversals

The "What Were You Thinking?" study provides a clear example of a developmental reversal. We would expect that the younger you are, the more rapidly you would answer the questions; but here, in fact, we see the opposite—the adults answer more rapidly and the adolescents answer more slowly. That's the developmental reversal. Taking more time to come up with an answer, as the adolescents do, is not what's expected based upon the popular theories of child development and the economics of decision making. The brain fMRI data supports the experimental observations. The adults are answering qualitatively, using automatic, quick, and unconscious thought processes; whereas the adolescents are answering quantitatively, using deliberate, slow, and conscious thought processes.

In an effort to explain why adolescents take more time to answer these high-risk questions, Abigail Baird, the chief author of the study, suggests: "It might look like they're being self-centered on the surface, but they're actually being hypervigilant, being aware of themselves in context, which is a really important part of learning about the world. You've got to consider the possibilities." That is, as our kids enter adolescence and start to chart their course for adulthood, they need to take all possible data into account; they consider more information—not less, like adults—so that they can learn about the world they will have to navigate independently in just a few years. They are more open to debate about how to proceed at nearly every decision point so that they can learn how to function successfully. They need to try things out and discover what does and doesn't work. As they age, their decision making in risky situations will become streamlined and automatic, and in ten years, they will answer these questions just like their parents do now. There is a risk, of course, that they will die trying to figure out the world and will not successfully reproduce. But as we discussed in chapter 4, that's a risk evolution is willing to take. Mother Nature will gladly sacrifice thousands to save millions.

The usual System 1/System 2 dichotomy doesn't account for developmental reversals. The late Herbert Simon (1916–2001), a multitalented scholar who won a Nobel Prize in economics, stated that "intuition is nothing more and nothing less than recognition," by which he meant practice. In Simon's mind, experts develop intuition because they've seen certain situations over and over, and so they've acquired "recognition" and, therefore, know how to respond rapidly. This would certainly make sense for some situations, but not many adults have ever been presented with a question like "Is it a good idea to set your hair on fire?" How in the world could they have acquired recognition for this type of scenario? To answer a question like that rapidly, you must have a gut response, an intuition that goes far beyond routine practice and into the realm of an internalized understanding of how the world works. In other words, our kids can have all the facts at their fingertips and still miss the meaning. As Valerie Reyna told me, "for adolescents who take risks, it's as though they know the price of everything, but the value of nothing."

> Our kids can have all the facts at their fingertips and still miss the meaning.

Paradigms Lost

Because we incorrectly believe that adults make safe decisions involving risk by engaging in a quantitative analysis using lots of information, we have mistakenly hammered our kids with details. We've exhaustively taught them that driving while drinking is risky, that having sex is risky, and on and on and on. But our adolescents know this already. They know it in spades and generally believe that bad outcomes are many times more likely than they actually are (see chapter 1). Until we appreciate how kids truly approach risk, until we incorporate modern knowledge of the adolescent brain, evolution, and the impact of peers into the design of our interventions, and until we change our paradigm of adolescent risk, we will continue to fund programs and policies that are ineffective. And our kids will continue to get hurt.

Not long ago, a nineteen-year-old patient of mine got into some legal trouble after he threatened to torch a young woman's car. Days before,

Carlo was having sex with this woman. He was using a condom, but the couple agreed partway through intercourse that he could take the condom off. One week later, the young woman told Carlo that she might be pregnant. For days Carlo tried to get clarification from her as to whether or not she was actually pregnant. He offered to pay for an abortion. "One day she was pregnant, and the next she wasn't," he told me. "She was jerking me around. I was getting really mad, so I sent her a text that I would torch her car if she didn't tell me the truth. I know it was stupid, and I never would have done anything. It was just a dumb threat." Carlo's text resulted in a restraining order, a fine, and nearly $5,000 in lawyer's fees.

When recounting the tale, Carlo told me that he knew his partner was not using any other form of birth control and that he very clearly understood the risks of taking off the condom while they were having sex. The $64,000 question is: "Why then did you take off the condom, Carlo?" "I actually thought a lot about it at that moment," he told me, "but I knew there was always Plan B or an abortion if she got pregnant." Carlo debated his options, considering Plan B and abortion, before taking off the condom. Both teens had all of the information they needed to make a safe and healthy decision, but they decided instead upon a risky path.

Carlo's story is another example of a developmental reversal. We expect that it's the adults who would weigh the risks and benefits of a condom, but, in fact, it's the adolescent who is looking at pros and cons. Would you have removed the condom? More to the point—would it even have been a point of discussion or internal dialogue? I don't think so. An adult would not engage in any sort of rational or conscious deliberation. The adult who doesn't want to get pregnant would wear the condom or not have sex. The decision is simple, binary, go or no-go. Adolescents and young adults generally weigh more information and take a great number of possibilities into account, which, again, often makes them very good multiple-choice test takers. But it doesn't make them good decision makers in risky situations.

Qualitative thinking helps adults stay risk averse. Adults don't make fine-grained distinctions between experimenting once or twice with a risk and experimenting more often. If doing something once can harm you, it's as much a risk to your health as doing something ten times. Adults employ gist thinking and know that since each time you have sex without a condom it's a risk, they won't ever engage in unprotected sex. To an adult, getting something is better than getting nothing, so sex with a condom is still better than no sex at all. But Carlo was thinking quantitatively, looking at the pros and cons, trying to maximize his gains, and responding to the age-old evolutionary drive for reward. As is typical of kids his age, he employed a verbatim analysis in concrete terms—he traded off the risk of pregnancy against the benefit of condom-free sex and removed the condom.

In an illustrative research study, adolescents and adults were instructed to watch a cloud of white dots on a screen moving against a black background. Although the dots seemed at first to be moving around at random, they were headed in a general direction. The participants were "incentivized" in this study with points for correctly determining which direction the dots were headed, and they were encouraged to earn as many points as possible. By now, you won't be surprised to learn that the adults in this study generally made more rapid decisions when large rewards (lots of points) were at stake. They were trying to capture at least *some* reward. By contrast, the adolescents typically took more time, waiting for more evidence to accumulate before deciding so that they could earn the *greatest possible* number of points. As with the "What Were You Thinking?" study, fMRIs of the experimental subjects found that areas of the brain associated with gathering data and making decisions (e.g., the intraparietal sulcus and dorsolateral prefrontal cortex) were more active in the adolescents than in the adults. That is, the adolescents were more quantitative in their decision making than the adults, who relied on a more qualitative, or gist, assessment. To an adult, some reward is better than no reward. The adult is thinking in absolute terms. Adolescents, on the other hand, are driven to maximize their rewards. To an adolescent, more reward is better than less reward. Adolescents think in relative terms, which slows down their thinking in risky situations and leads to bad choices.

In *Harry Potter and the Sorcerer's Stone*, Dudley Dursley nearly has a tantrum when he realizes that he has received only thirty-six presents for his eleventh birthday, "two less than last year." Dudley is employing quantitative reasoning using verbatim memory. He's thinking about precisely how many gifts he received last year, while not taking into account the quality, or gist, of last year's gifts compared to this year's more extravagant ones, like a new computer, a racing bike, and a second television. Instead, Dudley is trading off the magnitude of risk (e.g., having a full-on tantrum) against the possibility of more prizes (e.g., gaining more gifts). Children and adolescents are generally quantitative in their gambles— how many crayons, how many cookies, how many party invitations, how many friends, how many Instagram posts, and so on. A purely quantitative analysis, however, misses the forest for the trees.

With age, the brain lays down more white matter and becomes more efficient yet fixed. It becomes more difficult to learn new things, like languages, and quickly and easily consider all options. So advanced decision makers may not think out of the box all that easily, and this may be one reason that the young are so inventive. However, by homing in on essential patterns and not paying attention to verbatim details and extraneous cues, expert decision makers actually make better decisions *with fewer pieces of information*. Teens and young adults, by contrast, lack experience and tend to consider far too much information when making high-stakes decisions involving risk. They also typically have trouble regulating their emotions, understanding probability as it applies in the real world, and asserting themselves and their values when peers are present. They think in a quantitative way, evaluating every possible angle they can imagine. The irony, of course, is that most of our teachings and efforts to keep our kids safe are focused on improving their quantitative assessment of risks and benefits, which relies upon verbatim reasoning and weighing pros and cons. But the more our adolescents trade off risks and benefits or pros and cons, the more likely they are to rationalize and justify a decision that puts them at risk.

In one of his best-known songs, "Changes," David Bowie croons in the second verse that adolescents are fully aware of the changes they're experiencing. Well, Bowie was clearly no dummy. Teens and young adults know a whole lot more than we often give them credit for, particularly when it comes to risk. They've been listening to their parents and teachers and observing what's going on in their world. They know that HIV is real and that pregnancy can happen. They even believe these things are more common than they actually are. But unless they have built up considerable past experience and maturity, they will typically make very rational and quantitative assessments of how to behave in risky situations based upon verbatim, or literal, reasoning. Our greatest mistake in teaching adolescents about risk has been our tendency to rely upon the specific details and less upon *the gist*. Adolescents often stop listening to us because we hammer them with the same details and facts over and over again. Our goal must not be to simply stuff more and more knowledge about risky behaviors into our adolescents' heads. Rather, our goal must be to help our adolescents simplify and integrate what we teach them into an overall meaning—a global understanding that will keep them safe.

The really great news here is that while we cannot necessarily imbue adolescents with more experience or "hot-wire" their System 2, we can improve their pattern recognition, emotion regulation, understanding and proper use of risk statistics, and self-efficacy; in other words, we can emphasize those factors that can get them to gist long before they end their adolescence. Getting to gist earlier will help our adolescents improve their decision making in risky situations without waiting for them to accumulate years of hard-earned experience. We can also use everything we have learned about neurodevelopment, evolutionary biology, and peer effects to design strategies that will help our kids stay safe. And in the next three chapters, we'll talk about how to do just that.

CHAPTER 8

Not for the Faint of Heart

(or, What Parents Can Do to Reduce Risk Taking)

As the roaring of the waves precedes the tempest, so the murmur of
rising passions announces the tumultuous change . . . Keep your
hands upon the realm or all is lost.

—ROUSSEAU

ERIK ERIKSON, THE FAMOUS PSYCHOANALYST best known for his eight-stage model of psychosocial development, observed that during our adolescence we are faced with a profound "identity crisis," a term he coined to describe the transition from childhood into adulthood. The internal struggle to understand our past and the expectations that our parents and society have for us and to forge that into the person we want to be as adults is no easy task and filled with self-doubt and confusion. During our adolescence, we set our path for specialized schooling, future occupation, sexual identity, gender role, and political affiliation. Erikson said that early in adolescence we suffer from identity confusion because we are uncertain how to make these choices; this confusion continues until we truly know who we are and what we wish to be in the future. Conflict with parents is expected, Erikson and his mentors, like Anna Freud, posited, and not only unavoidable but necessary for healthy individuation from the parents. While these theories are appealing, Erikson, like many of the psychoanalysts who came before him, was talking perhaps more about himself and his own adolescent identity crisis, which he described as being on "the borderline between neurosis and adolescent psychosis."

I personally agree that many of us struggle with questions of identity at times during adolescence, but Erikson's observations and subsequent theories were largely based upon mentally ill and delinquent children and adolescents. In contrast to Erikson's ideas, when we finally got around to studying nonclinical populations of adolescents in the 1960s and '70s, as Lawrence Sterling observed, we found that the vast majority of teens are satisfied, even happy with the relationship they have with their parents. Sure, adolescents need to individuate from their parents, but it doesn't usually cause the intense and prolonged conflict that the early psychoanalysts predicted. In most of the families where significant conflict occurs during the teen years, in fact, there is a history of family troubles prior to adolescence.

When our kids are young, we need to make many choices for them. As they age toward the teenage years, we need to curate their choices. Adolescence is an enormous developmental opportunity. During these years, we must allow our kids to practice all of the many things that they will one day need to do independently as adults, but we must also continue providing close supervision. It's essential that we help our children establish self-efficacy and the ability to manage and regulate their behavior and emotions themselves. This means we must continue monitoring while at the same time shepherding them to self-discovery by giving them some room to explore—not an easy line to walk for a lot of us parents. Perhaps paradoxically, parents are frequently more stressed by the transition from childhood into adulthood than are adolescents themselves. Luckily, we now know how to help parents manage both their own emotions and their adolescents' behaviors.

"Just Right" Parenting

We accept without question that parents are the single greatest influence upon their child's development. As parents of young children, we make lots of choices that affect our kids—we choose their diet, how much they exercise, and their bedtime; we choose to stay with our spouse, raising the children in an intact family with two parents, or we choose to separate, sometimes causing our children to move between two homes; we choose to raise our children amidst great emotional conflict and fighting in the home, or in relative peace and harmony—but perhaps the most important choice we make in childrearing is the style with which we parent.

In 1966, UC Berkeley developmental psychologist Diana Baumrind eloquently described three distinctive parenting styles—permissive, authoritarian, and authoritative. Permissive parents make few demands upon their children and are "too easy." They rarely discipline their kids and are lenient, often indulgent, and frequently act more like a friend than a parent. Permissive parents may have low expectations and not believe their children to be capable of mature decision making and self-control. Alternatively, permissive parents may be raising their children solo, stretched to the brink by work and other commitments, unsure of their parenting skills, feeling guilty for making demands of their children, or simply distracted. Not infrequently, permissive parents have a solid education and financial means and choose to employ the same techniques in raising their children that have helped them to advance in life, such as empathy, curiosity, and novelty with little accompanying structure.

Authoritarian parents, on the other hand, are controlling, demanding, and "too hard." They require that their children follow strict rules or be punished. These parents are less responsive to their children and typically do not explain their reasoning. They expect obedience and are not happy to be questioned about their instructions. Authoritarian parents sometimes hail from the lower socioeconomic strata and tend to employ the same skills in childrearing that have helped them advance in life, such as discipline and firm guidelines.

By contrast, authoritative parents are warm and involved, yet firm and consistent in establishing guidelines and limits, and are "just right." They are in tune with their children's developmental level and have age-appropriate expectations. When Diana Baumrind first described these three parenting styles, she was clear that children raised in authoritative homes were better behaved than those raised in permissive or authoritarian homes. Fifty years later, we now also know that these same children grow into adolescents who perform better on virtually every psychological health metric studied. Kids raised in authoritative homes become adolescents who earn better grades, experience less anxiety and depression, demonstrate higher self-esteem, are more socially competent and self-reliant, and are far less likely to engage in antisocial behaviors like fighting, lying, theft, property damage, and alcohol and drug abuse. Even if alcohol and drugs become a concern, authoritative parents are much more effective at reducing substance abuse among their adolescents than permissive and authoritarian parents.

Authoritative parents have one additional skill that really matters. They are able to balance their active involvement in their children's lives, supervision of their children's activities, and the establishment of clear standards of behavior with granting increasing autonomy as their children age. This is not such an easy balance for many of us to achieve, but the benefits are well worth it. Children and adolescents raised in such a home perceive themselves more positively, feel more control over their lives, and take more pride in their efforts.

Parents may adopt these various styles unconsciously, emulating the behavior of their parents and friends, or consciously, based upon what they believe is best for their children. Whatever the reasons, permissive and authoritarian parents will have more trouble protecting their children from risky behavior, particularly as their children become adolescents. Permissive parents are easily manipulated when more directed parenting is called for, and authoritarian parents are so harsh and demanding that their children often become duplicitous, going behind their backs instead of facing the inevitable harsh consequences they're met with whenever they cross their parents.

Regardless of how much time we spend with our children, if we fail to parent *authoritatively*, balancing warmth and firmness, we put our kids in jeopardy. Studies of parents in China, Pakistan, Scotland, Australia, and Argentina support these findings, as do studies of parents of various ethnicities and all socioeconomic strata within the United States. These same authoritative traits are also effective for teachers, coaches, school principals and supervisors. So how do we help parents achieve authority with their children? Thankfully, we have an answer for that as well.

Parenting 101

I was driving through the countryside in Provence, France, with my pregnant wife, Alice, at my side and our two-year-old daughter, Parker, in a car seat behind me. We were spending the fall of 2000 in Geneva, Switzerland, where I was doing a research internship at the World Health Organization, writing a report about child and adolescent mental health policies worldwide. On weekends like this one, we would rent a car and drive out into the countryside to explore Europe. That day's drive had been longer than anticipated, and our daughter was getting restless. After singing countless songs and reciting *Madeline* and other favorites by heart, I took to placating her by taking my right hand off of the steering wheel and tickling her belly behind me. After a while, she started some silliness of her own by placing my fingers in her mouth. All was fine until she started nibbling on my fingers. It didn't hurt, but I told her to stop anyway. It was too distracting while I was driving, so I placed my right hand back on the wheel. Moments later she pleaded for my fingers, so I gave them back. Again, she bit, this time harder. Again, I removed my fingers, and once again she pledged not to bite me. Foolishly, I gave her my fingers a third time, and within a few minutes, she chomped down hard.

I immediately pulled the car over on the winding road's dirt shoulder. I abruptly grabbed Parker out of her car seat, screaming about how you NEVER BITE ANYONE, and put her on the ground beside the car in a small patch of flowers on the side of the road. I began pacing and mumbling profanities, sucking on my now bloody finger, and shouting at her that she was in a time-out. Since she had never been in a time-out before, and I had never put anyone in a time-out before, we were both a bit confused about the rules. Alice was trying to calm me down, as I continued on about NO BITING and YOU'RE IN A TIME-OUT, YOUNG LADY!

Parker meanwhile stayed pretty calm. She had never seen her father act so erratically, but it didn't seem to frighten her. Her mom was now smiling at her and hushing me as I ranted and raved. Parker was comfortably sitting safely in a patch of wonderfully scented flowers in one of the prettiest spots in the world looking out at hills and the vast French countryside. She picked a wildflower, smelled it, and reveled in getting just what she had wanted in the first place—out of the car.

For all sorts of reasons, parents sometimes yell at their children. We know a few things about yelling, however, that would be wise for all of us parents to bear in mind. When parents yell, kids don't always "hear" what's being said. They certainly grasp the emotion, but the words expressed within that emotion are often jumbled to their ears. Adults experience the same thing. Think about the last time you had an argument with a friend, coworker, or spouse. You probably spent a good deal of time talking about exactly "who said what" and had a hard time agreeing. That's because when our emotions rise, our threat response kicks in, and we go into survival mode. At those moments, we focus more on the emotional intensity of what's being said than on the exact words.

Unfortunately, research shows that harsh verbal discipline, characterized by frequent yelling, name-calling, and swearing at our children, increases the likelihood that they will misbehave and suffer depression in the years ahead. Uh-oh.

We returned to the United States in November, and I got back to my clinical work. Among the many challenges ahead, I realized that job number one for me was learning how to discipline a child. My first "time-out" had been a complete and utter failure. I was five years out of medical school at that time. I had finished my training in adult psychiatry and was halfway through my residency training in child and adolescent psychiatry; yet somehow I had no idea how to manage a disruptive child. I knew how to make a diagnosis of depression or ADHD or schizophrenia, sure, and I knew how to prescribe effective medications and do some psychotherapy. But other than giving lots of love and keeping her safe and warm and well fed, I didn't really have a clue as to how to manage my daughter's defiant behavior. I wasn't alone, of course. Children don't come with an instruction manual, and all parents struggle at times. We see it every day at the grocery store, at school drop-off, in the park, wherever. Luckily for me, I returned to my training program just in time to learn about parent management training.

Behavioral parent training, often referred to as parent management training, or PMT, is a well-established treatment that has been studied countless times and has excellent empirical support as an evidence-based approach to improving parenting practices. PMT teaches parents to be authoritative and gives them the skills necessary to produce major and sustained reductions in the disruptive behavior of their children. PMT relies upon basic behavior modification principles that work for both severely disruptive and typically developing children. Many books and videos are available to help parents learn these skills, and plenty of therapists are now trained in the core tenets, which can be mastered by parents in a matter of weeks but take a good amount of practice to get right. PMT is not designed specifically for adolescents, but the same techniques that work with young children are transferable to adolescents—and also work with our spouses, bosses, and supervisees. If we start using these behavior modification skills when our children are young, things will be a whole lot easier by the time they are teenagers.

The PMT techniques are timeworn and straightforward, and they incorporate much of what effective parents have been doing since the days of the caveman. But for many parents, myself included, the techniques are not always intuitive. Here are the skills that really matter:

- Positive Reinforcement—By using tactful praise, we focus on the good things our children do (recognizing their big, small, and even partial successes), which encourages them to do more of the same. When an adolescent earns an A on an exam, for example, she feels proud, empowered, and ready to study more for the next day. When she earns a poor grade, however, she feels discouraged, incompetent, and disinterested in the course. Every one of us wants to be praised by the people we care about, and adolescents are no exception. As parents, we often focus on the negative behaviors our kids engage in because those things stand out. Remember, we're evolutionarily designed to identify the threats and risks in our environment; for parents, this translates into recognizing the bad behavior of our children. As a result, we often don't think to praise our kids, even though they do tons of good things every day. By praising our children for their good behavior, we give them credit and positive attention for what they do right; in essence, praise tells our children how to behave, instead of how *not* to behave.

> Praise tells our children how to behave, instead of how *not* to behave.

Positive attention can take several forms, including not only praising, but also encouraging, acknowledging, thanking, and showing interest in our kids' hobbies, ideas, friends, and schoolwork. Positive reinforcement is a much more effective technique than punishment, in part because we have so many more options when we're being encouraging and positive than when we're punishing our kids. How many ways can you effectively punish your children? You can take something away, limit their privileges, or put them in time-out—that's about it. By contrast, we can positively reinforce and praise our children in myriad ways:

- We can praise them when they make a choice we like, such as finishing their homework before going out with friends.

- We can praise them when they say something funny, intelligent, kind, or thoughtful.

- We can praise them when they display a value we like, such as being generous with a friend or sibling.

- We can praise them when they refrain from a problem behavior and use their words instead of being physical.

- We can praise them when they exhibit mature behavior, such as starting their homework early and not waiting until the last minute.

- We can praise them when they perform quality work, such as when they wash the dishes well and don't leave the kitchen a mess.

Two more things about praise: First, remember that we aim to praise *behavior*, not personal qualities. "I like how you helped your sister with her homework" is a whole lot better and more precise than "You're such a good brother." We will get more of the behavior we want from our kids when we point out exactly what we like and stay away from global personal statements. Your son is always a "good" person, whether or not he volunteers to help his sister with her homework. Finally, our kids will be more encouraged to do as we wish if we praise *the process*, not just the completed behavior. When I say to my son, "Hey, the way you're setting up your books and computer on your desk is so cool, just like a real library," I'm observing what he's doing and encouraging him to keep it going.

- Effective Commands—By giving our children clear commands, we tell them precisely what we expect and what they need to do in order to earn our praise (and access to their privileges). There are two keys to giving effective commands: We need to command, not ask; and we need to be specific. Too commonly, we ask our children to clean their rooms or be home on time, instead of politely demanding those behaviors. "Please be home by ten" or simply "be home by ten" is short and sweet, right to the point, and leaves little wiggle room. "How about getting home by around ten?" is a whole lot different, implying there's room for debate or perhaps even seeming like the parent is asking for the child's permission. When we give effective commands (e.g., "put your clothes in the hamper," or "when your homework is done, you may go to John's house"), we make our expectations crystal clear and give our children their best opportunity to succeed because they know exactly what is expected from them. And, of course, once they do or start to do what's expected, we can begin to praise them with positive reinforcement.

- Selective Ignoring—Actively and selectively ignoring certain purposefully annoying or challenging behaviors that our children engage in can be a tough technique to master. We don't want to ignore our children, but rather their behavior that we don't like. Ignoring isn't particularly effective when used in isolation, but when followed by positive reinforcement for the behaviors that we *do* want, ignoring can be a very powerful form of setting limits. Try to think of ignoring as waiting for a behavior you really want, and then praising that behavior just as soon as it shows up. In the beginning, this approach may take some time, so you may need to plan accordingly—you might find yourself waiting a while for something to praise. It's important not to ignore dangerous, violent, or aggressive behavior, only that which we can safely ignore. Finally, try not to get angry or show any particular emotion while ignoring. It's an effective technique only if our kids really believe that we're removing our attention from their undesirable behavior.

- Scheduling—Knowing your adolescent's schedule takes a lot of the guesswork out of where they are and with whom they're spending time. This means that you can intervene if you believe they're too idle or spending time with troubled kids, both of which increase their risk-taking opportunities. You can also help them manage their time and be realistic about getting homework done, limiting screen time, and getting enough sleep.

- Rewarding Good Behavior—By establishing small rewards for desired behaviors, we can harness positive reinforcement and effective commands to direct, support, and reinforce adolescents in making good choices. For example, a parent may reward her adolescent if house rules are being respected (e.g., an extended curfew next Friday night to 10:30 p.m.) if the child is home by a curfew time of 10:00 p.m. for the first three weeks of the month. Even though the rewards are genuine (e.g., stickers for young children or privileges for adolescents), they are mere symbols used temporarily (for a few weeks or months) as a bridge until our children are able to do without the physical reward and appreciate the greater prize, namely the parents' (or peers' or society's) approval and appreciation of their good behavior. For some youth, it can also be useful to establish a token economy, or a system in which children and adolescents can earn points for good behavior that they can later cash in for small prizes or rewards.

A note about rewards—they shouldn't be huge or expensive. Rather, the best rewards involve activities that allow for shared, quality family time, like taking a bike ride with your child, watching a movie together, or baking cookies. Don't be fooled—this isn't bribery. Bribery comes before a behavior; rewards come after. By enticing our kids with small rewards, we can shape their behavior. Pretty soon they will link the natural, positive feeling that we all get from engaging in good behavior to the behavior itself, and the small reward will no longer be required.

- Limits and Consequences—In the same way that we can use small rewards, we can establish limits and consequences for our adolescents when they do not behave as we demand. For example, parents may limit their adolescent's privileges (e.g., tightening curfew to 9:00 p.m. for Saturday night or not allowing the child to go out at all) if the adolescent breaks curfew on Friday night. For younger children, punishments, such as time-out, and limiting access to desired activities, such as television, can be very effective at decreasing bad behavior.

Research on the use of rewards and punishments has found that they work best when positive reinforcement and rewards outweigh punishments and consequences by at least a ratio of *four to one*. Following a punishment, we must provide another opportunity soon after for our children to work their way back into our good graces and access the privileges they want. Likewise, overly harsh or restrictive punishments, such as taking away television privileges or anything our kids desire for more than twenty-four hours, are generally ineffective.

The goal of punishments is to set limits for our children, not to devastate them. I've worked with plenty of families who say that they've "taken away everything" from their child, but the bad behavior hasn't changed. I've even known some kids who have only a mattress and blanket in their bedroom because everything else has been removed. Believe me, these kids don't even begin to remember what they've done wrong; all they recall is that their parents are overly harsh and unforgiving. They give up trying to behave as their parents wish because they don't believe they will ever earn back their parents' respect and access the privileges they want; and so their bad behavior continues. After all, what do they have left to lose? To avoid these pitfalls, we need to use punishments sparingly and always provide numerous opportunities for our kids to earn back their privileges. After all, positive behavior is the goal—not retribution or exerting power for power's sake.

Parent management training is certainly not rocket science, but these simple techniques will save every parent's sanity time and time again if practiced and used consistently. More importantly, if we begin using these methods when our children are young, their behavior as adolescents will be much improved and less risky. They will be more likely to follow our direction because they know that positive reinforcement from parents (which, believe it or not, adolescents still do want) and enhanced freedoms and privileges are directly linked to how they behave and whether or not they meet our expectations.

PMT has also been shown to improve parent/child relations, reduce family conflict, enhance parents' problem-solving skills, and improve parents' attitudes toward their children. Children benefit by developing better self-efficacy in solving their own problems, feeling more socially competent, and even experiencing a greater attachment to school. Children whose parents use PMT are also less likely to be bullied. We're not sure why PMT has so many benefits. But it's my guess that by establishing clear guidelines and structure for our children and adolescents, we give them lots of opportunities to succeed as family members, friends, and students, which enhances their self-esteem and leads to all of these gains.

A DEVELOPMENTAL PROGRESSION FOR ANTISOCIAL BEHAVIOR

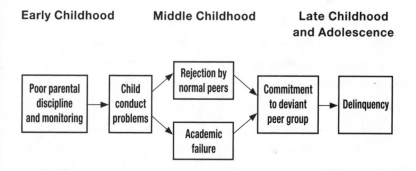

Adapted from Patterson, DeBarsche, & Ramsey, (1989)

Figure 8.1: One Model of the Development of Antisocial Behavior: This model does not, of course, directly incorporate all factors that contribute to the development of antisocial behavior, such as genetic vulnerability, neighborhood disorganization and violence, poverty, trauma, and so forth; however, many of these same genetic and environmental factors contribute to the deficiencies in discipline and monitoring that are observed among the parents of delinquent children and adolescents. (From Patterson et al, 1989.)

Research has convincingly demonstrated that parents who are ineffective at managing their children's behavior by age ten place their children at increased risk of antisocial and delinquent behavior. However, it's never too late for us to start using these strategies. We just need to be determined and willing to practice until we get it right. By improving parenting practices and increasing parent monitoring via instruction and coaching in PMT, we can help parents stop the onset or halt the progression of high-risk sexual behavior, academic failure, substance abuse, and other antisocial behaviors. On the other hand, models of antisocial behavior accurately forecast that poor parental monitoring and association with deviant peers in early adolescence are two strong predictors of delinquency by mid-adolescence (see figure 8.1).

Being There

It isn't always easy to talk with our kids. When they're young, they often want to tell us every excruciating detail about some person or event; but as they age, getting anything out of them can sometimes be like pulling teeth. Frequently, the more questions we ask, the less information they reveal. After a few minutes, we can start to feel like we're interrogating our kids more than we're having a conversation with them.

Some of the older generation of child psychotherapists used to talk about the "milk and cookies hour." Back in the day, therapists themselves would sometimes put out milk and cookies for their child patients during a session to make the therapy visit more tolerable, perhaps even something to look forward to. To this day, I will often take walks in the neighborhood or get snacks with my child and adolescent patients who tell me they "have nothing to say." Sure enough, just spending time with kids and being patient often leads to a conversation. Whether we start by talking about the weather or the taste of a cookie, soon we're discussing other things, like how it feels to be bullied or the frustration of not doing well in school.

I often start conversations with reluctant kids by asking open-ended questions like "What's going on?" or "How was school today?" If they shrug or give me brief answers, leaving the conversation back in my hands, I turn to more specific questions like "What are you studying in history?" or "What did you have for lunch today?" Or I may try to tap into something they enjoy or care about by instructing them with statements like "Tell me about your dog" or "Tell me about your brother." Over many years, I've learned that no matter what topic starts a conversation, it will sooner or later lead to an understanding of what matters to the adolescent and whatever is bugging him. Even what he had for lunch leads into who he ate with, where he ate, and what else was going on around him during lunch. When even direct questions won't work, we may play a game of chess or take a walk and get a snack. Whatever technique finally works, my job is to start by simply being there as an interested, caring, and willing adult. Fortunately, it works the same for parents.

Being there for our kids can happen many ways. Chatting, playing basketball or video games together, reading a story, making dinner, taking a walk, or any other shared activity results in the same wonderful gain—we learn about our kids and have the opportunity to do some great parenting. When my kids were in elementary school, my wife and I started a thirty-minute family reading time each night. We would all gather on the living room couch with our books and our beloved dog and read our books. We were role modeling for our children, showing them the value of reading, and they were getting their required reading for school done at the same time. Perhaps even better, once the reading time was over, we would often talk about what we'd just read, which would lead to discussions of what was happening at school and with friends. Finding a time to just "be" with your kids has enormous value.

Not surprisingly, the more we know about our children, the fewer risks they tend to take. Conversely, the less we know about our kids' whereabouts, activities, and friends, the more they tend to be involved

> The more we know about our children, the fewer risks they tend to take.

with alcohol, drugs, and antisocial behavior. Our continued monitoring into adolescence will further inhibit delinquent behavior, but, of course, our approach needs to change somewhat. When our children are young, they live in a benevolent autocracy at home, where parents set the rules and make most of the decisions. Over time, as our children become developmentally capable of making their own choices, we loosen the reins, but we still need to keep an eye on the horses.

A few years ago, my then fourteen-year-old son was out with friends at around 9:30 p.m. after they'd seen a movie. At the time, my son's weekend curfew was 10:00 p.m. We live in downtown New York City, just a few blocks from a city park. By day, the park is lovely and a great place to go and see all of humanity unfold before your eyes. By night, however, like many city parks it becomes a much different place, and drug sales and other unsavory business are easy to spot. Unsupervised wandering, whether it's in the streets or the city park, is associated with antisocial behavior. This explains what my son thought was my extreme reaction when he called and asked if I could extend his curfew that evening to allow him to stay in the park until 11:00 p.m. To be fair, I think I did overreact, but I know from personal experience and from the available research that no good comes from groups of adolescents wandering around unsupervised late at night.

There's a balance to be struck here, of course, between overpolicing our kids and trusting them to make good decisions. They need practice making decisions in risky situations, just like we need practice in monitoring their behavior. I advise parents to explain their reasoning to their adolescents. Bringing our kids into the discussion and explaining our rationale (even though they may disagree with us) shows that we're willing to collaborate, hear them out, and reason through our thought process. At the end of the day, you may still need to lay down the law, and they may not like it. But we cannot be as dogmatic with a fourteen-year-old as we can be with a six-year-old, and explaining ourselves shows that we respect them and want to keep lines of communication open.

The more adolescents perceive their parents to be trustworthy, accessible, and knowledgeable, in fact, the more they tend to share with their parents. And good communication between parents and teens helps to moderate risky behavior because parents can give advice and supervision. For example, having open discussions with our adolescents about sex and condom use leads our kids to believe that we are an accurate and reliable source of information about sex and pregnancy. In the absence of such conversations with parents, teens turn to peers, often emulating their behavior, and increasing the likelihood that they will engage in risky sexual behavior.

Since it's often very difficult for us to speak to our kids about health risks like drugs and sex, I strongly suggest you keep this in mind: Research shows that when we first remind our children of times when they were kind to other people, it confirms their self-esteem, which makes them more willing to listen to and remember our advice. So when you have these or any difficult conversations with your kids, it's a good idea to *start by speaking about the positives*, reminding them of something good or kind they've recently done.

Warm and supportive or "positive" parenting has been shown to benefit not only children's cognition, behavior, and psychological development, but also their brains. We've known for a few years that positive parenting during infancy results in beneficial effects that last throughout childhood, but we now know that at least some of those effects can also be achieved even after our kids are teenagers. In one study of nearly two hundred preteens, the primary area of the brain associated with threat and emotional reactivity (e.g., the amygdala) grew more slowly over the subsequent four years among those children whose mothers were frequently able to stay positive, warm, and supportive during conflicts with their teens. A slower-growing amygdala suggests that these children will suffer less anxiety and depression and have better self-control as they age.

Similar longitudinal research has found that teens raised by parents who employ positive techniques and have low levels of family conflict in the home have less demanding brain reward centers (e.g., the ventral striatum). This finding suggests that these adolescents will engage in less risk-taking behavior because they will be less sensitive to the rewarding effects of risk, perhaps because they find family and other interpersonal interactions sufficiently rewarding. In contrast, those teens who report more negative family experiences and a lack of parent support have more active brain reward centers and are more likely to take risks.

As with family support, adolescents who report high levels of peer support tend to take fewer risks, while chronic conflict with peers is associated with increases in risk-taking behavior. Likewise, greater conflict with peers is also associated with greater activation of the brain's reward centers, which increases risky behavior, while peer support lessens this effect.

Finally, research also shows that supportive families provide a buffering effect that protects adolescents against everything from common stressors like school and peers to not so common stressors like war. One study of more than 350 Israeli adolescents averaging fourteen years of age living near the Gaza Strip found that those who felt strong family support had lower rates of depression, aggression, and violent behavior one year later.

Why God Created the Fruit Bowl

In 2013, the United Nations shared a sobering statistic. Out of the 7 billion people estimated to live in the world, 6 billion have access to mobile phones, but only about 4.5 billion have access to a working toilet. Even in 1998, before widespread access to the Internet, video games, and mobile phones, a study of television screen violence reported that children in the United States see eight thousand murders and one hundred thousand other violent acts (including assault and rape) prior to middle school. More than a decade ago, a review of more than four hundred studies found a significant correlation between exposure to media violence (in TV, movies, video games, music, and comic books) and aggressive behaviors, aggressive thoughts, angry feelings, and physiological arousal. Although the magnitude of the effect on children was in the small to moderate range, it was stronger than the association between passive smoking and lung cancer.

Technology is everywhere, and we are increasingly learning that its effects are not benign. New research shows that undesirable changes are evident on brain scans and occur readily among adolescents with Internet and online gaming addiction. These effects include decreases in gray matter (neurons), reduced frontal lobe cortical thickness (the seat of the brain's CEO), impaired cognition and information processing, enhanced reward sensitivity and decreased sensitivity to loss, and neurological signs of cravings that are just like those found among people addicted to drugs. Heavy video game users have reductions in areas of the frontal lobe that manage emotion regulation and decision making.

But let's not lose hope. It seems that even temporarily removing media access from our children results in measureable social and emotional gains. One study took fifty-one preteens to an overnight nature camp for five days of school where screens were not allowed and compared them to fifty-four preteens who continued with their usual media practices. By the end of the week, the children who were deprived of screens were better able to recognize nonverbal emotional cues in other people, which translates into greater empathy. Similar experiments have shown that limiting screen time reduces childhood obesity; when our

> Fortunately, it appears that the negative effects of excessive screen time are reversible if we mandate regular breaks.

kids aren't glued to their screens, they engage in more physical activity and get more sleep. And any parent can tell you that their kids are generally "nicer" after a day in the country or playing sports or doing just about anything besides playing video games or watching television alone for a few hours. Fortunately, it appears that the negative effects of excessive screen time are reversible if we mandate regular breaks, which is precisely why God created the fruit bowl.

It's an unpopular job, but we've got to put some limits on our kids' use of smartphones, video games, and television. I advise parents that the phones go in the fruit bowl (or another convenient place) once the kids get home, staying there at least until the homework is completed. I know how difficult a task this is. My wife and I have struggled mightily with enforcing this rule, but it can make a real difference. Even without the brain scan research, we know that our kids are more irritable after a long period of time on screens, and we know that they become a whole lot nicer after a break. They need us to help them set some limits.

Here are a few basic guidelines I urge you to consider to limit the powerful and ever present impact of media on our children and adolescents:

1. No screen time until the homework and all chores are done.
2. Consider limiting screen time to only Friday afternoons through Sunday afternoons through the middle school years at least, unless the family watches a show or movie together during the week. Many families can comfortably maintain such a policy until their children are teenagers, and it will force your children

to engage in creative play with friends, be more physically active, and read.

3. Postpone giving your child a smartphone as long as humanly possible. They simply don't "need" that kind of exposure. (I know that if I had unfettered access to the world of the Internet when I was twelve or thirteen, I'm not sure I ever would have left my room.)

4. Once you give your child a smartphone, make it clear from the beginning that you own this device, which you're allowing your child to use. They can call it their phone, but you retain the right to take it away at any time for misuse or irresponsible behavior, or if you think it's getting in the way of schoolwork, chores, or any other school or family responsibility.

5. Keep all televisions in common areas like the family room, and never house a television in a child's bedroom. The temptation is simply too great, and any child will watch excessive amounts of television if given full access.

6. Always supervise your children when they're using computers. As with television, all computer activity should take place in the common areas of the home so that the kids cannot be online in the privacy of their bedrooms. If computers must be allowed in the bedrooms (such as laptops for homework as the kids get older), then the bedroom door must always stay open so that you can regularly make unscheduled visits to your children's rooms. I advise parents to continue enforcing this rule until the children complete high school.

7. Postpone allowing your children to join social media sites like Facebook, Instagram, Snapchat, and others until they are at least thirteen years old, which may still be too young for many. Once they join, require your children to "friend" you on these sites so that you can keep an eye on their activity and what they post.

8. Get the kids off of screens at least an hour before bed so that they can wind down. Focus on reading in the evening, drawing, puzzles, family games, conversation, or listening to music.

9. If your children must be on screens in the evenings before bed, have them sit at least five feet from the television; or, if they are using computers and smartphones, be sure they are using blue-light-blocking software (e.g., "f.lux" on computers or "night shift" on iPhones). The blue light released from electronic screens blocks melatonin and can hinder sleep. Blue-light-blocking software allows your child's natural melatonin to be released to promote sleep.

I realize that my suggestions may seem draconian to some parents, but the data on the potential negative effects of excessive screen exposure on our children are simply too persuasive to ignore. The American Academy of Pediatrics, in fact, advises that children under two years of age have absolutely no screen time and that children between two and six not be allowed any solo viewing. Children under six should not have access to virtual violence, even in cartoons, and total media time for all children is advised to be no more than two hours per day. Just to give these numbers some context, you should know that a national survey in 2013 found that children under one year of age were spending 58 minutes watching screens but only 19 minutes being read to daily. By two years of age, children were spending 118 minutes on screens but only 29 minutes reading.

Aristotle urged "moderation in all things," and never were these words more sage than with how we help our kids learn to manage screens. Just like we monitor alcohol and drug use, sleep, school and homework, curfew, exercise, nutrition, and friendships, we need to assertively monitor media exposure. Like any new technology, screens have real potential to help us. After all, I wrote this book on a computer. But we must not mislead ourselves—our kids don't "need" to be spending hours a day on screens watching movies for the tenth time, shooting monsters or people, or even figuring their way out of a maze. Beyond any necessary screen use for school or work, screen time is

> Our kids don't "need" to be spending hours a day on screens.

best viewed as a reward that parents control and share with their children, just as we allow our children to eat candy in moderation.

Reframing Reward

A few years ago, I was giving a talk about adolescent risk taking to the department of pediatrics at an academic medical center. During the question-and-answer period, an oncologist asked me about one of her patients. He was fifteen years old and in remission from acute lymphoblastic leukemia after receiving state-of-the-art treatment, but she was worried because he was no longer taking his medication daily. "If he stops taking his maintenance phase treatment," she said, "the leukemia may come back, and there will be nothing I can do. I tell him, and other patients like him, *Don't you see? If you don't take these medications every day, you may die.* But kids like him don't listen."

Acute lymphoblastic leukemia is a cancer of the white blood cells that mostly affects children and some elderly adults. Up until a few decades ago, it meant almost certain death. Today, however, the cure rate for those adolescents who take their treatment is around 90 percent. If you take all of your maintenance treatment, you have only about a 10 percent chance that the cancer will return. But if you skip your maintenance treatment more often than about once every ten days on average, the risk of recurrence doubles or even triples. And if you don't take the maintenance treatment at all, your risk of recurrence is about 80 percent.

Although adults aren't always great at finishing their oral antibiotics for an infection or taking their antihypertensive every day as prescribed, they're a whole lot better at taking their chemotherapy or transplant antirejection drugs than adolescents. So back to the well-meaning pediatric oncologist who was in despair—she had tried everything, told her patients "a million times" that they must take their medication daily or face a possible return of the cancer and death. "What can I do," she asked me, "with a kid like this?"

The first thing I suggested to the oncologist was to think about where adolescents are at developmentally. I reminded her that adolescents are driven intensely by the desire for reward, given the neurodevelopmental imbalance between their emotional brain and prefrontal cortex, and the fact that adolescents have more circulating dopamine in their brains than at any other time of life. I wasn't surprised, I told her, that she found fear to be an ineffective strategy in motivating adolescents to take their medication. I suggested, instead, that she appeal to the adolescent brain and focus on immediate reward.

> Appeal to the adolescent brain and focus on immediate reward.

"What does an adolescent want?" I asked. "To drive a car, to spend time with friends, to go to amusement parks, to skateboard, to date, to do well in school?" I posed. "So these are the things I would focus on."

I advised the oncologist to look at the *immediate rewards* that her patient wants and then collaborate with his parents and the entire treatment team to provide access to those rewards that are acceptable to the parents when their child takes his medication. Threatening adolescents with death is not terribly effective in most cases. Remember, they already be-lieve they're not invincible. But appealing to their big neuronal reward center, the ventral striatum, is often a useful approach. Parents can do the same thing at home. We will get further with our kids by *helping them see the benefits of making good choices* than we will with the drawbacks of making bad ones. Here are a few examples of what we call "positive op-posites":

- Do say: "Study hard in school so that you can apply to any college you like," but don't say: "If you don't study hard, you won't get into a good college."

- Do say: "Drive safely tonight, so you can use the car next week," but don't say: "If you don't drive safely, you might get hurt."

- Do say: "Take your allergy medicine so you can play baseball to-morrow," but don't say: "If you don't take your allergy medicine, your allergies will only get worse."

A positive opposite tells a child what to do, instead of what not to do. By focusing on shared values that parents and their adolescents both em-brace, like being a good friend, positive opposites can encourage safe be-havior. If your teen is going out with a group of friends or attending a party, for example, encouraging restraint and sobriety is not likely to be very effective. In other words, "don't drink" is likely to fall on deaf ears. But you may motivate your daughter to keep from drinking (or to limit her drinking) by tapping into the values of friendship and loyalty. By staying sober, she can help and protect her friend, for example, who often drinks to excess and gets into trouble.

Since social success is so important to teens, another approach to lim-iting drinking is pointing out that when people get drunk, they often embarrass themselves terribly. A twenty-year-old patient of mine, in fact, recently stopped drinking at parties because she just couldn't stand "making a fool of [herself]" any longer. But it took until she was twenty, and a lot of psychotherapy, to get there; perhaps she could have arrived at this decision sooner had she worked through this issue at home when she was a teen.

Studies of adolescents with cancer suggest that those who don't take their chemotherapy maintenance medications may not fully understand the details of their illness as well as those who take their medications regularly. Some of these adolescents may also not be sufficiently future oriented, while others may be in denial about the true nature of their illness. Undoubtedly, it's essential to educate these kids and their families about the illness. But appealing to the adolescent brain's drive for reward is also a reasonable strategy, which is predicated upon our understanding of developmental neurobiology. It's a good start and well worth trying, but there's much more we can do.

Would I Lie to You?

When I talk with adolescents about risk, I always keep in mind one important fact: By and large, they don't want to lie to their parents. Of course, they sometimes feel compelled to lie or tell only some of the truth, but given a choice, adolescents would almost always rather be honest with their parents. Being truthful with your parents has great value to most kids, and now and again it's useful to remind them of that. If you don't engage in risky behavior, I tell my patients, you won't have to lie to your parents, and that will feel good. And the more you tell the truth, I add, the more you will earn the trust of your parents, which will lead to more privileges.

Conversely, it's incumbent upon us as parents to acknowledge and appreciate, no matter how difficult it is, when our kids are telling the truth. Remember, they don't want to lie, so we need to try to make it possible for them to be truthful with us. The truth, however, is often difficult for parents to take and can be pretty shocking at times. It may also make you fear that you haven't done a good job as a parent, which may in turn make you feel sad, anxious, or even angry at your child. When our children tell us the truth, it doesn't mean that we cannot still punish them. But it might mean that we want to start by acknowledging that we understand just how difficult it is to be truthful, and how maturely and admirably they're now behaving. This sort of appreciation is a real self-esteem booster for our children and will make it easier for them to accept any reasonable consequence that follows.

The Need for Speed

Our job as parents is to help keep our kids' minds open, engaged, and safe. But no matter what we do, adolescents are sometimes going to choose risk. Our goal, then, is to shift the risk paradigm from one of fear to one of opportunity. We can achieve this goal by encouraging our kids to participate in well-regulated risky behavior, like rock climbing, white-water rafting, and skateboarding with adequate protective gear and adult supervision, instead of leaving them to their own devices where they might choose unprotected sex or drunk driving. We can take them and their friends to amusement parks and let them spin themselves into a frenzy on rides that we wouldn't touch with a ten-foot pole; we can take them to concerts and DJ parties, where we can supervise them from a distance; or we can take them go-karting, where they can drive a well-regulated course. By providing our kids with meaningful challenges that engage their risky brains, we appease their "need for speed" and help them establish new skills and neural connectivity, all of which will enhance their problem-solving skills, emotion regulation, and self-efficacy.

Getting Back to Gist

Although it may seem like swimming upstream against millennia of natural selection, we *can* educate our children to think in terms of gist.

Our goal here is to steer adolescents toward categorical thinking and away from deliberate calculation. In other words, we want to teach our children to think qualitatively (e.g., "it only takes once to get hurt"; "driving drunk is a bad idea") and not quantitatively (e.g., "don't overdo it"; "a couple of drinks before driving is probably okay"; "it will probably be all right if I pull out in time"). Here are seven strategies supported by Valerie Reyna and Charles Brainerd's fuzzy-trace theory that can help our kids grasp the gist of the risks they face.

Analogies

Parents can present their adolescents with analogies that help frame decision making in terms of gist or the bigger picture. A frequently used example is the following sentence: "Would you play Russian roulette for one million dollars?" To most adults, there is no amount of money that makes playing Russian roulette worth the risk, but remember that our adolescents are weighing pros and cons. Here's a few more: "Would you have unprotected sex?" and "Would you steal the answer key for a perfect score on the SAT?" Again, adults understand that unprotected sex is not worth the risk of pregnancy and sexually transmitted illness and that no grade is worth stealing for, so most adults will answer these sorts of questions immediately and behave accordingly. Adolescents, however, tend to consider the alternatives. So our job as parents is to present these sorts of scenarios to our adolescents *before* they encounter them and to help our kids *practice* safe responses. We can reason through why they answer as they do, but our focus should be less on the reasoning and more on helping them to develop a gut or gist understanding that Russian roulette results in death, unprotected sex results in pregnancy and sexually transmitted illness, and theft results in guilt and punishment—and that it's just not worth the risk. "But not every time," your adolescent responds. "Right," you say, "not every time, *but once is all it takes.*" Instilling this big-picture perspective will save them a great deal of internal debate, hand-wringing, and anxiety as they try to process the degree of risk in every questionable life situation—and more importantly, it will help them walk away from risky scenarios the way most adults would.

Statistical Gist

Some of the smartest people I know have trouble splitting the bill in a restaurant or calculating the tip. If you're one of these people, or know someone who is, it turns out that you're not alone. For many people, just the word "math" causes immediate worry. One of the most common problems people have with math is understanding ratios, which is sometimes called "denominator neglect." For example, would you rather choose a lottery ticket from a pile where one in ten is a winner or nine in one hundred are winners? More people than you might imagine select the second pile, even though the likelihood of winning from the first pile is 1 percent greater. This happens when people think only about the numerator (the first number in a ratio) and neglect the denominator (the second number in the ratio).

I mentioned in chapter 1 that the likelihood of pregnancy from one episode of unprotected intercourse averages about 5 percent, or one in twenty. Although adolescents typically estimate the likelihood to be much, much higher, even an estimate of 90 percent isn't enough to stop many adolescents from having unprotected intercourse. This is, in part, because they neglect the denominator. They think only about the first number, the one in twenty, which sounds pretty low; or the 5 percent, which sounds like a small percentage. In order to counter this effect, we must explain risk in such a way that kids can grasp the gist. If one of my patients tells me that he or she is having unprotected sex, I lay it out like this: Let's say you have unprotected sex once a week. By the end of twenty weeks, you will definitely be pregnant. It may happen the first time, the tenth time, or the twentieth time, but it *will* happen. If we speak about statistics in this way, we can help adolescents grasp the gist that adults already understand, which is that having unprotected intercourse just once can get you pregnant, and that it's simply not worth the risk.

Specific Emotional Cues

Because emotions so often get the best of adolescents before they can even stop to think about what's really going on, we need to help them develop cues to identify when their emotions are carrying them away. For example, when an adolescent I'm seeing tells me she's having sex with her boyfriend, among all of the other issues we discuss, I also make sure to ask about contraception. All too often I find that she is inconsistent in its use. So in addition to addressing the denominator neglect, I also ask very matter-of-factly, "What will you do if you get pregnant?" In response, I most often hear, "I don't know." I then say, "Let's talk about it." Adolescents generally try to avoid this discussion, but I'm relentless. And as we walk painstakingly through each step of what happens next (e.g., "How do you tell your parents? Do you have the baby or get an abortion? What do you say to your friends? Do you graduate on time? What happens to the gymnastics team?" etc.), a light always goes on in their heads. The emotional *feeling*, not just the abstract *thought*, of what it would be like to actually get pregnant starts to sink in. This technique can counter an adolescent's sense of ambiguity or uncertainty about the possible outcomes of a risky behavior, and I find kids to be much more realistic and grounded about their choices after this sort of conversation.

The most meaningful emotional cues to mature decision making are personal. So when having a discussion with an adolescent about driving drunk, the risks need to be customized to them (e.g., "What would happen if you're pulled over by a police officer? How long would it be before you could drive again? What would that do to your performance in the school play next week and going to junior prom in May?").

Research shows that when we ask people to think about all of the reasons that a given outcome might affect them personally, or when we ask them to go through a series of steps that could lead to such an outcome, they perceive a greater likelihood of this outcome actually happening to them, which helps to counter any optimistic bias they may have.

Planning Decision Pathways

We have always put a lot of emphasis upon risk/benefit analysis, and we teach our kids that they should weigh the pros and cons of every important decision they make. Even in psychotherapy, we often teach adolescents to think about the pluses and minuses of any given choice before they act. Unfortunately, as we've already discussed, if we encourage adolescents to weigh the pros and cons *at moments of risk*, like when they're drunk and considering whether or not to drive home, they are more likely to justify a bad decision. Risk/benefit discussions can be used to our advantage, however, if we have them *before* our kids are faced with a risky situation, when they're in a state of "cold" cognition.

Parents can prepare their adolescents for the inevitability of risky situations by helping them plan responses before they find themselves knee-deep in doubt and peer pressure. Given how present alcohol and drugs are in our world, for example, we can pretty much guarantee that our adolescents will at least occasionally find themselves at a party or other gathering where these substances are present. Although most of us wouldn't condone such parties, we also recognize that our kids need strategies to stay safe at these moments. Our efforts then should be aimed at planning decision pathways so that our kids are ready for these situations when they arise.

Most parents talk with their kids about never, ever driving while drinking or being in the car with a drunk or stoned driver. But we can go further by role-playing how they would turn down a ride from a friend who has been drinking. Role-playing sounds corny, I know, but turning down a ride takes a lot of self-esteem and so requires lots of practice. Parents can use other strategies as well, such as encouraging their adolescents to call them for a safe ride home if they drink or use drugs, with a guarantee that the parents won't "explode" with anger, but that they will speak with their child the next morning about their behavior and possibly even apply consequences.

A few years back, my then seventeen-year-old daughter attended a small gathering of friends at a house in the country where I suspected there might be alcohol at some point during the day. Before she left, we rehearsed what she would do if she had even a sip of alcohol—we agreed that she would not leave the house. Under no condition, except for a fire or some equal tragedy, was she to leave the house. We also agreed that she would call me and that I would drop whatever I was doing and pick her up immediately if she felt unsafe at any time (without fear of retribution or punishment). I insisted that she pledge to me before she left that she would not reconsider this decision. I'm a realist, and I know my daughter. She's a good student, a trustworthy friend, a responsible girl, and still she might attend a gathering of similar teens where there could be alcohol. I can live with that. But I can't live with her drinking and driving. Neither can she.

Helping our adolescents plan out decision pathways ahead of time will lower their anxiety and help them feel more in control. We know that having better decision-making abilities as early as age ten or eleven is correlated with having fewer troubles with peers, better conduct, and greater emotional stability in adolescence. It makes perfect sense. Just think about how much better and more relaxed you feel when you go into a difficult emotional situation, like asking your boss for a raise, when you've rehearsed what you're going to say and how you're going to behave. Let's give our kids the same opportunity to practice for their difficult moments.

Red Alerts

Adolescents can be taught to recognize and avoid situations where they face risk. In New York City, for example, teens talk about attending a "free," which is a party at someone's home when the parents are away. If your adolescent attends a free, there's virtually no doubt that she will be exposed to alcohol and marijuana, and perhaps other drugs as well. A free is a red alert—if your teen attends, there's a good chance she may drink or smoke weed. If our kids aren't ready for that type of exposure, we need to monitor and limit their access. Similarly, if your daughter has a boyfriend, but she isn't ready to have sex (and/or you aren't ready for her to), teach her that being home, or anywhere, totally alone with her boyfriend is a red alert. The more opportunity they have to be totally alone, the greater the likelihood that they will have unprotected sex. I advise parents to identify the red alerts that their children are likely to face and then do everything possible to avoid them before they happen. Red alerts are nonstarters, and they mean that risk and danger are imminent, about to happen, so get out; they don't mean "proceed with caution." Remember that you can role-play with your kids how to avoid these and other risky situations. Repeated practice leads to improved self-efficacy.

Role Modeling

As parents, we must be conscious of the fact that our children are always watching and learning from us. How we choose to speak, how often we use profanity, how much our anger gets away from us, how much time we spend looking at screens, how often we yell, and how we treat our spouse and others—all of these factors and more affect our children as they mature. We also need to remember that we're far from the only influence on our children. When our kids see things in media or online, they're being affected whether they realize it or not. The good thing is that we can choose to share positive media images that role model healthy behaviors by sharing movies, books, and television shows with them that provide teachable moments. We can also process the negative images they see. When my kids and I watch a movie where a physically strong character smokes cigarettes, for example, I usually make a small comment about how someone who smokes that much wouldn't really look that fit and be able to run that fast. Talking with our kids about their experiences, both the real-life ones and those they experience in media, helps them to make sense of the world and develop the immediate, gist responses that will help them stay safe.

Frequent Reminders

Even though our kids may say that we sound like a broken record, we are wise to remind them often that we're aware of the risks they face and to offer them ideas for how to manage those risks. Even adults don't always remember to employ their knowledge and safety strategies when they're not cued or reminded of things that can help them, so don't be afraid to tell your kids that you understand what they're going through and that you have some strategies to help them stay safe. It's a good idea to change up your words and exact delivery of the messaging now and again so that they don't tune you out, but keep it up. They need the frequent reminders.

Pithy phrases that parents sometimes use as their kids head out the door include "make good choices" and "use good judgment." Parents can even have fun with their kids and use silly catchphrases like "buckle up for safety," "safe driving is no accident," or "only you can prevent forest fires." However, the key here isn't a slogan, but rather providing good information that encourages our kids to avoid risks. "Sweetheart," you might say before your child heads out to a friend's house on a Saturday night, "do not get into the car tonight with someone who has been drinking or using drugs; nothing is worth that amount of risk. Remember, it only takes one slip behind the wheel to get hurt, permanently disabled, or killed. If anyone has anything at all to drink or smoke to-night, please call me, and I'll pick you up. No blame, just safety."

Since 2008, I've hosted a nationally broadcast radio call-in show every Friday morning, called *About Our Kids*, on the SiriusXM satellite radio network's Doctor Radio channel. I sometimes joke on the show that I was just about the perfect parent until I had kids. The advice I've laid out in this chapter is well supported by lots of evidence. Adopting these practices will make a meaningful difference in the lives of parents and their children and adolescents, but I know from personal experience that these guidelines aren't always easy to follow and don't always make us popular with our kids. What I can promise you is that once your kids cool down and are no longer in a state of "hot" cognition (like they are the minute you turn off the television, or when you insist that they come home by curfew even though they tell you that their friends are allowed to stay out later), they will settle down and be thankful, whether they tell you or not, for giving them structure, support, and safety.

CHAPTER 9

The Hidden Curriculum

(or, What Schools Can Do to Reduce Risk Taking)

*Education is what remains when one has forgotten
what one has learned in school.*

—ALBERT EINSTEIN

WHEN I ASK PARENTS WHAT they want for their kids by the time they finish high school, I absolutely never hear, "I want him to be great at geometry," or "I want her to really understand Shakespeare." Instead, they say things like, "I want him to have confidence in himself," or "I want her to be fair-minded and thoughtful." According to Gallup Polls, more than 90 percent of American adults concur, stating that acceptance of people of different races and ethnic backgrounds, honesty, caring for family and friends, democracy, and moral courage should be taught in public schools. What do you want for your children? Are they learning these things in school?

Based upon my clinical and personal experience with parents and schools, I believe there's a real disconnect between what parents want for their children and what most schools typically provide. Of course, all parents want their children to learn the necessary reading, writing, and arithmetic, but we also want them to gain skills in citizenship, teamwork, and empathy. Academic skills are important for our children's future, but no more important (perhaps even less important) than self-efficacy and emotion regulation skills for getting a good job and raising a family. Undoubtedly, mastering academic material empowers our children, but not all children are naturally good students, which leaves a lot of disempowered kids on the sidelines. Similarly, some of these desirable character traits can be nurtured through involvement in sports, the arts, and after-school clubs, but extracurricular activities incorporate only a minority of kids. If we really want to enhance our children's self-esteem, wellness, and future prospects, we must be purposeful about teaching resilience in school.

As we discussed in chapter 1, resilience is a multifaceted construct, generally thought of as our ability to maintain emotional control and persevere when confronted with life's challenges. Fortunately, we're now learning that resilience can be directly taught in the classroom, where it's often referred to as "character education." This can take many forms and has increasingly been employed to improve children's organizational skills, executive functioning, impulse control, empathy, sense of purpose, communication skills, and self-efficacy, while decreasing their anxiety and elevating their moods. Tried-and-true low-tech methods include meditation, aerobic exercise, distress tolerance skills, healthy nutrition, anger management, and goal setting.

> Resilience can be directly taught in the classroom.

We've spent the last hundred years focusing psychology into a science of what goes wrong—what's bad, negative, or the matter with us. There is good reason for this: As a species, we are primed for disaster. We are evolutionarily geared to look out for stress and to identify threats so that we can survive in a frequently hostile environment. We are not designed to look for positives. This made great sense for eons, but it doesn't make as much sense today. The deficit model looks at "what's wrong" with our kids, instead of what is right and how we can take advantage of their strengths and make them more resilient.

When you walk into a high school, chances are pretty good that one of the first things you'll see is something about the sports teams. In the lobby of my high school was a large glass case filled with football trophies. The same is pretty much true in most schools to this day. What does this say about the priorities of our schools? It tells us that sports really matter, maybe even more than academics.

What about early high school start times? More than 40 percent of high schools in the United States start classes before 8:00 a.m., but repeated studies have demonstrated that delaying the high school start time by as little as thirty or sixty minutes provides big advantages for teens, such as better grades, less depression, improved decision making, and fewer automobile accidents. Some of the most common reasons cited for early high school start times are the cost of transportation (e.g., the earlier the buses start rolling, the more kids can be picked up and the less traffic they hit) and, again, sports (e.g., later school start times mean a delay in practices and games and later nights for parents). Transportation costs and sports programming are important considerations, but the primacy of these factors unveils the hidden curriculum. We say we prioritize reading, writing, and arithmetic at school—that's the stated curriculum, even though most parents would like character education to be a greater priority. The hidden curriculum, however, is keeping the costs low and the competitive sports teams on top.

The Triumvirate of Good Health

While we cannot ward off all illness and disability, there are a few straightforward things that each of us can do to enhance our physical and emotional health and longevity—obtain sufficient exercise, eat a balanced diet, and get adequate sleep. I call these factors the triumvirate of good health and address them with every patient I see. Unfortunately, our schools all too often aren't doing their part to help our kids stay on top of these three essential factors.

When I was in elementary school, we had morning recess and a long lunch so that we could play after we ate. How much time do your kids get for recess? In New York City public schools these days, there is no recess (although the children generally do get some time to play after lunch). At my kids' New York City public elementary school, in fact, the children weren't even allowed on the jungle gym during recreation time because the school was frightened that a child would get hurt and the school would be sued. Do your kids walk to school? I did, and you probably did too. But these days our kids are increasingly bused or driven to school. In middle and high school, I had a forty-five-minute period for gym most every day. New York City public school kids today commonly get two to three forty-minute periods of gym each week. How active are your kids?

Recess and regular physical education classes have enormous physical benefits for our children, but more than that, they have been shown to enhance cognitive and academic development, along with social and emotional functioning. New research has even found that exercise can alleviate clinical depression in some adolescents. The vast majority of American parents believe in the value of recess and gym class but acknowledge that schools don't provide their children with sufficient daily physical activity.

The problem typically begins in preschool. Parents' desire for their children to be "school ready," along with parent and teacher concerns about the children being injured during physical play, have led to significant decreases in the physical activity of our children at the earliest ages. Developmental experts suggest that preschool should be about make-believe, telling and listening to stories, conversation, physical activity, and exploration of the natural world.

"If you look across the animal kingdom," says Alison Gopnik, professor of psychology at UC Berkeley, "you'll find that the more flexible an adult is, the longer that animal has had to be immature."

> If we don't give kids time to explore, play, and be physical, we set them up for real problems.

Dr. Gopnik is reflecting upon the same idea we discussed in chapter 3—namely, that by granting our children and adolescents more time to explore, play, question, and learn about their world, we extend the amount of time that it takes for their brain to fully prune and the white matter to completely set, giving them a more plastic, or flexible, brain and thereby enhancing their adaptability as adults. If we don't give kids time to explore, play, and be physical, we set them up for real problems.

As we discussed in chapter 4, more than one-third of children and adolescents in the United States are currently overweight or obese. Healthy weight range is based on a calculation called the body mass index (BMI). The Centers for Disease Control and Prevention defines overweight children and adolescents as those who are between the 85th and 95th percentile of BMI for their age, and obese children and adolescents as those above the 95th percentile. However, tipping the scales isn't happening only in America—obesity has now become a worldwide epidemic, and over 30 percent of the world's population, or 2.1 billion people, are believed to be overweight or obese. In developed countries, over 22 percent of girls and about 24 percent of boys are overweight or obese on average (though the United States seems to be leading the pack), and even in the developing world, where food can be scarce at times, about 13 percent of both boys and girls are overweight or obese.

Insufficient exercise isn't the only thing that contributes to the rise in obesity. Given all that we know about nutrition, it's a shame that we just can't seem to feed our children as we would like. Whether it's because we're busy parents, or raising our kids solo and just don't have time to prepare fresh meals, the reality is that kids are eating more fast food, more processed food, and more artificial food than ever before. Disappointingly, this happens both at home and at school.

Over 5 billion lunches were served in U.S. public schools in 2014, nearly three-quarters of which were offered free or at a reduced price. Nearly 20 million children in the United States get a free lunch at school every day. In 2014, the U.S. Department of Agriculture spent $16 billion, just under 0.5 percent of the federal budget, feeding these children a free breakfast and lunch. By the time labor costs are accounted for, schools in the United States have about $1.50 of funding from the Department of Agriculture for each lunch they provide, and there's only so much healthy nutrition $1.50 can buy you. As poverty climbs in the country, the number of children and adolescents receiving a free breakfast and lunch at school is growing rapidly. So what are we feeding our kids?

Although there are limits put on certain nutrients, including fat and sodium, we all know that today's school lunches are not the best nutrition we can provide for our children. In large part, this is because in order to save money, schools use primarily prepackaged foods, generally supplied by industrial food corporations that use more preservatives, emulsifiers, and artificial flavors and colors than most of us like our kids eating. While we don't know that all of these food additives are bad for our children, they certainly aren't necessary and good for our children. Plus, virtually all of this food comes prepackaged in potentially hormone-disrupting plastics (see chapter 4) that are typically placed in microwaves for heating on-site, where they can leach into the food even more readily. You might think that with all of our emphasis on local food, farmers' markets, and farm to table we would have shared the benefits of good nutrition with those to whom it matters most, our children. But, in fact, we've not come a long way from our own childhood days in the school cafeteria, and the menu items remain much the same—pizza, hamburgers, fried chicken, sandwiches, and mac and cheese. Take a look at your child's school lunch menu—I don't think you'll like what you see.

Some school districts have begun to take on nutrition, and the School Lunch Initiative in Berkeley, California, is a good example. The curriculum teaches elementary school students about nutrition, as they also learn to garden and cook. The students who go through the program become more knowledgeable about nutrition and are more than twice as likely as kids who don't go through the program to improve their eating habits.

Just as important to our children's healthy development as exercise and nutrition, if not more, is adequate and refreshing sleep. As we've already discussed in chapter 3, however, adolescents all too often don't get the sleep they need, which leads to loads of neurocognitive and behavioral problems as well as an increased likelihood of risky decision making. The CDC, in fact, now advises that high school not start prior to 8:30 a.m., but fewer than one in five American high schools adhere to this recommendation. And if all of the neuropsychological and behavioral problems weren't enough to convince you of our kids' need for more sleep, insufficient sleep also causes our bodies to produce more ghrelin (the hormone that signals hunger) and less leptin (the hormone that signals fullness). In other words, the less sleep our kids get, the more calories they eat, which, of course, further contributes to the epidemic of obesity.

All told, not achieving adequate exercise, nutrition, and sleep can make for a series of crippling impairments that increase the likelihood of risky behavior: lethargy, inattention, memory impairments, poor verbal fluency, computational difficulties, decreased creativity and abstract-problem-solving abilities, impulsivity, impaired decision making, and obesity and its attendant low self-esteem. The good news is that schools can actually do a lot to address these problems.

Exercise and sports programs keep our kids active and should be available daily for every child, not just those on the competitive sports teams. Starting high school later in the morning, at 9:00 or 10:00 a.m., would accommodate our teens' natural circadian rhythm instead of working against it and increase their sleep by more than an hour a day in most cases, helping to reduce bad decision making and risky behavior. Delaying the school start time will also keep our high school students in class later in the afternoon, giving them less unsupervised time during which they can engage in risk taking. Limiting school lunch portion sizes and providing kids with fewer prepackaged and more fresh foods, perhaps by engaging local farms and providers, will help to reduce obesity, enhance our kids' self-esteem, and save a lot of health care dollars due to the negative effects of obesity, hypertension and other heart disease, and diabetes as they age. Most importantly, these efforts will improve our children's concentration and mood, academic performance, overall physical health, coping skills, stress management, and social engagement with family and peers, all of which are associated with improved self-esteem and resilience to anxiety, depression, and substance abuse.

An Eleven-Letter Word

I frequently receive calls from middle and high schools about the struggles that their students are having. Depression, anxiety, agitated and aggressive behavior, and drugs and alcohol typically top the list of concerns. When I talk to the teachers and parents and the students themselves, I hear about how stressed they are, overwhelmed by schoolwork and other commitments, and often not sleeping well.

Based on my training and experience as a child, adolescent, and adult psychiatrist, and as a father of two teens, I know that a fifty-something-year-old man giving middle or high school students a talk about drugs and alcohol, no matter how engaging, doesn't generally make much of a difference in their behavior. But my conversations with teachers and parents are always intriguing. At the end of the day, most parents and teachers and teens themselves know that the real problem they struggle with isn't actually marijuana or alcohol or any of the other drugs with which teens may experiment. Likewise, they know that the real problem isn't sex or sexually transmitted infections. No, they know exactly what lies at the core of these problems and just what to call it—an eleven-letter word we all know as "adolescence."

When schools ask me to give the student body a talk about the perils of substance abuse, it's not because they are convinced that anything I say will change their students' behavior; rather, it's because they feel they must do something, anything, to help the students manage their stress in more productive ways.

We clearly don't need the same old warnings about drugs and alcohol, like "Just say no," and "This is your brain on drugs." What we truly need has relatively little to do with drugs and alcohol. What our teens and young adults need are tools to manage their stress, skills to help them tolerate the vicissitudes of their moods, means of improving their communication with parents and peers, and more sleep. And this is something we should all be able to really get behind.

Teaching Resilience

In 2005, an incredible opportunity came my way when I was invited by the NYU College of Arts and Science to develop a novel mental health education program for undergraduate students. Most undergraduate psychology departments are really good at teaching students about perception, memory, cognition, and personality, and NYU is no exception. But few psychology departments teach undergraduates about clinical care, or how we diagnose and treat mental illnesses like depression and schizophrenia. In 2006, my team at the NYU School of

Medicine launched the department of Child and Adolescent Mental Health Studies within the College of Arts and Science at NYU. CAMS, as it's known on campus, is now one of the largest undergraduate academic programs at NYU, with well over four thousand students enrolled annually in nearly fifty unique courses. Within the CAMS department we teach not only courses that you would expect to find in a clinical psychology program, like child development and psychopathology, but also courses on sleep, happiness, sexual identity, morality, children's literature, divorce, love, and a whole lot more.

Once I began working directly with college students every day, it quickly became evident to me how much they struggle with anxiety, peer pressure, sadness, getting adequate sleep, drug and alcohol use, and time management. So it was only a matter of time before I landed upon the idea for a course focused on enhancing resilience. As a physician I know that one of the best ways to help people achieve a desired change is first to teach them the behavior and then to give them lots of practice at it outside of the clinic or classroom in real-life settings. One of the many idiosyncratic phrases often overheard in the halls of medical schools is "see one, do one, teach one." It applies when learning to draw blood or arterial blood gases, do a lumbar puncture, place a nasogastric tube, suture a wound, or any of the many hundreds of skills that medical students and residents learn throughout their education and training. Doctors have observed that the best way to learn is by practicing and then teaching others.

Edgar Dale was a twentieth-century expert in education. He is the creator of the Cone of Learning, as displayed in figure 9.1. Dale's cone basically says that we learn more from active engagement, by doing, than we do from sitting passively and observing. Dale wasn't convinced that the percentages assigned to various learning styles were entirely accurate. In fact, he knew that what his Cone of Learning suggests is actually something that has been common wisdom for thousands of years. As Confucius said:

I see and I forget, I hear and I remember, I do and I understand.

CONE OF LEARNING
(EDGAR DALE)

After 2 Weeks we tend to remember		Nature of Involvement	
10% of what we READ	Reading	Verbal Receiving	PASSIVE
20% of what we HEAR	Hearing Words		PASSIVE
30% of what we SEE	Looking at Pictures		PASSIVE
50% of what we HEAR & SEE	Watching a Movie / Looking at an Exhibit / Watching a Demonstration / Seeing it Done on Location	Visual Receiving	PASSIVE
70% of what we SAY	Participating in a Discussion / Giving a Talk	Receiving/ Participating	ACTIVE
90% of what we SAY & DO	Doing a Dramatic Presentation / Simulating the Real Experience / Doing the Real Thing	Doing	ACTIVE

Figure 9.1: The Cone of Learning: The Cone of Learning, sometimes called the learning retention pyramid, displays how much we remember based upon our involvement in the learning process. The percentages are widely debated, but the general trend appears valid. The more we engage or do with our learning, the more we tend to retain. (Percepsys Performance, Inc., 2017)

I believed that we could teach our NYU undergraduates to be more resilient, and since resilient adolescents manage risk better, there is no better use of our efforts. Studies have shown that characteristics like being good at managing emotions, having good impulse control, showing empathy toward others, having a sense of purpose in life,

> Resilient adolescents manage risk better.

and feeling self-efficacious, or believing that you have some control over your own life, result in higher levels of resilience among adolescents. And we know that a high level of social-emotional skill among kindergarten children is predictive of higher levels of education and employment, along with lower levels of criminal activity, substance abuse, and mental health difficulties, decades later in adulthood. But could we teach undergraduates these kinds of skills in the classroom?

Based upon Dale's cone and my training as a physician, I surmised that the college students would learn and retain the resilience material best if they applied their knowledge directly. So in the fall of 2011, my colleague Ursula Diamond and I launched a two-semester CAMS course called Risk and Resilience in Urban Teens: Mental Health Promotion and Practicum. In the fall semester we taught the undergraduates about resilience and risk-taking behavior among adolescents. In the spring semester, we taught them a curriculum we had developed that addressed cognitive distortions, stress management and reduction, drug and alcohol use, sleep hygiene, interpersonal communication, adolescent decision making, and organizational skills. Our students then delivered this ten-session curriculum at a local high school.

In our second year, after working out the kinks, we studied the effects our risk and resilience class had had on the college students. We compared the students in the intervention (the CAMS risk and resilience class) to college students who weren't in the intervention (but who were taking another CAMS class).

We learned something very important from our study: By teaching a semester-long course to undergraduates, we were able to improve their coping skills, reduce their dysfunctional attitudes, and lower their perceived degree of stress in a big way. These findings were not only statistically significant; they were, as behavioral programs go, moderate to large in magnitude. The students who took our class became much more resilient than the average NYU student. We observed our findings at the end of the first semester, and they held in place by the end of the second semester, after the college students had taught the high school students. The changes were not only meaningful. They were lasting.

The real question that remains unanswered, of course, is whether the gains our NYU students made by the end of the year will hold up five years from now. Will they have a higher graduation rate than students who didn't take our class? Will they handle the inevitable breakups better? Will they be more optimistic when they don't get into their first or second choice of graduate school? Will they exercise regularly and prioritize sleep and good nutrition? Will they get sick less often? Will they use fewer drugs and less alcohol than other college graduates? Will they become less depressed or anxious when confronted with life's challenges? These tough questions will only be answered by longer, more expensive studies. But we have every reason to believe that by teaching students how to manage their dysfunctional attitudes better, reduce the stress they feel, and rely on improved coping skills, we're helping them to manage the unavoidable difficulties ahead.

The Science of Happiness

Teaching resilience and health promotion practices can help to reduce risky behavior, and school is the place to start. It's only in the classroom that our children are truly a captive audience. Even teaching these skills briefly to high-risk high school students has been shown to significantly reduce the odds of depression, anxiety, and behavior problems up to two years later. And reducing negative moods and anxiety, along with behavior problems, means less risk taking. As we gather more and more data on the benefits of health promotion and disease prevention programs, it seems increasingly like educational malpractice when we don't teach these concepts at school.

Here's where I often like to start when I work with kids in schools. Take a look at the list in figure 9.2. Now circle every emotion that you've felt so far today.

Figure 9.2. Emotion Identification

DAILY EMOTIONS

How many of these emotions have you felt today?

Afraid	Disappointed	Indifferent	Serious
Alienated	Distrustful	Insecure	Shy
Amazed	Embarrassed	Insulted	Silly
Amused	Enthusiastic	Interested	Smart
Angry	Excited	Jealous	Stupid
Annoyed	Frightened	Lonely	Surprised
Ashamed	Frustrated	Loving	Sympathetic
Bitter	Guilty	Lustful	Tired
Bored	Happy	Nervous	Trusting
Calm	Hesitant	Proud	Uncomfortable
Confident	Hopeful	Regretful	Upset
Confused	Hurt	Sad	Vengeful
Curious	Impatient	Satisfied	Worried

How many emotions did you identify? Are you surprised? Most of us feel many more emotions than we might imagine during a day, or merely over the course of a few hours. But research shows that adolescents experience an even wider range of moods and emotions than adults, as well as higher highs and lower lows, along with more frequent mood switches throughout the day. Just imagine how our tweens and teens must feel when they come home from school or work, having gone through the volatility of so many emotions in a day, feeling like a pinball in a machine of moods.

Fortunately, there's a lot that our schools can do to help our kids understand and manage their moods. Starting at a young age, we can teach our children about how their brains work, so they will develop more em-pathy for themselves and others, which generally leads to less blaming and negative emotion. They will also come to understand that their brains, and therefore their moods, can actually get better with practice. We call this a "growth mindset," and many studies have demonstrated that it can be a powerful effect with lasting impact (something we will talk about more in chapter 10). And if we add instruction in the cognitive behavior techniques that we employ in psychotherapy for children and adolescents who face depression and anxiety, we will actually be pro-viding our kids with the keys to a happier life.

Remember the cognitive triangle from chapter 5? It shows us vi-sually how our feelings, thoughts, and behaviors all influence one an-other. If your child feels depressed, it does little good to simply tell her to feel better. Since thoughts, feelings, and behaviors are all intertwined and influence one another, however, influencing one of these factors will influence the others. In other words, the cognitive triangle teaches us that by changing our behavior and our thoughts, we can change our feelings.

> By changing our behavior and our thoughts, we can change our feelings.

Changing our behavior isn't always easy, but it's doable and teachable to kids in school. For example, when we're sad, we tend to isolate ourselves, but we feel better when we go out with friends or spend time with family. This simple behavior change of getting together with others instead of isolating ourselves is actually drawn from a technique that therapists call "opposite action"; that is, doing the opposite of what we would otherwise tend to do when we're in a bad mood. Getting back to the things we enjoy, and making sure that we engage in hobbies and activities outside of school and work, surely makes us happier and more productive; but more often than not, when we feel bad, we tend to stop doing these things, which only makes us feel worse. Other behavioral activation techniques that help to reduce stress and improve mood include getting regular exercise and sufficient sleep, as discussed above. Deceptively simple, I know, but highly effective.

Likewise, it's not always easy to change our thinking, but challenging our thoughts turns out to be a very effective technique for reducing anxiety and negative moods. Imagine a teenage girl whom we'll call Julia who is not "tagged" in a Facebook photo on a friend's page, even though every other teen in the photo is. Julia may react strongly to seeing this photo, believing that she was purposefully not tagged, which may lead to feelings of hurt and anger along with fantasies of revenge. Thinking back to chapter 5, it would seem that Julia is experiencing a number of cognitive distortions: (1) She may be *filtering*, or magnifying the negative details while blocking out all of the positive aspects; after all, even though she wasn't tagged, she was in the photo that her friend posted. (2) She may be *mind reading*, or presuming to understand why her friend didn't tag her in the photo and strongly suspecting that she was purposefully left off. Or (3) she may be *personalizing*, or thinking that her friend didn't tag her because of something Julia recently said or did. Our thoughts, just like our behaviors, have a direct influence on how we feel. So if Julia is overly influenced by these distorted thoughts, she may spend the next few hours or days feeling just miserable.

If Julia has been taught to recognize her cognitive distortions, however, she may think about this experience entirely differently and feel a whole lot better. By teaching Julia about filtering, mind reading, personalizing, and other cognitive distortions, we can help her question her thoughts. And fewer negative thoughts means less bad moods, less anxiety, and a decreased likelihood of risk-taking behavior.

One quick method for challenging a troubling thought is the triple-column technique (see figure 9.3). This method requires that we first identify a worrisome thought, then decide if the thought constitutes a cognitive distortion, and finally combat any distortions by "talking back," or challenging the thought. We can also think of "talking back" as advice we might give to a friend. We are often a lot nicer to our friends than we are to ourselves, so this method really resonates with some kids.

Figure 9.3. The Triple-Column Technique

Searching automatic thoughts for signs of cognitive distortions and then "talking back" is a powerful tool in helping reduce anxiety and improve mood.

AUTOMATIC THOUGHT	COGNITIVE DISTORTIONS	TALK BACK (OR ADVICE FOR A FRIEND)
He ignored my text message. He must be mad at me for something.	Filtering Mind reading Blaming	"Maybe he's just busy or distracted by some of his own troubles."
I wasn't invited to the party. I must have done something wrong. She must hate me.	Filtering Mind reading Personalization	"Maybe it was just a mistake. She can be so absentminded sometimes."

The science of happiness doesn't stop with emotion identification and cognitive behavioral training. Teaching social skills to those who struggle with friendships can enhance resilience. Making certain that we identify as early as possible those children who have emotional and behavioral troubles like ADHD, depression, and anxiety, along with those who have trouble learning, will allow us to intervene and provide special education services, therapy, and medication as necessary to help keep those kids on track. We know that adolescents with these sorts of troubles also frequently struggle with self-esteem and engage in higher rates of risky behavior and drop out of school more often, so early identification and treatment of affected kids can make a big difference.

And there is still more we can do. While subject-specific health promotion interventions at school, like sex education and bullying prevention programs, are only sometimes effective, more broad-based risk reduction efforts can address many of the behaviors in which our kids engage, like sex, drugs, and bullying. Enhanced monitoring in middle and high school where high-risk behaviors take place (like behind the wood shop or out on the athletic fields), training teachers and staff when and how to intervene when disruptive behavior is evident, and establishing clear school policies for how to handle bullying and risky behavior at school can be effective. And meaningful extracurricular activities, along with mandated community service hours for high school students, may allow us to harness some of the intense adolescent emotion and channel that energy into productive civic engagement.

There are also a whole host of other practical skills that we can teach our children and adolescents in school that will serve them well throughout their lives. It's remarkable, when you think about it, that we don't generally teach proper sleep hygiene, nutrition, goal setting, and communication skills in school; *but these concepts can be taught and practiced, and our kids will get better at them.* We can also teach our adolescents behavior modification principles, like the behavioral parent training we discussed in chapter 8, which will help them to be more successful in all of their personal and work relationships.

Schools and parents don't always see the value of incorporating these character education efforts into our kids' schooling because we become consumed with our desire for our kids to advance academically. And, frankly, we don't have one tried-and-true curriculum that we know works in middle and high school to effectively transmit this information and consistently change behavior. But some studies, like ours with the

NYU undergraduates, have been effective; and these efforts are worthwhile because we know that neuroscience-informed interventions can improve adolescents' emotional stability, and emotionally healthy kids engage in less risky behavior. When we change our behavior, our thoughts, our sleep, and even our breathing, we reduce risk and change ourselves for the better.

Barely Breathing

Take a deep, relaxing breath. Now exhale slowly. Do that three times. Now close your eyes and do it three more times. How do you feel?

Restful breathing is another proven strategy that we can use to enhance our resilience. In San Francisco, a handful of middle and high schools have incorporated one fifteen-minute period of meditation and breathing into the beginning and end of each day, and the results have been simply remarkable. After a few months of the breathing program, suspensions at Visitacion Valley Middle School dropped by 79 percent, attendance increased to 98 percent, and the grade point average increased by 0.4 points. At San Francisco's Burton High School, once known as "Fight School," the breathing program led to a 75 percent reduction in suspensions and a major increase in the school's state academic ranking. All this from slowing down and taking a few breaths. In our hurried and harried world, it seems that our kids have been barely breathing.

Similar school-based efforts all over the world have employed mindfulness meditation with great benefits for students. Mindfulness, often defined as "paying attention in a particular way: on purpose, in the present moment, and nonjudgmentally," represents what is sometimes called the "third wave" of psychological therapies. Freudian-influenced psychoanalysis and insight-oriented psychodynamic psychotherapy were the first wave; cognitive behavior therapy (CBT), using techniques like opposite action and the triple-column technique, was the second wave; and now mindfulness is the third wave.

Whenever we feel anxious and worried, it's always about something from the past (e.g., "Did I hurt his feelings?" "Did I screw things up with my teacher?") or the future (e.g., "What if I don't do well on this exam?" "How am I going to pay for college?"). To address this past/future orientation that we all experience at times of high anxiety, mindfulness teaches us to be in the moment, focusing on the here and now. Mindfulness practices teach us to be simply aware of our thinking, instead of trying to restructure and change the thoughts that bother us. We learn that thoughts are just thoughts; they are not who we are, but rather temporary ideas in our head. We learn to quiet our mind; and we learn that negative, perseverative, and obsessional thoughts are transient, and that "this too shall pass."

Mindfulness practices typically start with learning to breathe, as the kids in San Francisco did. Invariably, I work on breathing with my patients who struggle with anxiety. Restful breathing is a great way to settle your body, slow things down, and relax when you feel stressed. When we breathe slowly and deeply, it slows down our heart rate, which helps us calm down and makes us feel less anxious. Our heart and respiratory rate can act like a barometer for our stress level. Ironically, when we're stressed, we often change our breathing radically, which causes us to feel more jittery and irritable.

Restful breathing, sometimes called belly breathing, requires that you push your diaphragm (the large muscle at the bottom of your lungs) down into your abdomen. This method allows the most air to enter your body with the least amount of physical effort. Breathing this way causes your belly to rise and fall with each breath, while your chest stays still. When you find your chest rising and falling dramatically as you breathe, it's usually because you're taking very deep breaths due to strenuous exercise or emotional distress; that is, any time you need to pull lots of air into your body quickly. But using our chest muscles to breathe costs a lot of energy and only brings in a bit more air. It's not worth expending the energy unless you absolutely need the air. Restful breathing calms down the entire nervous system, and one of the greatest things about this method is that it's portable and goes wherever we go. It's best if we practice this technique when we're not feeling stressed, so that it works well when we really need it.

RESTFUL BREATHING EXERCISE

Practicing this simple exercise a few times each day can help us to calm our nervous system and reduce the impact of stress on our bodies and minds.

1. Lean back in your chair with both feet planted flat on the floor.
2. Place one hand on your belly and one hand on your chest.
3. Inhale slowly and deeply through your nose or mouth into your belly so that you push out the hand on your belly as much as feels comfortable—like you're inflating a small balloon; then exhale. The hand on your chest should be pretty much still, while the hand on your belly should rise and fall with each breath. Try taking a few slow and steady breaths like that.
4. As you breathe in, say to yourself, "I am here." Breathe in for about five seconds. As you exhale, say to yourself, "I am calm." Continue taking long, slow, deep breaths that inflate and deflate your belly. Focus on the sound and feeling of breathing as you become more and more relaxed. Every time that your mind wanders onto something else, gently bring the attention back to your breathing.
5. Continue deep breathing for a couple more minutes.

Mindful Eating

Mindfulness doesn't stop with breathing, of course, and there are many other practices that we can employ in schools to help our kids feel more calm and focused for the tasks at hand. Eating, for example, can be a mindful activity. How often do you power through your meals, distracted by watching the television or reading a book or engaging in a stimulating conversation, not really even noticing what you're ingesting? Try this experiment next time you sit down to eat: First, look at the food you're about to eat. Take a really good, long look. What is its shape and consistency? What color is it? How much space does it take up? Where does it shine and reflect the light? Second, listen to your food. What sound does it make as you touch it, or rub your fork, knife, or spoon over it? Third, take some time to smell your food. Is the smell familiar? Is it pleasing? Does it make your mouth water? Fourth, place some of the food into your mouth and feel it pass your lips and move onto your tongue. Move it around in your mouth. Do different parts of your tongue taste the different flavors, like salty and sweet? Take some time to chew the food and let it move around in your mouth—enjoy every bit of flavor you can. Finally, swallow the food and feel how it moves down your esophagus, observing how your entire mouth and neck work together to bring the food into your body. Starting each meal in this way not only slows us down, it also can help to make us more appreciative of and grateful for the food we are eating.

Gratitude

Gratitude, or feeling grateful for our food, our friends, the natural world, and anything else that is meaningful to us, has been repeatedly shown in studies to be another important practice that we can employ in reducing stress and improving mood. The research protocols in these studies are quite basic and generally only require that participants keep a gratitude journal in which they write down daily or every few days the things for which they feel grateful. Such simple experiments have consistently found that participants observe an increase in positive emotions and smiling, and a reduction in anger and other negative emotions. And as we discussed in chapter 8, more positive emotions and less stress and anger mean less active brain reward centers and threat detection areas, which translates into less risk-taking behavior.

Mindfulness demands that we purposefully pay attention to whatever we're doing at any given moment. This can take a lot of effort, particularly for adolescents, who have so many things on their mind, but the rewards can be substantial. And who needs that more than our kids? Reduced anxiety and stress, improved mood, better concentration and memory, weight loss, reductions in anger, and enhanced mood stability have all been reported in studies of adults and adolescents who regularly practice mindfulness. The techniques include not only mindful breathing and eating, but also yoga, mindful walks, scanning our body for signs of tension, and focusing on a single part of the body, such as a hand or the soles of the feet, and becoming entirely engrossed in and aware of how that part of the body feels in all respects for minutes at a time. Mindfulness is beneficial for everyone, and there are no age limits. The earlier we start, the better. Furthermore, by using mindfulness at home, parents have a wonderful opportunity to role model and teach emotion regulation practices to their children.

Although we don't understand the precise neural mechanisms that underlie mindfulness, there is no doubt that it alters the brain. Neuroimaging studies have demonstrated that mindfulness practices increase activation within the prefrontal cortex (the brain's CEO and center of attention, working memory, organization, and decision making) and decrease activation within the amygdala (the brain's threat detection center) in as little as a few weeks to a few months. In other words, mindfulness practices appear to stabilize and enhance executive functions and cognitive control while limiting the impact of negative emotions on attention, memory, organization, and decision making; all of which can help to improve academic performance and reduce risk taking.

The Failure of Health Class

Remember health class? How embarrassing was that—listening to teachers talk about body parts, sex and sexually transmitted infections, drinking and drugs? Every single kid in my ninth grade class treated it like a big joke, and it pretty much was. The teacher uncomfortably lectured us about the dangers of sex and drugs. It seems that things haven't changed much in the past forty years or so. Tina Fey satirized health class in the 2004 film *Mean Girls*, when Coach Carr tells the kids, "Don't have sex, because you will get pregnant and die."

Talking about sex in schools is the right thing to do. Here's what we know: First, abstinence-only education doesn't work. Telling adolescents to not have sex or to wait until marriage has no effect. Second, teaching kids about contraception doesn't increase the likelihood that they will have sex. And third, making condoms available in schools doesn't increase sexual activity, but it does increase condom use among the adolescents who have sex. The data from the United States, Canada, and Europe couldn't be clearer.

Likewise, we can do better with our drug prevention efforts. Universal prevention programs that provide general drug education for teens and tweens by and large haven't been effective at reducing drug use and have oftentimes made things worse. Perhaps a better approach is to target those kids who are at high risk of alcohol and substance abuse for a more intensive intervention. The Jesuits have an old maxim: "Give me a child until he is seven, and I will give you the man." While not perfect, the truth is that past behavior commonly predicts future behavior; remember, as we discussed in chapter 8, in most of the families where major conflict occurs during the teen years, there is a family history of troubles prior to adolescence.

Identifying ninth-grade adolescents with a high risk for addiction and mental health problems and providing them with even a brief targeted intervention has been shown to significantly reduce the odds of drinking, binge drinking, and the severity of problem drinking by about 30–40 percent for up to two years. The tools for identifying high-risk kids and helping to prevent alcohol and drug use aren't yet perfect, but by finding those kids with risky personality traits like sensation seeking, impulsivity, anxiety, and hopelessness, we will almost certainly do a whole lot better than most prior prevention programs have. An added benefit of targeting high-risk adolescents is what's called the "herd effect." Since high-risk kids are, unfortunately, often role models to their lower-risk peers, when the high-risk kids drink less, typically the lower-risk kids (or the "herd") follow suit.

In reality, health classes commonly try to help our kids improve their decision making by teaching them to weigh the pros and cons of any potentially risky behavior. Unfortunately, as we now know, encouraging a quantitative assessment or risk/benefit analysis often results in our kids making worse decisions when faced with a risky choice. Health class as it's being taught today may be putting our kids at greater risk, but we can do better.

How Do You Get to Carnegie Hall?

Karen Adolph studies how infants and toddlers learn to move, and what she has discovered is incredibly instructive for those of us who work with risky adolescents—basically, getting good at anything takes a lot of practice. In learning to walk, Dr. Adolph's research has shown, the typical toddler takes 2,368 steps, equal to 701 meters, or the length of nearly eight American football fields, and falls seventeen times each hour.

When multiplied by six hours, which is equivalent to about half of a toddler's waking day, that's about 14,000 steps, forty-six football fields, and more than one hundred falls per day. Who knew?! Toddlers must really want to learn to walk because falling a hundred times each day is uncomfortable and frustrating. But we only become efficient walkers by practicing over and over again. It's the same for learning to speak—by three years of age, middle-class infants have heard over 30 million words. And for learning to see—by four months of age, infants have made somewhere between 3 million and 6 million eye movements.

Most parents want schools to teach their children to be honest, accepting, caring, and courageous, but chemistry and history can only take us so far in this direction. In the not too distant past, young children prepared for their future by learning to hunt and prepare food early in life. Today's kids have precious little opportunity to practice the kinds of tasks that teach caregiving and responsibility for others; the kinds of skills that they will need to perform effectively as grown-ups. My sisters and I used to babysit for neighborhood kids all of the time. However, my teenage daughter has only babysat a few times, and my teenage son has never babysat. Although I never had a paper route, one of my closest childhood friends had one, and sometimes I substituted for him. By the age of fourteen, I was a paid summer camp counselor for younger kids, a job I kept for four more summers. But most of these jobs today are held by adults, and pretty much all our kids do is go to school, do homework, spend time on screens, and maybe have an extracurricular activity or two.

You would be hard-pressed to find an adolescent these days who doesn't know that regularly eating high-fat foods and not exercising results in weight gain. And I dare you to find a teenager who doesn't know that condoms protect against pregnancy. But still our kids overeat and have unprotected sex. Why? Because knowledge is only a part of the puzzle. Knowing that cigarette smoking causes cancer and emphysema

> Knowledge is
> only a part
> of the puzzle.

might dissuade a few kids from smoking, but remember, our kids already believe they're not invincible. And most fifteen-year-olds can't even begin to imagine how lung cancer will feel at fifty-five. In order to help our kids change their behavior, or not pick up unhealthy behaviors like smoking to begin with, they need to have *an emotional connection* to the behavior change; they need to *feel* it's really important to do or not to do something.

My patient Olivia is a case in point. Olivia's parents smoked cigarettes when she was younger. They were chain-smokers. She remembers how her dad would tire on the ball field when they would play catch together. She remembers how her parents smelled like smoke. When Olivia was in her teens, her father developed emphysema; when Olivia was a young adult, her father died of cancer. As much as Olivia admired her father, she never even considered smoking, given what she'd seen growing up. The emotional salience of getting sick from cigarettes really stuck with Olivia, and that, along with the knowledge that smoking kills, enabled her to stay away from tobacco. But the emotional connection to smoking for some kids is exactly the opposite. Smoking looks cool. Smokers seem unafraid of consequences. And for these reasons, smoking can enhance a young teen's social standing.

Helping children and adolescents develop an emotional connection to the desired behavior brings us right back to gist. I encourage you to take another close look at the strategies described in the final section of chapter 8 ("Getting Back to Gist"). These approaches, which can be taught at home and in school, are all about helping our kids to develop a solid emotional grasp of potentially harmful situations and then rely upon this internalized understanding, or gist, to override their tendency to overthink in risky situations.

As we've discussed, adolescents are driven by hormones to gain elevated peer status. They are supersensitive to rewards and feel true pain when peers exclude them. The only way we can combat these forces and guide our kids toward choosing healthy behaviors is to help them find meaningful challenges that are emotionally salient, and then give them loads of practice at these tasks. Repeated practice shapes the brain, but the kids first need to feel a genuine connection to the behavior changes that we're trying to help them accomplish. Having a patient who is dying of lung cancer due to cigarette smoking speak at your school may influence a few kids; but giving our adolescents the opportunity to volunteer at a nursing home and become personally connected to that same patient is a much more powerful lesson.

We desperately need to support our schools in doing a better job of helping all of our youth develop healthy habits. Research clearly shows that our children will be less likely to take unnecessary risks when they are emotionally stable and believe that they are able to positively affect their future. Establishing daily exercise programs, improving school breakfasts and lunches, and adjusting school start times are a start. Incorporating character education, or resilience training—e.g., emotion identification, cognitive behavior therapy techniques, breathing, mindfulness, goal setting, and communication and social skills—is also necessary to help reduce risk, and our efforts in this regard must not be fleeting. We need to give our children lots of practice in these skills and make them a regular part of elementary, middle, and high school classes each year.

In the small country of Iceland, this common-sense approach has been applied to after-school activities and yielded huge benefits over the past fifteen years. The Youth in Iceland program has worked with local communities to build extensive after-school programs in sports, music, dance and art. They have taught parents the value of spending time with their children, given low-income families money in the form of a "Leisure Card" to pay for recreational activities together, and passed laws prohibiting teens aged thirteen to sixteen from being outside after 10:00 p.m. in winter and after midnight in summer. The percent of fifteen- and sixteen year-olds who "often" or "almost always" spend time with their parents on weekdays has doubled from 23 to 46 percent, and the percent involved in sports at least four times each week has gone from 24 to 42 percent. Even more important, the percent who have been drunk in the past month has plunged from 42 percent in 1998 to just 5 percent in 2016; those who have ever smoked marijuana has tumbled from 17 percent to 7 percent; and those smoking cigarettes daily has dropped from 23 percent to 3 percent.

You might worry that providing character education in schools and offering extensive after-school activities will take away from much-needed teaching and homework time—most of us parents do. But the fact is that we could even lengthen the school day if we needed to (it's not like we need our kids hanging out for more hours at the mall each day), and we can cut back a bit on homework to give them more time to participate in valued school and after-school activities that will further teach life skills. In the lower grades, homework is most meaningful when it focuses on improving reading and general study skills and establishing good habits. In the higher grades, middle and high school, homework has real value and can advance our kids' learning of complex material. But this holds only up to a point. My kids' and patients' high school homework burden has become so onerous, often three to four hours each day, that their teachers frequently don't even check the work—the teachers are assigning so much homework, in fact, that they don't even have time to review if the kids get it right or wrong! In other words, homework isn't doing its actual job, which is to help our kids learn. The best research we have on homework suggests that thoughtful assignments (e.g., introducing new content, reinforcing recently learned skills, and allowing students to explore their own interests) that students can actually complete and that the teachers will actually review is the best use of our efforts. If

you're looking for a rule of thumb about the amount of homework assigned, one of the lead researchers in this area has suggested about ten
minutes per grade per day, or about two hours for a twelfth-grade student
and one hour for a sixth-grade student.

As a psychiatrist, I often remind my patients that we can change ourselves into something better but that change rarely occurs overnight. We
have to really want to make these changes, and we need to feel an intense
emotional connection to the outcome we desire—to feel less depressed
and anxious, to lose weight, to do better in school, to build a better relationship with our parents, to stop smoking cigarettes, or to stop drinking
alcohol and using drugs. Change takes time and happens in small steps,
within a trusting relationship, and where there are lots of opportunities
to practice the new skills and approaches. As we begin to make small
changes, we will start to reap their benefits, and it's those rewards that
will further encourage us to keep moving in the new direction. The real
key here is having an emotional connection to the behavior change and
lots of opportunity to practice so that it becomes a habit.

We expect schools to give our children a solid academic foundation, but
there is always a hidden curriculum. Cultural beliefs and societal expectations, values, and norms are the unintended lessons that find their way
into every reading, problem set, essay, and sports activity. If your children
are reading books primarily written about characters who are white, for
example, whether we like it or not they're being taught that white people
are somehow more important than other ethnic groups. Or consider the
often-disproportionate attention schools give to annual statewide standardized tests. If you're a child in school during the months leading up to
the testing, you are likely to become convinced that your test performance
is the school's most important measure of your success; more important
than your behavior, your thoughtfulness toward others, even your

intellect. And certainly we've all written an essay that's more about what we think the teacher wants us to write than about what we believe and wish to write.

Every time we make our teenagers start school at 7:30 a.m., we're telling them in no uncertain terms that we don't care too much about their natural circadian rhythm. We're telling them that we'd rather their education be convenient for parents and teachers than the best it can be for their learning, health, and welfare. Similarly, when we leave character education, or resilience training, out of the curriculum, we're telling our kids that their wellness and emotional regulation are not among our primary concerns. That's the hidden curriculum.

Our schools can do a lot more to support our children's health, happiness, and resilience, all of which will help reduce adolescent risk taking. As parents, we have a major role in helping our schools find a better balance between academics, exercise, nutrition, and sleep, and we have a role in modeling this balance at home for our children as well. Schools must be purposeful about teaching self-efficacy and emotional self-regulation skills like mood and anxiety management, mindfulness, and restful breathing. Schools must incorporate more group projects and creative problem-solving exercises that emphasize collaboration and shared responsibility instead of competition and rote memorization. Schools must expand the scope of required readings and assignments so that they're actually teaching those values that most parents say they want our schools to teach. And schools must give our kids lots and lots of practice with these skills so that they will have what they need to succeed in their future.

CHAPTER 10

The Big Picture

(or, What Society Can Do to Reduce Teen Risk Taking)

I skate to where the puck is going to be, not where it has been.

—WAYNE GRETZKY

I HAD A RUDE AWAKENING A few months after my daughter, Parker, turned twelve years old. The two of us were walking on a small street in downtown New York City just a few blocks from our home on a hot, midsummer Saturday afternoon. Baseball was blaring on the TV in the local bars, and the young men were spilling onto the street with beers in hand. As Parker and I approached, they caught her in their gaze, undoubtedly noticing her tank top, shorts, and long flowing hair. They averted their eyes only when we got close enough for them to notice her tender age, along with my glaring disapproval of their gawking. I realized at that moment that whether or not my daughter and I were ready for it, the world was beginning to see her as a woman.

We often equate adolescence with being an older teenager, but the reality is that most girls are knee-deep in puberty by about thirteen (although boys typically trail girls by two or three years). This means that by the time girls are thirteen and boys are fifteen or sixteen, their bodies and brains are in the midst of major changes. They're experiencing tremendous physical growth; girls are being hit on by (often older) teenage boys for the first time; and their brains are awash in hormones. It's during these preteen and early teen years, as puberty is really taking hold, that our kids first come face-to-face with risks like drugs, tobacco, alcohol, driving, and sex, most often long before they're ready to take on such big challenges. It's also during these years that we commonly see the emergence of substance abuse and psychopathology, like depression and anxiety. If we wait to intervene until our kids hit this mid-adolescent period, which extends from around thirteen until about nineteen and is generally the most dangerous time for adolescents, we put ourselves well behind the eight ball and have a hard time protecting them from risk.

The best way for us to reduce risk taking among adolescents is to focus on prevention before they hit the teen years. Preventing our kids from risk can be achieved by many of the efforts we've already discussed in the last two chapters, such as teaching young parents how to use behavioral parenting skills; monitoring our kids' activities and spending quality time with them; managing screen time; using gist-based parenting strategies; emphasizing the triumvirate of health; and teaching resilience in schools. The earlier we start with these efforts, the greater the benefits our kids will reap. There's also a lot we can do as a society to prevent adolescent risk taking. In this chapter, we'll talk about the importance of diagnosing and treating kids with emotional, behavioral, and learning disorders; supporting a so-called growth mindset for our most vulnerable children; developing evidence-based mentorship programs; teaching our kids media literacy; delaying their exposure to alcohol, tobacco, and drugs as long as possible; and mandating graduated driver's licensing. While some of these societal fixes can be put in place right away, others will require significant policy changes and a major overhaul of long-established systems.

Perhaps one of the most important things we can do to prevent risk-taking behavior is reduce poverty. I recognize that taking on poverty is a daunting task, but what we've learned about poverty and its effects on children and adolescents in the last thirty years is highly instructive for those of us who are trying to keep kids safe. Adolescent risk taking is particularly associated with conditions of poverty and being the child of parents who themselves are hindered by its effects. Having nowhere to go after school but a disorganized and dangerous neighborhood further contributes to setting up our most vulnerable kids for trouble. In fact, when middle-aged adults are exposed to the same poverty conditions, they often show similar levels of crime, accidents, homicide, motor vehicle fatalities, and other behavioral problems that we commonly associate with adolescents. The take-home point is that at the end of the day, poverty probably trumps every other societal factor that contributes to dangerous risk-taking behavior among our children.

Toxic Stress

In the 1990s, Vincent J. Felitti and Robert F. Anda launched what has become one of the most important public health studies of the past fifty years. The Adverse Childhood Experiences (ACE) Study sought to identify how many adults experienced trauma as children and the effects it had on their development. Felitti and Anda classified traumatic exposures as being due to abuse, neglect, or being raised in a significantly dysfunctional household—things like growing up in extreme poverty, witnessing or being the victim of domestic or neighborhood violence, parental substance abuse and mental health problems, death of a parent, or a parent being jailed. Many thousands of adolescents and adults have since been studied over the past thirty years, and we've learned that the greater the number of ACEs to which children are exposed, the more likely they are to develop common health problems like hypertension, obesity, and diabetes as adults. We've also learned that the more ACEs a child has, the more likely he or she is to eventually start smoking, attempt suicide, become an alcoholic, inject street drugs, get a sexually transmitted disease, be violent, have more marriages, experience more depression, be absent more from work, and on and on.

Growing up in poverty is an adverse experience in and of itself, but it also increases the likelihood of exposure to other ACEs. Stated another way, the most vulnerable among us with the fewest resources are the most likely to be exposed to further traumas and to suffer their effects the most. Children exposed to two or more ACEs are more than twice as likely to repeat a grade in school; more than four times as likely to bully others; and eight times as likely to have behavioral problems.

Children raised in impoverished environments feel a lot of stress. Their home environments are unpredictable; they suffer abuse and neglect; and they may often go hungry, unsure of when they will have their next meal. Children chronically exposed to this level of adversity often develop what we call "toxic stress." You can think of it like this: When you start your car in the morning, you might rev the motor for a few minutes to warm it up. Our bodies do precisely the same thing each morning. As we awaken, our stress hormone levels increase to kick-start our heart rate and blood pressure, increasing our circulation and giving us the jolt we need to get up and on with our day. But imagine what happens when you rev the motor all day long because you never know when you will need that jolt. This is what it's like for kids exposed to toxic stress—their young bodies are always vigilant, on the lookout for threat, and primed for action. In the short run, this sort of vigilance provides a clear advantage because the child's fight-or-flight system is always ready to go, prepared to protect him from further harm. In the long run, however, maintaining such a high level of vigilance disrupts brain development and other organ systems and eventually leads to a whole variety of behavioral, emotional, and physical health problems.

In the United States, the richest country in the world by far, over one in five children live below the federal poverty line. By the time these kids start school, they generally score one-half to one full standard deviation below other children on most standardized academic achievement tests. These findings are, unfortunately, not surprising, given that growing up in an impoverished environment often means less opportunity to spend time with parents and other good role models, fewer places to learn and play safely, and more unmonitored screen time.

Unfortunately, poverty's toxic stress has also been associated with changes in the brain. One study found that the size of a child's amygdala (the brain's threat hub) is inversely correlated with the number of years that the child's parent has been educated, and that greater family income is positively correlated with a child's hippocampal volume (a key long-term memory structure that is particularly vulnerable to stress). In other words, growing up in poverty may cause brain changes that put children at risk. The same research has also found that growing up in a higher socioeconomic bracket without the stress of poverty is associated with protracted brain gray matter pruning, which typically leads to greater plasticity and adult adaptability. Toxic stress operates on the brain and body, crippling our children's ability to regulate their emotions. Thankfully, children's brains are malleable, so we must not accept that those who grow up in poverty are doomed.

Research shows that resilience, just like we talked about in chapter 9, can moderate the impact of adverse childhood experiences. The ability to stay calm and emotionally in control in the face of challenges provides our children with a firewall that won't keep out all toxic stress but will help to minimize its impact. And we can enhance resilience by giving our kids more quality time with parents, teachers, religious leaders, and other mentors who can enrich frontal cortical brain growth by teaching children skills and helping them to become passionate about school, hobbies, and interests. These factors will help to improve our adolescents' ability to control their emotional brains and engage in less risk.

Although poverty is not likely to be eradicated any time soon, there is a great deal we can do as a society right now, this very minute, that will help keep our kids safe. We can enhance after-school and weekend programming in poor neighborhoods so that high-risk kids have a safe place to recreate, receive tutoring, and be mentored. We can tackle solicitous advertising and how we market products like alcohol and cigarettes that put our children at risk, and we can support laws that limit access to these goods. And we must make mental health services readily available so that those kids who are suffering and at risk can receive the help they need before becoming totally derailed.

Early and Often

Once upon a time, we thought that children were immune to mental illness, but those naive days are now long gone. Today, across all socio-economic strata we reliably diagnose autism as early as eighteen months, and studies from both the United States and Europe show surprisingly high rates of mental illness even in preschool children, aged two to five. In some studies, the rate of anxiety among preschool children approaches 10 percent, while the frequency of ADHD and oppositional defiant disorder each hover around 5 percent. Unfortunately, we often take a "watch-and-wait" approach to these children and their struggles. "Oh, he'll grow out of it," we say. But they don't. Without intervention, these preschool children don't generally show improvement in their behavioral and emotional problems, and, even worse, they pick up more diagnoses as they age—the four-year-old who struggles with anxiety becomes depressed by age ten; the toddler with ADHD becomes intensely oppositional and defiant by age seven; and the child who showed significant learning problems at age five is completely out of his league in the classroom by age eight.

By the time our children reach eighteen, more than one in five have had a diagnosable emotional or behavioral condition. Half of these kids, or at least one in ten, suffer major functional impairments due to their condition, like failing in school or having no friends. And if we don't address these disorders early, like during the preschool years, they only get worse with age. Between thirteen and eighteen, up to one in three adolescents has a diagnosable anxiety disorder, one in five has a disruptive behavior disorder, one in six has major depressive disorder, and one in ten has a substance use disorder. One in four adolescents has used an illicit drug within the past thirty days, and more than one in five have engaged in binge drinking (e.g., consumed five or more alcoholic drinks in two hours) within the past fourteen days. Recall from chapter 1 that over half of all children are exposed to trauma, which further increases their likelihood of risk taking, substance abuse, mental illness, smoking, sexually transmitted diseases, and obesity. When you add it all up, nearly half of all adolescents develop a psychiatric condition, and one in five is in severe emotional distress.

Youth who struggle with major mental illness are not only more likely to drop out of school, become incarcerated, get pregnant, and drive drunk, they are also more likely to attempt suicide. Even children and adolescents with very common and seemingly benign troubles like ADHD face more than twice the risk of tobacco and drug dependence, and over 80 percent of children with ADHD will carry that diagnosis and/or another psychiatric problem into adulthood. And adults with ADHD still aren't off the hook—they have more problems maintaining employment, an increase in sexual and reproductive risks, more motor vehicle accidents and traffic violations, higher rates of substance abuse, and more accidents than those without a diagnosis of ADHD.

School is our kids' workplace, and it's there that we should be providing mental health care. But fewer than 10 percent of the eighty thousand public schools in the United States provide comprehensive mental health services. Equally concerning is the fact that although we

> Only about one in five youth with a diagnosable mental illness receives care.

now have many effective treatments for the mental disorders that ail our children, only about one in five youth with a diagnosable mental illness receives care, and among these children, only 2 percent receive a treatment known to be effective. We must do better.

Mental illness doesn't go away if we "watch and wait." Our kids don't magically grow out of these problems, and untreated, these disorders and the associated problems they cause propel our children toward risky behavior. As a society, we need to establish a broader network of mental health clinics in schools. We also need to do a better job of caring for the mental illness of parents by investing more in our community mental health centers. Children suffering from mental illness commonly have parents who also suffer, and we know that these adults will be much more effective parents if they receive the treatment they need. Furthermore, treating the parents has been shown to reduce the distress among mentally ill children. If we don't start investing more in our efforts to identify and treat mental illness in children and parents, we are dooming our children to repeat the mistakes of prior generations. And although we may not be able to set up an efficient network of mental health clinics in all schools right away, a change in mindset will get us started.

Changing Mindset

Nelson Mandela famously said, "Education is the most powerful weapon which you can use to change the world." Through universal education, we provide all individuals with the chance to learn, establish a good career, and achieve social equality. Unfortunately, however, many of us hold negative stereotypes about various individuals' ability to learn and take advantage of educational opportunities. Not surprisingly, these stereotypes also affect the very people we stereotype.

Just as our society may stereotype minority and low-income individuals as bad students, lazy, or not intellectual, so may minority and low-income individuals pigeonhole themselves. Research has shown that you don't even need to believe the stereotype to have it affect your performance; you only need to be aware of it. Studies of black Americans, for example, have found that simply knowing about negative stereotypes suggesting black students are not as intellectual as white students can be psychologically intimidating. This effect is called "stereotype threat," and it's known to cause both worse academic performance and reduced interest in school among affected individuals. Fortunately, we can do something about it.

Over the past decade, studies of middle school, high school, and college students have shown that both academic and social resilience can be enhanced by helping people to change their mindset. The key is teaching students that intelligence is malleable and can grow. If we think of intelligence as fixed and unchanging, then we can easily become discouraged because we think of our opportunities as predetermined; there is simply nothing we can do but live out our destiny. So if we do poorly on a test, it only confirms our negative beliefs about our limited ability. And if we are a member of a minority group or hail from a low socioeconomic rung of society, academic struggles further feed into the stereotype threat that we feel every day. A few too many of these experiences, and we stop caring about school. Likewise, if we believe that we will always be bullied or victimized by our peers or excluded from social groups because that's just who we are and our personality is unchangeable, then we are likely to continue to feel on the outs and to struggle more with each passing day. But as we've discussed repeatedly throughout this book, the brains of children and adolescents are inherently changeable, and we have seen amazing improvements in self-efficacy with even modest changes in mindset.

When adolescents are taught that their brains can change and that they are not doomed to repeat the past, they become more resilient. Interventions that emphasize this type of growth mindset (as opposed to a so-called fixed mindset) have sometimes yielded huge results, including measurable improvements in grade point average, college retention, happiness, and social belonging. Participants also show reduced self-doubt, less physical illness, and fewer visits to the doctor. These interventions are helpful for all adolescents but are particularly effective for racial minorities, who disproportionately suffer from stereotype threat. And all this from programs that range from a few hours to a few weeks long. Is there anything more valuable?

These "light-touch" interventions, as they are sometimes called, rely upon two key components. In the first step, participants are taught that the brain changes during adolescence and that continued education and learning build new neural connections and pathways, resulting in a more efficient brain. Various studies have employed lectures, videos, and personal success stories to effectively get this idea across. In the second step, the participants are encouraged to internalize this concept by either writing a letter to a younger student who is having academic difficulties or by writing an essay or making a brief video to share with others about their own experiences and newfound potential in light of this understanding. It's just like the old "see one, do one, teach one" discussed in chapter 9. The best way to internalize something is to teach it.

Studies of the growth mindset have taught us that overpraising mediocre schoolwork or making the work less challenging for vulnerable students often further discourages them and confirms that they are bad students who will never show improvement. They are left with the feeling that they may as well just give up. Instead, the goal is for teachers to maintain high standards by critically evaluating students' assignments, but with an emphasis upon the fact that the teacher believes that the student is capable of reaching these standards and expectations. Students must, of course, be given the resources and support to reach the academic standards, and praising student *effort*, not just the final outcome, results in still better academic performance.

Alternatively, adolescents who hold on to a fixed mindset continue to struggle academically and socially. They become convinced that things will never change. These adolescents also report a greater desire for revenge after conflict with a peer, and they are more likely to retaliate aggressively when bullied. Wouldn't you probably do the same, if you thought things would never change?

Interventions that enhance a growth mindset are steeped in cognitive psychology. They are brief and stealthy. Adolescents respond better, in fact, when they don't know the purpose of the intervention. And because these efforts tap into repetitive processes (e.g., students are constantly being assigned academic work), they allow for improvements to accumulate over time, as adolescents become more and more confident in their ability to do better.

Mentorship Matters

Mentorship is a popular concept. Millions of children and adolescents are mentored in school and community-based programs all over the world. In the United States, mentorship has even made it onto a postage stamp. Have you ever been mentored? What did you gain from the experience? We can all imagine the benefits—advice, support, inspiration, improved access to resources, and enhanced opportunities. Some mentoring programs of children and adolescents have shown significant benefits, including fewer unexcused school absences, better grades, higher rates of school graduation and employment, improved self-esteem and mental health, superior physical health, and decreases in problem behaviors. The reality, however, is that the impact of most mentoring programs is small because they are not built upon what we now know works. The good news is that mentoring programs that adopt research-based "best practices" are up to three times more effective in meeting their goals.

Best practices for mentorship programs focus on education, purposeful planning, and appropriate expectations. Effective efforts begin with recruitment of mentors and screening of mentees. Adults who hail from helping professions generally make better mentors. And as with growth mindset interventions, high-risk youth, for whom lower socioeconomic status is a good indicator, get the most out of mentoring. When adolescents have a mentor or an adult in their life from whom they can seek help and advice, they are less likely to engage in high-risk behaviors like using drugs, smoking cigarettes, having sex, and carrying a weapon. Those children who are already having academic or behavioral troubles, however, fare less well in mentoring programs. So, again, our goal is to identify those kids at high risk and get them into mentoring relationships as early as possible.

Matching mentors and mentees based upon common interests, proximity, availability, and similar characteristics is also associated with success. Additional key features of effective programs include: (1) continual training for mentors; (2) organized activities for mentors and mentees; (3) clear expectations regarding the frequency of meetings (e.g., weekly face-to-face for at least two hours is a good guidepost); (4) meeting outside of school, like in the community or at the mentor's workplace; (5) longer-lasting relationships (e.g., relationships lasting at least one year have better outcomes); (6) support and involvement of the mentee's parents; (7) continued monitoring of the mentor/mentee relationship by the responsible agency; (8) goal setting; and (9) shared engagement in community service projects. Clearly, not all mentoring programs are the same, so if we invest in these efforts, let's follow the evidence laid out here and do it right.

Don't Mess with Texas

Looking out my daughter's bedroom window right now, I see a large beer advertisement on a billboard. I've never liked that one of the first things my kids see each morning is an oversized commercial, but it's nearly impossible for parents to limit exposure to ads. Middle school students who report greater exposure to alcohol advertising are more likely to drink alcohol in high school than those who report less exposure. Big surprise? Of course not—more than $21 billion is spent in the United States each year on tobacco and alcohol advertising for one simple reason. It works. By some estimates, advertising is thought to be responsible for up to 30 percent of teen alcohol and tobacco use.

Remember, tobacco is the single greatest cause of death among adults in the United States and most countries, and tobacco addiction effectively always starts in adolescence. And let's not forget that thousands of kids die every year in automobile accidents, many of whom drink before they get behind the wheel.

Not long ago, my wife and I were sitting outside enjoying a meal at our favorite neighborhood diner. As we ate, a large truck drove by with an advertisement displayed on its side. The ad was for a new brand of tequila, and a famous actor and his business partner, who co-own the company, were riding their motorcycles past Mexican agave fields in their shirt-sleeves without helmets nor a care in the world. Let's unpack that ad for minute: The image constitutes an attractive high-definition photo with tequila bottles, beautiful wood barrels for aging the spirits, a ridiculously successful and handsome actor known the world over, and gorgeous classic motorcycles being ridden without any safety equipment. When I came home, I found the ad online and showed it to my then fifteen-year-old son and asked him what he thought of the two men in the photo. "I think they're pretty cool guys," responded Julian. And there you have it.

It was all I could do to stop myself from jumping up and down. "Cool guys?! They're just regular old businessmen, and they clearly care for nobody but themselves!" Okay, I'm paraphrasing.

But the reality is that the actor and his buddy do look cool, riding their vintage motorbikes. "Dad, they're obviously just sitting on the bikes against a green screen," said my media-savvy son upon closer inspection of the photo. Regardless, I said, it's disgraceful that role models for adolescents and young adults all over the world would encourage risky behavior just so they can line their pockets with more cash. Riding a motorcycle without a helmet is a personal decision, but we must convince our kids that it's a stupid one. Drinking and driving kills, and that's not cool. When we see irresponsible, risk-promoting ads, we must point out real-life implications to our children. After my tirade, Julian said, "I got you, Dad. It is a pretty dumb ad when you look at it that way." Thank you, Julian.

> When we see irresponsible, risk-promoting ads, we must point out real-life implications to our children.

Just north of Mexico, Texas was having a big problem with litter on its highways in the 1980s, caused mainly, it was determined, by men aged eighteen to thirty-five. More than twenty-five thousand motor vehicle accidents are caused by trash each year on U.S. roadways, so the Texas Department of Transportation decided to tackle the problem with an advertising campaign. In 1986, the slogan, "Don't Mess with Texas," went prime time. Over the next four years, litter on Texas highways fell by 72 percent. What began as an ad campaign has become, over the last thirty years, a cultural identity and proclamation of Texas bravado that can still be found today everywhere from stadiums to saloons to political conventions to automobile bumpers. The ad infused young men with pride in their homeland and a desire to keep it clean. It had a cool factor that was just like the careless actor and his pal on the motorcycles peddling tequila, except that in this case the ad was supporting a value that we *want* for our children.

Media Literacy

Here's something that doesn't stop children and adolescents from smoking: Telling them that tobacco is bad for them. Antismoking ads supported by Big Tobacco as mandated by the Tobacco Master Settlement Agreement of 1998 (which required the largest U.S. tobacco companies to pay for, among other things, antismoking advertisements) employing slogans like "Think. Don't smoke," or "Tobacco is whacko if you're a teen," are generally ineffective. Even worse, some research suggests that these ads are counterproductive and actually encourage kids to start smoking because they emphasize being independent, tough, and thinking for yourself—just what adolescents typically want to believe about themselves. But there's nothing new under the sun—tobacco companies have a long history of manipulating adolescents.

The Marlboro brand made its debut in 1924 as a filtered cigarette marketed to women. "Mild as May," stated the copy, right alongside attractive women with cigarettes perched gently between their fingers and lips. Back in the 1920s, smoking filtered cigarettes was seen as not very manly, so women were the primary sales target for Marlboro, which held less than 1 percent of the cigarette market share in the United States until the 1950s. Then an amazing thing happened. As knowledge of the ills of smoking became better recognized, filters became more acceptable among male smokers, and the Marlboro Man was born. Within one year, Marlboro became the fourth-bestselling brand of cigarettes in the country.

The first Marlboro Men were sailors, mechanics, weightlifters, and the like. They were no-nonsense characters and fierce smokers. The

Marlboro Man campaign was one of the earliest entries into the advertising trend known as lifestyle branding, which promotes products and services based upon who the consumer wants or imagines himself to be. Once the ad teams chose the cowboy as their new Marlboro Man, however, all bets were off.

Cowboys embody virility, independence, and strength—what adolescent male doesn't want to think of himself this way? The ironic thing is that cowboys by and large aren't even cigarette smokers; those who use tobacco tend to prefer chewing it, which is a whole lot easier to manage in your mouth than lighting cigarette after cigarette while herding cattle on horseback. But accuracy has never been the dominion of advertisers, and the Marlboro cowboys flat-out stole the rodeo. Since 1972, Marlboro has been the bestselling cigarette brand in the world with annual sales of over $25 billion.

Telling kids that cigarettes cause lung cancer, emphysema, chronic bronchitis, heart disease, and a veritable who's who of other grizzly illnesses simply doesn't stop them from smoking tobacco. What does seem to work is approaching them just like I did with Julian when talking about the tequila ad. When you show kids that they're being taken advantage of by unscrupulous companies that are actually making them into pawns by stealing their money and health, that they're being made to look more like fools than cools, then you give them the backbone to stand up for themselves and make a healthy choice. The Marlboro Man is trying to convince our kids that smoking is cool and makes you a rebel. But the companies that manufacture and market cigarettes are the furthest thing possible from rebels—they're big, ultrawealthy, and superconservative.

Parents, schools, and the media all need to take a stand against any company that is poisoning our kids and setting them up for a life of addiction and misery, but we must not be puritanical about it. Of course smoking kills. Every child and adolescent knows that, but our kids are striving for reward and social status. So we must create a social context in which kids admire healthy patterns of behavior, like sticking it to the tobacco man, because it's hard for a teen to ignore anything that increases or decreases his or her social status.

The most effective antismoking advertisements are those in which the truth is told. Some of that truth is the real story behind our role models, like the fact that the original men who portrayed the cowboy Marlboro Man have all died of smoking-related illnesses. Some of that truth is what happens to smokers, like the CDC's 2012 "Tips from Former Smokers" campaign, which depicts chronic smokers as they go about their day putting in false teeth and placing their hand over their neck stoma so they can speak, while eking out their last breaths connected to an oxygen tank. And some of that truth must come from parents, schools, and the media itself by exposing the tobacco companies for just what they are really all about—making addicts of our kids and laughing all the way to the bank.

The American Academy of Pediatrics has issued a policy statement recommending a ban on all tobacco advertising in the media, along with clear limits on alcohol advertising, and removing solicitous substance-related exposures on television and in PG-13 and R-rated movies. That's a good start. Beyond advertising and media, we should raise the minimum legal age for purchase of tobacco products to twenty-one, which would take us past the teen years, when most kids start smoking. We must outlaw the sale of alcohol, tobacco, and marijuana (where it's legal) within a reasonable distance (at least one thousand feet) of all schools and public parks. We must empower the police to crack down on merchants who sell alcohol and tobacco to underage adolescents, and we need stiff penalties for offenders. We need to keep taxing tobacco and alcohol products as much as we can so that they are simply too expensive for kids to purchase. And we need to teach media literacy in schools so that our kids can see how the advertisers are emotionally manipulating them to buy products that will ruin their lives.

Can We Teach Our Kids to Drink Responsibly?

Each year, around five thousand adolescents under the age of twenty-one die in the United States due to alcohol-related causes. Nearly 40 percent of these deaths involve motor vehicles. Alcohol use among adolescents is also associated with drowning, suicide, homicide, falls, burns, alcohol poisoning, and a slew of other serious but nonfatal outcomes. And although alcohol may make us feel disinhibited and less anxious at first, it's actually a central nervous system depressant, and continued use only worsens anxiety and depression. Alcohol also, of course, is commonly implicated in physical and sexual assaults and the spread of sexually transmitted infections.

Given these risks of accident, illness, and addiction, it's unfortunate that adolescents are generally less sensitive to the acute "hangover" effects of alcohol, compared to adults. So the morning after that bender, your adolescent just won't feel as achy, sleepy, or nauseated as you would if you had imbibed the same. This is really too bad because it can fool our kids into thinking that alcohol isn't that toxic. In fact, adolescents are *more* sensitive than adults to the neurotoxic effects of alcohol, such as memory deficits and changes in brain volume. So when it comes to alcohol, adolescents get less of a warning signal but experience more harm.

Okay, so alcohol causes a slew of problems, particularly in young people, and giving them unfettered access to alcohol seems unwise. Yet if parents don't teach their kids to drink, who will? Do we really want to suddenly unleash our kids on bars when they turn twenty-one? How did you learn to drink responsibly?

You might be thinking that we would be better off following the

European model, where the legal minimum drinking age is usually sixteen to eighteen. Don't those kids have fewer problems with alcohol? If only. Surprising as it may seem, the vast majority of countries where kids have legal access to alcohol at a younger age actually have higher rates of alcohol use, intoxication before age thirteen, and binge drinking. In a 2007 comparative study, for example, 33 percent of American fifteen- and sixteen-year-olds reported drinking in the past thirty days, while 80 percent of Danish, 70 percent of British, and 63 percent of Italian teens in that age group acknowledged the same. Only Iceland (where the legal drinking age is twenty) had a lower rate than the United States, at 31 percent. And while 18 percent of American teens reported becoming intoxicated in the past thirty days, 49 percent of Danish, 33 percent of British, and 22 percent of German and Swiss teens had one too many themselves. Similarly, 22 percent of American teens reported binge drinking in the past thirty days, while 60 percent of Danish, 57 percent of German, 34 percent of Italian, and 28 percent of French did the same.

The unfortunate reality is that we have no tried-and-true method of teaching adolescents how to drink responsibly, so the only conclusion to be drawn at present is that we're better off restricting access to alcohol for adolescents. To date, studies designed to teach adolescents how to drink responsibly have failed. Moreover, teaching adolescents about "responsible use" plays right into their quantitative tendency to overthink, weigh the pros and cons, and come out drunk. What should that legal age be? Hard to say—there's no magic in eighteen or twenty-one. But it's clear that the longer we can keep adolescents away from alcohol and drugs, the less likely they are to have a motor vehicle accident or become addicted.

Social Norms Marketing

In a survey of college students in the mid-1980s, Wesley Perkins and Alan Berkowitz found that adolescents commonly have exaggerated beliefs

> Adolescents commonly have exaggerated beliefs about the behaviors of their peers.

about the behaviors of their peers, or their "social norms." It's remarkable that even today with online access to unheard-of amounts of information at their fingertips, undergraduates still haven't a clue what their peers are actually up to.

According to the American College Health Association's spring 2016 report, for which over ninety-five thousand students were surveyed in anonymity, undergraduates remain totally baffled about who does what. Only 9 percent of college students smoked a cigarette in the past thirty days, but they perceive that 74 percent of their peers did. Only 4 percent used an electronic cigarette in the past thirty days, but they believe that 72 percent of their peers did. Only 4 percent used a hookah or water pipe to smoke tobacco in the past thirty days, but they believe that 66 percent of their peers did. Numbers climb for alcohol and marijuana, of course, but still their perceptions are way off. While 64 percent of college students drank some alcohol in the past thirty days, they believe that 94 percent of their peers did. Meanwhile, only 19 percent smoked marijuana in the past thirty days, but they believe that 85 percent of their peers did.

Social norms marketing suggests that if adolescents really knew how few of their peers are using drugs and alcohol, then they too would follow the crowd and use these things less frequently and in lesser amounts. So far, interventions employing social norms marketing among college students have had mixed results in reducing alcohol use—it's clear that social norms marketing can change students' misperceptions, but only some studies have shown that it can change their drinking behavior. Still, we will never go wrong by making sure that adolescents understand the real numbers and how the media often frames statistics to make things seem more sensational and newsworthy. In my work with patients, families, and students, I find this approach very useful.

The media has a tendency to express worrisome behaviors in terms of how many people are doing something risky, like smoking marijuana or having sex. According to social norms marketing, this approach can make kids feel left out and think that these behaviors are what they themselves ought to be doing. But we can also look at things the other way—instead, we can look at how many people are *not* doing something (which generally is half or more). This is an important message when discussing risk.

When we ask, for example, "How many high school seniors have tried marijuana?" the answer is around 45 percent in the United States. That sounds like a big number, so what is a teenager to think? "Half of my peers have tried weed! What's wrong with me that I haven't yet tried it?" How would you feel if someone told you that 45 percent of your peers had driven a Ferrari, and you hadn't? You'd probably feel left out too, but adolescents, given the incredible impact of the peer effects that we discussed in chapter 5, feel that many times over. But ask the question another way—"How many high school seniors have not tried marijuana?"—and you get 55 percent. Now more than half of their peers haven't smoked weed, and they're no longer in the minority if they haven't tried it. While addressing statistics in this way is less dramatic and undoubtedly pulls in lower television ratings, it's a whole lot more health promoting. This is another reason that we need to teach our kids media literacy.

Backseat Parenting

What's the most dangerous thing that you do these days? For most of us, it's driving. How many times have you almost nodded off or actually fallen asleep at the wheel? It's amazing how calm we are when driving down the highway at fifty-five miles per hour, knowing that one wrong move can lead to instant death. Yet it's ironic that we can be so relaxed doing something so complex like driving down the freeway, when simply standing and speaking in front of ten peers can completely unnerve us and make us feel intense anxiety. The fear of being judged negatively by others, what scientists call "social-evaluative threat," is a major contributor to the peer effects that we discussed in chapter 5 that so powerfully influence our adolescents when behind the wheel in the presence of peers.

The most dangerous time in an adolescent's life is the first two years after he or she receives a driver's license. Adding peers to the mix only increases that risk. With one nonfamily passenger in the car of an adolescent driver, the risk of a motor vehicle accident increases by 44 percent. That risk is doubled when a second passenger is added to the car and quadrupled when three or more come along for the ride. Not surprisingly, high-risk adolescent drivers are three times more likely to report that their parents don't monitor their driving closely.

While we're not yet sure how to teach adolescents to use alcohol safely, we certainly know how to teach them safe driving. And as we discussed in chapter 2, routine driver's education classes are not sufficient. Instead, we need to support graduated driver's licensing programs, which work by granting adolescents enhanced driving privileges as they gain increased experience and competence. Most American states currently have some version of a graduated pathway to licensing young drivers, and it's a great example of how an apprenticeship model can be successfully used to teach our kids how to manage risky situations.

Graduated licensing typically begins with obtaining a learner's permit at age sixteen. For the next twelve months, a parent or guardian must be in the car whenever the teen is driving. The Insurance Institute for Highway Safety recommends at least seventy hours of supervised driving before graduating to intermediate licensing at seventeen, at which time the adolescent can drive alone but may not drive at night after 8:00 p.m. or with nonfamily teen passengers. Finally, at age eighteen, adolescents may obtain an unrestricted driver's license.

Graduated driver's licensing programs address the major risks with teen drivers—peers and nighttime. Inexperienced drivers have more accidents, but those rates increase even more when teens are driving in the dark (particularly given how underslept most adolescents are) or when their peers are in the car.

Adorable babies grow into curious children and then risky teens and young adults. It's unavoidable but predictable. So let's take Wayne Gretzky's advice and skate to where the puck will be. Let's rely upon prevention and be proactive. We're only kidding ourselves if we choose to believe that our adolescents won't face risky situations each day. Instead of waiting for those risks to happen, we can anticipate the dangers and be ready for them. Thankfully, there's a lot our society can do to help keep our kids safe.

We must identify and treat our children's emotional, behavioral, and learning disorders at the earliest of ages, and this means putting proper mental health services into schools and providing adequate community-based services for parents. We must support our schoolteachers in learning techniques that support a growth mindset and making sure they have the time to employ these methods in the classroom. We can design evidence-based mentorship programs, and we can teach our children media literacy both at home and at school. Equally important, we can use our understanding of child and adolescent development to support clear limits on the advertising and glorification of products that harm our adolescents, like alcohol and tobacco. There's also a lot of room for innovative advertisers to use role models who will make healthy choices seem cool to teens. We definitely need to support our law enforcement agencies in holding retailers accountable for selling to minors, and we should continue to support and enhance graduated driver's licensing and similar apprenticeship programs at every turn. These societal fixes will save adolescent lives and years of disability, and they will save us lots of money in the long run.

Looking at the big picture means thinking from a public health perspective. That is, how can we prevent adolescents from taking risks? The strategies offered in this chapter focus on society-level efforts that in some cases may lead to big gains and in other cases may move the needle only slightly in the direction of health promotion and risk reduction. But even social programs that lead to just a small degree of change can have beneficial effects on millions of adolescents and change their lives forever.

Final Note

SEVEN YEARS AGO, I SET out to write a comprehensive but user-friendly guide about tween, teen, and young adult risk-taking behavior for parents, teachers, and policy makers. In the intervening years, I have thought a lot about how I would like to position these ideas. I've read large amounts of original scientific research, interviewed dozens of scientists, and jotted down volumes of notes. But, in fact, this book began years earlier, starting with the many questions I've had about my own childhood and upbringing and my concerns about how to raise my own children. I hope that my translation of both science and personal experience as a clinician, parent, and former adolescent myself contributes to a better understanding of these challenging years. More importantly, I hope that this knowledge and the strategies we've discussed for reducing risk will act as a guide and toolkit for implementing solutions at home, in school, and within society at large.

When you add it all up, adolescents are primed for risk, but for good reason. They are exquisitely designed to be successful in the natural environment where our species evolved. But we've come a long way, and today many of our kids' innate tendencies put them at great risk of bad outcomes, disability, and death. My understanding of the research literature along with my personal and professional experience have convinced me that now is the time to rethink our approach to adolescent risk taking. We must stop relying on ineffective programs that are based upon hunches and old ideas and theories. Instead, we must utilize what we now know about why adolescents take risks and how they make decisions so that we can build evidence-based programs that will reduce risk-taking behavior in our homes, schools, and communities.

The strategies discussed within these pages will not alone guarantee our success. But they will absolutely help us to ameliorate a great deal of today's adolescent risk-taking behavior. I hope that this book will be a rallying cry in the effort to keep our kids safe.

SELECTED BIBLIOGRAPHY

THE BIBLIOGRAPHY INCLUDES MANY OF the most relevant research articles, books, and websites that served as references for this book. This material will be particularly useful for those who would like to delve deeper into the content within these pages. Additional references, source material, and tools for addressing risk and resilience with adolescents can be found on my website: drjesspshatkin.com.

INTRODUCTION

Freud, A. (1958). "Adolescence." *Psychoanalytic Study of the Child*, 12, 255–278.

Steinberg, L., E. Cauffman, J. Woolard, S. Graham, and M. Banich (2009). "Are Adolescents Less Mature than Adults?: Minors' Access to Abortion, the Juvenile Death Penalty, and the Alleged APA 'Flip-Flop.'" *American Psychologist* 64(7), 583–94. doi:10.1037/a0014763.

CHAPTER 1

Fuller, R. B. (1981). *Critical Path*. New York: St. Martin's Press.

Risk Happens

Fact Sheets—Underage Drinking. (2016, October 20). Retrieved January 30, 2017, from https://www.cdc.gov/alcohol/fact-sheets/underage-drinking.htm.

Forhan, S. E., S. L. Gottlieb, M. R. Sternberg, F. Xu, S. D. Datta, G. M. McQuillan, et al. (2009). "Prevalence of Sexually Transmitted

Infections Among Female Adolescents Aged 14 to 19 in the United States." *Pediatrics* 124(6), 1505–1512.

Kann, L., E. O. Olsen, T. McManus, et al. (2016). "Sexual Identity, Sex of Sexual Contacts, and Health-Related Behaviors Among Students in Grades 9–12—United States and Selected Sites, 2015." *MMWR Surveillance Summaries* 65(SS-9), 1–202. http://dx.doi.org/10.15585/mmwr.ss6509a1.

Sexual Risk Behaviors: HIV, STD, and Teen Pregnancy Prevention. (2016, July 18). Retrieved January 30, 2017, from https://www.cdc.gov/healthyyouth/sexualbehaviors.

Shatkin, J. P. (2015). *Child and Adolescent Mental Health: A Practical All-in-One Guide*. New York: W. W. Norton.

Wasserman, D., Q. Cheng, Q., and G.-X. Jiang. (2005). "Global Suicide Rates among Young People Aged 15–19." *World Psychiatry* 4(2), 114–120.

Youth Risk Behavior Surveillance System (YRBSS). (2016, August 11). Retrieved January 30, 2017, from https://www.cdc.gov/healthyyouth/data/yrbs.

The Myth of Adolescent Invincibility

Elkind, D. (1967). "Egocentrism in Adolescence." *Child Development* 38(4), 1025–1034. doi:10.2307/1127100.

Kanner, L. (1943). "Autistic Disturbances of Affective Contact." *Nervous Child: Journal of Psychopathology, Psychotherapy, Mental Hygiene, and Guidance of the Child* 2, 217–250.

Medicine: "The Child Is Father." (1960, July 25). Interview. *Time*. http://autismedsp5310s20f10.pbworks.com/f/Time-The+Child+Is+Father.pdf.

Everything Right Is Wrong Again

Fischhoff, B., W. B. Bruin, A. M. Parker, S. G. Millstein, and B. L Halpern-Felsher. (2010). "Adolescents' Perceived Risk of Dying." *Journal of Adolescent Health* 46(3), 265–69. doi:10.1016/j.jadohealth.2009.06.026.

Quadrel, M. J., B. Fischhoff, and W. Davis. (1993). "Adolescent (In) vulnerability." *American Psychologist* 48(2), 102–116.

Reyna, V. F., and F Farley. (2006). "Risk and Rationality in Adolescent Decision Making." *Psychological Science in the Public Interest* 7(1), 1–44. doi:10.1111/j.1529-1006.2006.00026.x.

Kids Say the Darnedest Things

Biggs, M. A., and D. G. Foster. (2013). "Misunderstanding the Risk of Conception from Unprotected and Protected Sex." *Women's Health Issues* 23(1), 1–7.

Colombo, B., and G. Masarotto. (2000). "Daily Fecundability: First Results from a New Data Base." *Demographic Research* 3.

HIV Risk Behaviors. (2015, December 4). Retrieved January 30, 2017, from https://www.cdc.gov/hiv/risk/estimates/riskbehaviors.html.

Pregnancy and Childbearing among U.S. Teens. (2014, July). Planned Parenthood. Retrieved January 31, 2017, from https://www .plannedparenthood.org/files/2013/9611/7570/Pregnancy_And _Childbearing_Among_US_Teens.pdf.

Lake Wobegon

Dunning, D., C. Heath, and J. M. Suls. (2004). "Flawed Self-Assessment." *Psychological Science in the Public Interest* 5(3), 69–106. doi:10.1111 /j.1529-1006.2004.00018.x.

Kruger, J., and D. Dunning. (1999). "Unskilled and Unaware of It: How Difficulties in Recognizing One's Own Incompetence Lead to Inflated Self-Assessments." *Journal of Personality and Social Psychology* 77(6), 1121–1134. doi:10.1037//0022-3514.77.6.1121.

Risk and Resilience

Blum, R. W., and F. Qureshi. (2011). "Morbidity and Mortality among Adolescents and Young Adults in the United States." Retrieved April 6, 2017, from http://www.jhsph.edu/research/centers-and-institutes

/center-for-adolescent-health/_images/_pre-redesign/az/US%20Fact %20Sheet_FINAL.pdf.

From Juvenile Delinquency to Young Adult Offending. (n.d.). Retrieved January 30, 2017, from https://www.nij.gov/topics/crime/Pages /delinquency-to-adult-offending.aspx#reports.

Kochanek, K. D., S. L. Murphy, J. Xu, and B Tejada-Vera. (2016). National Vital Statistics Reports: Deaths: Final Data for 2014. Centers for Disease Control and Prevention, National Center for Health Statistics. Retrieved January 31, 2017, from https://www.cdc.gov/nchs/data /nvsr/nvsr65/nvsr65_04.pdf.

Masten, A., J. Herbers, J. Cutuli, and T. Lafavor. (2008). "Promoting Competence and Resilience in the School Context." *Professional School Counseling* 12(2), 76–84. doi:10.5330/psc.n.2010-12.76.

Mortality among Teenagers Aged 12–19 Years: United States, 1999–2006. (2010, May 5). Retrieved January 30, 2017, from https://www.cdc .gov/nchs/products/databriefs/db37.htm.

Murray, C. J., and A. D. Lopez. (1996). *The Global Burden of Disease: A Comprehensive Assessment of Mortality and Disability from Diseases, Injuries, and Risk Factors in 1990 and Projected to 2020.* Cambridge, MA: Harvard School of Public Health.

Olsson, C. A., L. Bond, J. M. Burns, D. A. Vella-Brodrick, and S. M. Sawyer. (2002). "Adolescent Resilience: A Concept Analysis." *Journal of Adolescence* 26, 1–11.

Ten Leading Causes of Death and Injury. (2016, February 25). Retrieved January 30, 2017, from https://www.cdc.gov/injury/wisqars /leadingcauses.html.

The Adolescent Paradox

Friedman, H. (1990). "Adolescent Health: Promise and Paradox." In H. M. Wallace and K. Giri (eds.), *Health Care of Women and Children in Developing Countries.* Oakland: Third Party Publishing.

Justice, N. C. (n.d.). FBI Arrest Statistics: 1994–2012. Retrieved February 8, 2017, from http://ojjdp.gov/ojstatbb/ezaucr/asp/ucr_display.asp.

CHAPTER 2

Earl, E. (ed.). (1867). *The Iliad of Homer*, Volume II. Third Edition from the Fifth Revised English Edition. New York: Charles Scribner & Co.

My Goal Is 100 Percent Not to Get Hurt

Counts, J. (2012, December 2). "Son Prayed for Safety, but Chose Not to Wear a Motorcycle Helmet; Now Parents' Grief Is Doubled." Retrieved January 30, 2017, from http://www.mlive.com/news/index.ssf/2012 /12/son_prayed_for_safety_but_chos.html.

I D.A.R.E. You

Kann, L., T. McManus, W. A. Harris, et al. (2016). "Youth Risk Behavior Surveillance—United States, 2015." *MMWR Surveillance Summaries*, 65(SS-6), 1–174. doi: http://dx.doi.org/10.15585/mmwr.ss6506a1.

Pan, W., and H. Bai. (2009). "A Multivariate Approach to a Meta-Analytic Review of the Effectiveness of the D.A.R.E. Program." *International Journal of Environmental Research and Public Health* 6(1), 267–277. doi:10.3390/ijerph6010267.

Singh, R. D., S. R. Jimerson, T. Renshaw, E. Saeki, S. R. Hart, J. Earhart, and K. Stewart. (2011). "A Summary and Synthesis of Contemporary Empirical Evidence Regarding the Effects of the Drug Abuse Resistance Education Program (D.A.R.E.)." *Contemporary School Psychology* 15, 93–102.

Welcome to the MTF Website. (n.d.). Retrieved January 30, 2017, from http://www.monitoringthefuture.org.

D.A.R.E. Devils

AAG Robinson and OJJDP Acting Administrator Slowikowski Discourage the Use of Scared Straight Programs. (2011, February 1). Retrieved

February 1, 2017, from https://www.ojjdp.gov/enews/11juvjust /110201.html.

Finckenauer, J. O. (1982). *Scared Straight! and the Panacea Phenomenon.* Englewood Cliffs, NJ: Prentice-Hall.

Klenowski, P. M., K. J. Bell, and K. D. Dodson. (2010). "An Empirical Evaluation of Juvenile Awareness Programs in the United States: Can Juveniles be 'Scared Straight'?" *Journal of Offender Rehabilitation* 49 254–272.

Petrosino, A., C. Turpin-Petrosino, M. Hollis-Peel, J. G. Lavenberg. "Scared Straight and Other Juvenile Awareness Programs for Preventing Juvenile Delinquency: A Systematic Review." *Campbell Systematic Reviews* 2013:5. doi: 10.4073/csr.2013.5.

Less than Zero

"Are Zero Tolerance Policies Effective in the Schools?: An Evidentiary Review and Recommendations. (2008)." *American Psychologist* 63 (9) 852–862. doi:10.1037/0003-066x.63.9.852.

Losen, D. J., and R. J. Skiba. (2010). *Suspended Education Urban Middle Schools in Crisis.* 1–24.

Drive Time

Arrazola, R. A., T. Singh, C. G. Corey, et al. (2015). Tobacco Use Among Middle and High School Students—United States, 2011–2014. Retrieved February 1, 2017, from https://www.cdc.gov/mmwr /preview/mmwrhtml/mm6414a3.htm?s_cid=mm6414a3_w.

Breuner, C. C., and G. Mattson. (2016). "Sexuality Education for Children and Adolescents." *Pediatrics* 138(2). doi:10.1542/peds.2016-1348.

Fryar, C. D., M. D. Carroll, and C. L. Ogden. (2014). "Prevalence of Overweight and Obesity Among Children and Adolescents: United States, 1963–1965 Through 2011–2012." *National Center for Health Statistics,* 1–6.

Keyes, K. M., J. Maslowsky, A. Hamilton, and J. Schulenberg. (2015). "The Great Sleep Recession: Changes in Sleep Duration Among U.S. Adolescents, 1991–2012." *Pediatrics* 135(3), 460–468. doi:10.1542/peds.2014-2707.

Kohler, P. K., L. E. Manhart, and W. E. Lafferty. (2008). "Abstinence-Only and Comprehensive Sex Education and the Initiation of Sexual Activity and Teen Pregnancy." *Journal of Adolescent Health* 42(4), 344–351. doi:10.1016/j.jadohealth.2007.08.026.

Mayhew, D. R. (2007). "Driver Education and Graduated Licensing in North America: Past, Present, and Future." *Journal of Safety Research* 38(2), 229–235. doi:10.1016/j.jsr.2007.03.001.

National Health Education Standards. (2016, August 18). Retrieved February 1, 2017, from https://www.cdc.gov/healthyschools/sher/standards/index.htm.

Physical Education Profiles, 2012: Physical Education and Physical Activity Practices and Policies among Secondary Schools at Select US Sites. (2014). Centers for Disease Control and Prevention, U.S. Department of Health and Human Services.

Vernick, J. S., G. Li, S. Ogaitis, E. J. Mackenzie, S. P. Baker, and A. C. Gielen. (1999). "Effects of High School Driver Education on Motor Vehicle Crashes, Violations, and Licensure." *American Journal of Preventive Medicine* 16(1), 40–46. doi:10.1016/s0749-3797(98)00115-9.

Youth Physical Activity Guidelines Toolkit. (2015, August 27). Retrieved February 1, 2017, from https://www.cdc.gov/healthyschools/physicalactivity/guidelines.htm.

After Midnight

Brown, B. B. (1990). "Peer Groups and Peer Cultures." In S. S. Feldman and G. R. Elliott (eds.), *At the Threshold: The Developing Adolescent*, 171–196. Cambridge, MA: Harvard University Press.

Larson, R. W., M. H. Richards, G. Moneta, G. Holmbeck, and E. Duckett. (1996). "Changes in Adolescents' Daily Interactions with Their

Families from Ages 10 to 18: Disengagement and Transformation."
Developmental Psychology 32(4), 744–754. doi:10.1037/0012-1649.32.4.744.

CHAPTER 3

Bechara, A., A. R. Damasio, H. Damasio, and S. W Anderson. (1994).
"Insensitivity to Future Consequences Following Damage to Human
Prefrontal Cortex." *Cognition,* 50(1–3), 7–15. doi:10.1016/0010
-0277(94)90018-3.

Kotowicz, Z. (2007). "The Strange Case of Phineas Gage." *History of the
Human Sciences* 20(1), 115–131. doi:10.1177/0952695106075178.

A Brain Owner's Guide

Heller, A. S., and B. Casey. (2015). "The Neurodynamics of Emotion:
Delineating Typical and Atypical Emotional Processes during
Adolescence." *Developmental Science* 19(1), 3–18. doi:10.1111/desc.12373.

Temporarily Closed for Construction

Giorgio, A., K. Watkins, M. Chadwick, et al. (2010). "Longitudinal Changes
in Grey and White Matter During Adolescence." *NeuroImage* 49(1),
94–103. doi:10.1016/j.neuroimage.2009.08.003.

Guyer, A. E., J. S. Silk, and E. E. Nelson. (2016). "The Neurobiology of the
Emotional Adolescent: From the Inside Out." *Neuroscience &
Biobehavioral Reviews* 70, 74–85. doi:10.1016/j.neubiorev.2016.07.037.

Shulman, E. P., A. R. Smith, K. Silva, G. Icenogle, N. Duell, J. Chein, and
L. Steinberg. (2016). "The Dual Systems Model: Review, Reappraisal,
and Reaffirmation." *Developmental Cognitive Neuroscience* 17, 103–117.
doi:10.1016/j.dcn.2015.12.010.

Somerville, L. H., R. M. Jones, and B. Casey. (2010). "A Time of Change:
Behavioral and Neural Correlates of Adolescent Sensitivity to
Appetitive and Aversive Environmental Cues." *Brain and Cognition*
72(1), 124–133. doi:10.1016/j.bandc.2009.07.003.

Better Than Expected

Galvan, A. (2010). "Adolescent Development of the Reward System." *Frontiers in Human Neuroscience.* doi:10.3389/neuro.09.006.2010.

Spear, L. (2000). "The Adolescent Brain and Age-Related Behavioral Manifestations." *Neuroscience & Biobehavioral Reviews* 24(4), 417–463. doi:10.1016/s0149-7634(00)00014-2.

Wahlstrom, D., P. Collins, T. White, and M. Luciana. (2010). "Developmental Changes in Dopamine Neurotransmission in Adolescence: Behavioral Implications and Issues in Assessment." *Brain and Cognition,* 72(1), 146–159. doi:10.1016/j.bandc.2009.10.013.

Twenty-Something

Arnett, J. J. (2014). *Emerging Adulthood: The Winding Road from the Late Teens Through the Twenties.* New York: Oxford University Press.

Dufouil, C., A. Alperovitch, and C. Tzourio. (2003). "Influence of Education on the Relationship Between White Matter Lesions and Cognition." *Neurology* 60(5), 831–836. doi:10.1212/01.wnl.0000049456.33231.96.

Noble, K. G., M. S. Korgaonkar, S. M. Grieve, and A. M. Brickman. (2013). "Higher Education is an Age-Independent Predictor of White Matter Integrity and Cognitive Control in Late Adolescence." *Developmental Science* 16(5), 653–664. doi:10.1111/desc.12077.

Four Days in Verona

Dahl, R. E. (2004). "Adolescent Brain Development: A Period of Vulnerabilities and Opportunities. Keynote Address." *Annals of the New York Academy of Sciences* 1021(1), 1–22. doi:10.1196/annals.1308.001.

The Sleepy Brain

Banks, S., and D. Dinges. (2007). "Behavioral and Physiological Consequences of Sleep Restriction." *Journal of Clinical Sleep Medicine* 3(5), 519–528.

Beebe, D. W. (2011). "Cognitive, Behavioral, and Functional Consequences of Inadequate Sleep in Children and Adolescents." *Pediatric Clinics of North America* 58(3), 649–665. doi:10.1016/j.pcl.2011.03.002.

Danner, F., and B. Phillips. (2008). "Adolescent Sleep, School Start Times, and Teen Motor Vehicle Crashes." *Journal of Clinical Sleep Medicine* 4(6), 533–535.

Matricciani, L. A., T. S. Olds, S. Blunden, G. Rigney, and M. T. Williams. (2012). "Never Enough Sleep: A Brief History of Sleep Recommendations for Children." *Pediatrics* 129(3), 548–556. doi:10.1542/peds.2011-2039.

McKnight-Eily, L. R., D. K. Eaton, R. Lowry, J. B. Croft, L. Presley-Cantrell, and G. S. Perry. (2011). "Relationships Between Hours of Sleep and Health-Risk Behaviors in US Adolescent Students." *Preventive Medicine* 53(4–5), 271–273. doi:10.1016/j.ypmed.2011.06.020.

Owens, J. (2014). "Insufficient Sleep in Adolescents and Young Adults: An Update on Causes and Consequences." *Pediatrics* 134(3). doi:10.1542/peds.2014-1696.

Sadeh, A., R. Gruber, and A. Raviv. (2003). "The Effects of Sleep Restriction and Extension on School-Age Children: What a Difference an Hour Makes." *Child Development* 74(2), 444–455. doi:10.1111/1467-8624.7402008.

"School Start Times for Adolescents." (2014). *Pediatrics* 134(3), 642–649. doi:10.1542/peds.2014-1697.

2014 Sleep in America Poll—Sleep in the Modern Family. (2015). *Sleep Health*, 1(2). doi:10.1016/j.sleh.2015.04.013.

The Addicted Brain

Chen, C., C. L. Storr, and J. C. Anthony. (2009). "Early-onset Drug Use and Risk for Drug Dependence Problems." *Addictive Behaviors* 34(3), 319–322. doi:10.1016/j.addbeh.2008.10.021.

Di Chiara, G., and A. Imperato. (1988). "Drugs Abused by Humans Preferentially Increase Synaptic Dopamine Concentrations in the Mesolimbic System of Freely Moving Rats." *Proceedings of the National Academy of Sciences of the United States of America* 85(14), 5274–5278.

Fowler, J. S., N. D. Volkow, C. A. Kassed, and L. Chang. (2007). "Imaging the Addicted Human Brain." *Science & Practice Perspectives* 3(2), 4–16.

Hingson, R. W., T. Heeren, and M. R. Winter. (2006). "Age at Drinking Onset and Alcohol Dependence." *Archives of Pediatrics & Adolescent Medicine* 160(7), 739. doi:10.1001/archpedi.160.7.739.

How Age Affects Car Insurance Costs. (n.d.). Retrieved February 7, 2017, from https://www.valuepenguin.com/how-age-affects-auto -insurance-costs.

Lopez-Quintero, C., J. P. de los Cobos, D. S. Hasin, M. Okuda, S. Wang, B. F. Grant, and C. Blanco. (2011). "Probability and Predictors of Transition from First Use to Dependence onNnicotine, Alcohol, Cannabis, and Cocaine: Results of the National Epidemiologic Survey on Alcohol and Related Conditions (NESARC). *Drug and Alcohol Dependence*, 115(1–2), 120–130. http://doi.org/10.1016/j.drugalcdep.2010.11.004.

Phillips, P. E., G. D. Stuber, M. L. Heien, R. M. Wightman, and R. M. Carelli. (2003). "Subsecond Dopamine Release Promotes Cocaine Seeking." *Nature* 422(6932), 614–618. doi:10.1038/nature01476.

Volkow, N. D. (2004). "Imaging the Addicted Brain: From Molecules to Behavior." *Journal of Nuclear Medicine* 45(11), 13N–24N.

2013 National Survey on Drug Use and Health: Mental Health: Detailed Tables. (2014). Rockville, MD: Substance Abuse and Mental Health Services Administration, Center for Behavioral Health Statistics and Quality.

CHAPTER 4

Casey, B. J., L. H. Somerville, I. H. Gotlib, et al. (2011). "Behavioral and Neural Correlates of Delay of Gratification 40 Years Later." *Proceedings of the National Academy of Sciences of the United States of America* 108(36), 14998–15003. http://doi.org/10.1073/pnas.1108561108.

Mischel, W., O. Ayduk, M. G. Berman, et al. (2010). "'Willpower' over the Life Span: Decomposing Self-Regulation." *Social Cognitive and Affective Neuroscience* 6(2), 252–256. doi:10.1093/scan/nsq081.

Engineered for Success

Casey, B. J., S. Getz, and A. Galvan. (2008). "The Adolescent Brain." *Developmental Review* 28(1), 62–77. http://doi.org/10.1016/j.dr.2007.08.003.

Tymula, A., L. A. Rosenberg Belmaker, A. K. Roy, L. Ruderman, K. Manson, P. W. Glimcher, and I. Levy. (2012). "Adolescents' Risk-Taking Behavior Is Driven By Tolerance to Ambiguity." *Proceedings of the National Academy of Sciences of the United States of America* 109(42), 17135–17140. http://doi.org/10.1073/pnas.1207144109.

Van den Bos, W., and R. Hertwig. (2017). "Adolescents Display Distinctive Tolerance to Ambiguity and to Uncertainty During Risky Decision Making." *Scientific Reports* 7, 40962. http://doi.org/10.1038/srep40962.

Fear Factor

Burke, A., F. Heuer, and D. Reisberg. (1992). "Remembering Emotional Events." *Memory & Cognition* 20(3), 277–290. doi:10.3758/bf03199665.

Cahill, L., B. Prins, M. Weber, and J. L. McGaugh. (1994). "ß-Adrenergic Activation and Memory for Emotional Events." *Nature* 371(6499), 702–704. doi:10.1038/371702a0.

Casey, B. J. (2015). "Beyond Simple Models of Self-Control to Circuit-Based Accounts of Adolescent Behavior." *Annual Review of Psychology* 66(1), 295–319. doi:10.1146/annurev-psych-010814-015156.

Hare, T. A., N. Tottenham, A. Galvan, H. U. Voss, G. H. Glover, and B. J. Casey. (2008). "Biological Substrates of Emotional Reactivity and Regulation in Adolescence During an Emotional Go-Nogo Task."

Biological Psychiatry 63(10), 927–934. http://doi.org/10.1016/j.biopsych
.2008.03.015015.

Masataka, N., S. Hayakawa, and N. Kawai. (2010). "Human Young Children
as Well as Adults Demonstrate 'Superior' Rapid Snake Detection
When Typical Striking Posture Is Displayed by the Snake." *PLoS ONE*
5(11). doi:10.1371/journal.pone.0015122.

Pattwell, S. S., S. Duhoux, C. A. Hartley, et al. (2012). "Altered Fear Learning
Across Development in Both Mouse and Human." *Proceedings of the
National Academy of Sciences of the United States of America* 109(40),
16318–16323. http://doi.org/10.1073/pnas.1206834109.

Spielberg, J. M., T. M. Olino, E. E. Forbes, and R. E. Dahl. (2014). "Exciting
Fear in Adolescence: Does Pubertal Development Alter Threat
Processing?" *Developmental Cognitive Neuroscience* 8, 86–95. http://doi
.org/10.1016/j.dcn.2014.01.004.

You're Soaking in It

Boksem, M. A., P. H. Mehta, B. V. Bergh, et al. (2013). "Testosterone Inhibits
Trust but Promotes Reciprocity." *Psychological Science* 24(11), 2306–
2314. doi:10.1177/0956797613495063.

Eiland, L., and R. Romeo. (2013). "Stress and the Developing Adolescent
Brain." *Neuroscience* 249, 162–171. doi:10.1016/j.neuroscience
.2012.10.048.

Eisenegger, C., J. Haushofer, and E. Fehr. (2011). "The Role of Testosterone
in Social Interaction." *Trends in Cognitive Sciences* 15(6), 263–271.
doi:10.1016/j.tics.2011.04.008.

Goodman, E., B. S. McEwen, L. M. Dolan, T. Schafer-Kalkhoff, and N. E.
Adler. (2005). "Social Disadvantage and Adolescent Stress." *Journal of
Adolescent Health* 37(6), 484–492. doi:10.1016/j.jadohealth.2004.11.126.

Lupien, S. J., B. S. McEwen, M. R, Gunnar, and C. Heim. (2009). "Effects of
Stress Throughout the Lifespan on the Brain, Behaviour and Cognition."
Nature Reviews Neuroscience 10(6), 434–445. doi:10.1038/nrn2639.

Maroun, M., and S. Wagner. (2016). "Oxytocin and Memory of Emotional Stimuli: Some Dance to Remember, Some Dance to Forget." *Biological Psychiatry* 79(3), 203–212. doi:10.1016/j.biopsych.2015.07.016.

Nagasawa, M., Mitsui, S., S. En, et al. (2015). "Oxytocin-Gaze Positive Loop and the Coevolution of Human-Dog Bonds." *Science* 348(6232), 333–336. doi:10.1126/science.1261022.

Rilling, J. K., and L. J.Young. (2014). "The Biology of Mammalian Parenting and Its Effect on Offspring Social Development." *Science* 345(6198), 771–776. doi:10.1126/science.1252723.

Shamay-Tsoory, S. G., and A. Abu-Akel. (2016). "The Social Salience Hypothesis of Oxytocin." *Biological Psychiatry* 79(3), 194–202. doi:10.1016/j.biopsych.2015.07.020.

Precocious Puberty

Biro, F. M., M. P. Galvez, L. C. Greenspan, et al. (2010). "Pubertal Assessment Method and Baseline Characteristics in a Mixed Longitudinal Study of Girls." *Pediatrics* 126(3). doi:10.1542/peds. 2009-3079.

Cesario, S. K., and L. A. Hughes. (2007). "Precocious Puberty: A Comprehensive Review of Literature." *Journal of Obstetric, Gynecologic & Neonatal Nursing* 36(3), 263–274. doi:10.1111/j.1552-6909.2007.00145.x.

Childhood Obesity Facts. (2017, January 25). Retrieved February 7, 2017, from https://www.cdc.gov/healthyschools/obesity/facts.htm.

Greenspan, L., and J. Deardorff. (2014). *The New Puberty: How to Navigate Early Development in Today's Girls.* New York: Rodale.

Kelly, Y., A. Zilanawala, A. Sacker, R. Hiatt, and R. Viner. (2016). "Early Puberty in 11-Year-Old Girls: Millennium Cohort Study Findings." *Archives of Disease in Childhood.* doi:10.1136/archdischild-2016-310475.

Oakley, A. E., D. K. Clifton, and R. A. Steiner. (2009). "Kisspeptin Signaling in the Brain." *Endocrine Reviews* 30(6), 713–743. doi:10.1210/er.2009-0005.

Roy, J. R., S. Chakraborty, and T. R. Chakraborty. (2009). "Estrogen-like Endocrine Disrupting Chemicals Affecting Puberty in Humans—a Review." *Medical Science Monitor* 15(6), 137–145.

Steingraber, S. (2007, August). The Falling Age of Puberty in U.S. Girls: What We Know, What We Need to Know. Retrieved from http:// www.breastcancerfund.org/assets/pdfs/publications/falling -age-of-puberty.pdf.

The Trade-off

Aidoo, M., D. J. Terlouw, M. S. Kolczak, et al. (2002). "Protective Effects of the Sickle Cell Gene Against Malaria Morbidity and Mortality." *The Lancet* 359(9314), 1311–1312. doi:10.1016/s0140-6736(02)08273-9.

Krawczak, M., J. Schmidtke, A. Trefilov, and J. Berard. (2005). "Male Reproductive Timing in Rhesus Macaques Is Influenced by the 5HTTLPR Promoter Polymorphism of the Serotonin Transporter Gene." *Biology of Reproduction* 72(5), 1109–1113. doi:10.1095/ biolreprod.104.038059.

Pier, G. B., M. Grout, G. Meluleni, et al. (1998). "Salmonella Typhi Uses CFTR to Enter Intestinal Epithelial Cells." *Nature* 393(6680), 79–82.

The Most Valuable Player

Average Player Age in MLB by Team 2016. (2016). Retrieved February 7, 2017, from https://www.statista.com/statistics/236223/major-league -baseball-clubs-by-average-age-of-players.

Miglio, A. (2013, July 16). "For Quarterbacks, the NFL Is No Country for Old Men." Retrieved February 7, 2017, from http://bleacherreport.com /articles/1702238-for-quarterbacks-the-nfl-is-no-country-for-old-men.

CHAPTER 5

Colten, M. E., and S. Gore. (1991). *Adolescent Stress: Causes and Consequences.* New York: Aldine de Gruyter.

We Need the Eggs

Larson, R. and L. Asmussen. (1991). "Anger, Worry and Hurt in Early
   Adolescence: An Enlarging World of Negative Emotions." In M. E.
   Colton and S. Gore (eds.). *Adolescent Stress: Causes and Consequences*
   (pp. 21–41). New York: Adline de Gruyter.

Thinking Errors

Beck, A. T. (1963). "Thinking and DepressionI. Idiosyncratic Content and
   Cognitive Distortions." *Archives of General Psychiatry* 9(4), 324–333.
   doi:10.1001/archpsyc.1963.01720160014002.
———. (1964). "Thinking and Depression II. Theory and Therapy." *Archives
   of General Psychiatry* 10(6), 561–571. doi:10.1001/archpsyc.1964.01720
   240015003.

The Heat of the Moment

Alvarez, L. (2012, May 23). "Hazing Ritual of a Band Is Described in
   Documents." Retrieved February 8, 2017, from http://www.nytimes
   .com/2012/05/24/us/documents-describe-fatal-hazing-ritual
   -at-florida-am.html.
Cherney, E. (2015, June 26). "Three Ex-FAMU Students Sentenced to 10
   Years' Probation in Fatal Hazing Case." Retrieved February 8, 2017,
   from http://www.orlandosentinel.com/news/famu-hazing-band
   /os-famu-hazing-sentencing-20150626-story.html.
Dreher, J., P. J. Schmidt, P. Kohn, D. Furman, D. Rubinow, and K. F. Berman.
   (2007). "Menstrual Cycle Phase Modulates Reward-Related Neural
   Function in Women." *Proceedings of the National Academy of Sciences*
   104(7), 2465–2470. doi:10.1073/pnas.0605569104.
Gardner, M., and L. Steinberg. (2005). "Peer Influence on Risk Taking, Risk
   Preference, and Risky Decision Making in Adolescence and

Adulthood: An Experimental Study." *Developmental Psychology* 41(4), 625–635. doi:10.1037/0012-1649.41.4.625.

Logue, S., J. Chein, T. Gould, E. Holliday, and L. Steinberg. (2013). "Adolescent Mice, Unlike Adults, Consume More Alcohol in the Presence of Peers than Alone." *Developmental Science* 17(1), 79–85. doi:10.1111/desc.12101.

O'Brien, L., D. Albert, J. Chein, and L. Steinberg. (2011). "Adolescents Prefer More Immediate Rewards When in the Presence of their Peers." *Journal of Research on Adolescence* 21(4), 747–753. doi:10.1111/j.1532-7795.2011.00738.x.

Puts, D. A. (2005). "Mating Context and Menstrual Phase Affect Women's Preferences for Male Voice Pitch." *Evolution and Human Behavior* 26(5), 388–397. doi:10.1016/j.evolhumbehav.2005.03.001.

Weigard, A., J. Chein, D. Albert, A. Smith, and L. Steinberg. (2013). "Effects of Anonymous Peer Observation on Adolescents' Preference for Immediate Rewards." *Developmental Science* 17(1), 71–78. doi:10.1111/desc.12099.

Life in the Fast Lane

Albert, D., J. Chein, and L. Steinberg. (2013). "The Teenage Brain: Peer Influences on Adolescent Decision Making." *Current Directions in Psychological Science* 22(2). doi:10.1177/0963721412471347.

Carney, C., D. McGehee, K. Harland, M. Weiss, and M. Raby. (2015). "Using Naturalistic Driving Data to Assess the Prevalence of Environmental Factors and Driver Behaviors in Teen Driver Crashes." AAA Foundation for Public Safety.

Chein, J., D. Albert, L. O'Brien, K. Uckert, and L. Steinberg. (2010). "Peers Increase Adolescent Risk Taking by Enhancing Activity in the Brain's Reward Circuitry." *Developmental Science* 14(2). doi:10.1111/j.1467-7687.2010.01035.x.

Shope, J., and C. Bingham. (2008). "Teen Driving Motor-Vehicle Crashes and Factors That Contribute." *American Journal of Preventive Medicine* 35(3). doi:10.1016/j.amepre.2008.06.022.

Sticks and Stones

Dewall, C. N., G. MacDonald, G. D. Webster, et al. (2010). "Acetaminophen Reduces Social Pain." *Psychological Science* 21(7), 931–937. doi:10.1177/ 0956797610374741.

Harris, M. J. (2009). *Bullying, Rejection, and Peer Victimization: A Social Cognitive Neuroscience Perspective.* New York: Springer.

Masten, C. L., N. I. Eisenberger, L. A. Borofsky, J. H. Pfeifer, K. McNealy, J. C. Mazziotta, and M. Dapretto. (2009). "Neural Correlates of Social Exclusion During Adolescence: Understanding the Distress of Peer Rejection." *Social Cognitive and Affective Neuroscience* 4(2), 143–157. doi:10.1093/scan/nsp007.

Eisenberger, N. I. (2013). "An Empirical Review of the Neural Underpinnings of Receiving and Giving Social Support." *Psychosomatic Medicine* 75(6), 545–556. doi:10.1097/psy.0b013e31829de2e7.

Eisenberger, N. I., J. M. Jarcho, M. D. Lieberman, and B. D. Naliboff. (2006). "An Experimental Study of Shared Sensitivity to Physical Pain and Social Rejection." *Pain* 126(1), 132–138. doi:10.1016/j.pain.2006.06.024.

Breakfast at Gregory's

Gentile, D. A., R. A. Reimer, A. I. Nathanson, D. A. Walsh, and J. C. Eisenmann. (2014). "Protective Effects of Parental Monitoring of Children's Media Use." *JAMA Pediatrics* 168(5), 479. doi:10.1001/ jamapediatrics.2014.146.

Lenhart, A. (2012, March 19). Teens, Smartphones and Texting. Retrieved February 8, 2017, from http://www.pewinternet.org/2012/03/19/teens -smartphones-texting.

Rideout, V. (2016). "Measuring Time Spent with Media: The Common Sense Census of Media Use by US 8- to 18-Year-Olds." *Journal of Children and Media* 10(1), 138–144. doi:10.1080/17482798.2016.1129808.

Rideout, V. J., U. G. Foehr, and D. F. Roberts. Generation M2, Media in the Lives of 8- to 18-Year-Olds. A Kaiser Family Foundation Study. January 2010. Retrieved March 1, 2017 from https://protect-us .mimecast.com/s/9Xe1BRCDE1kacz?domain=kaiserfamilyfoundation .files.wordpress.com.

Sherman, L. E., A. A. Payton, L. M. Hernandez, P. M. Greenfield, and M. Dapretto. (2016). "The Power of the Like in Adolescence." *Psychological Science* 27(7), 1027–1035. doi:10.1177/0956797616645673.

Monkey See, Human Do

Glantz, S. A., A. Iaccopucci, K. Titus, and J. R. Polansky. (2012). "Smoking in Top-Grossing US Movies, 2011." *Preventing Chronic Disease 9.* doi:10.5888/pcd9.120170.

Hazan, A. R., H. L. Lipton, and S. A. Glantz. (1994). "Popular Films Do Not Reflect Current Tobacco Use." *American Journal of Public Health* 84(6), 998–1000. doi:10.2105/ajph.84.6.998.

Morgan, D., K. A. Grant, H. D. Gage, et al. (2002). "Social Dominance in Monkeys: Dopamine D2 Receptors and Cocaine Self-Administration." *Nature Neuroscience* 5(2), 169–174. doi:10.1038/nn798.

Primack, B. A., M. A. Dalton, M. V. Carroll, A. A. Agarwal, and M. J. Fine. (2008). "Content Analysis of Tobacco, Alcohol, and Other Drugs in Popular Music." *Archives of Pediatrics & Adolescent Medicine* 162(2), 169. doi:10.1001/archpediatrics.2007.27.

Results from the 2007 National Survey on Drug Use and Health: National Findings. (2008). NSDUH Series H-34, DHHS Publication No. SMA 08-4343. Rockville, MD: Substance Abuse and Mental Health Services Administration, Office of Applied Studies.

Roberts, D. F., P. G. Christenson, L. Henriksen, E. Bandy, H. D. Jessup, and J. Abdul-Wahid. (1999). "Substance Use in Popular Music Videos." *PsycEXTRA Dataset.* doi:10.1037/e375462004-001.

Thompson, K. M., and F. Yokota. (2001). "Depiction of Alcohol, Tobacco, and Other Substances in G-Rated Animated Feature Films." *Pediatrics* 107(6), 1369–1374. doi:10.1542/peds.107.6.1369.

CHAPTER 6

Caution to the Wind

Armitage, C. J., and M. Conner. (2001). "Efficacy of the Theory of Planned Behaviour: A Meta-Analytic Review." *British Journal of Social Psychology* 40(4), 471–499. doi:10.1348/014466601164939.

Carpenter, C. J. (2010). "A Meta-Analysis of the Effectiveness of Health Belief Model Variables in Predicting Behavior." *Health Communication* 25(8), 661–669. doi:10.1080/10410236.2010.521906.

Rosenstock, I. M. (1974). "Historical Origins of the Health Belief Model." *Health Education & Behavior* 2(4), 328–335. doi:10.1177/109019817400200403.

Willing and Able

Loewenstein, G. (1996). "Out of Control: Visceral Influences on Behavior." *Organizational Behavior and Human Decision Processes* 65(3), 272–292. doi:10.1006/obhd.1996.0028.

Marczinski, C. A., M. T. Fillmore, M. E. Bardgett, and M. A. Howard. (2011). "Effects of Energy Drinks Mixed with Alcohol on Behavioral Control: Risks for College Students Consuming Trendy Cocktails." *Alcoholism: Clinical and Experimental Research* 35(7), 1282–1292. doi:10.1111/j.1530-0277.2011.01464.x.

Marczinski, C. A., M. T. Fillmore, A. L. Henges, M. A. Ramsey, and C. R. Young. (2012). "Mixing an Energy Drink with an Alcoholic Beverage Increases Motivation for More Alcohol in College Students." *Alcoholism: Clinical and Experimental Research* 37(2), 276–283. doi:10.1111/j.1530-0277.2012.01868.x.

Winkielman, P., K. C. Berridge, and J. L. Wilbarger. (2005). "Unconscious Affective Reactions to Masked Happy Versus Angry Faces Influence Consumption Behavior and Judgments of Value." *Personality and Social Psychology Bulletin* 31(1), 121–135. doi:10.1177/0146167204271309.

Cartesian Dualism

Kahneman, D. (2011). *Thinking, Fast and Slow.* New York: Farrar, Straus and Giroux.

CHAPTER 7

The Friendly Skies

Dreyfus, S. E. (2004). "The Five-Stage Model of Adult Skill Acquisition." *Bulletin of Science, Technology and Society* 24(3), 177–181. doi:10.1177/0270467604264992.

When Less Is More

Goldman, L., E. F. Cook, P. A. Johnson, D. A. Brand, G. W. Rouan, and T. H. Lee. (1996). "Prediction of the Need for Intensive Care in Patients Who Come to Emergency Departments with Acute Chest Pain." *New England Journal of Medicine* 334(23), 1498–1504. doi:10.1056/nejm199606063342303.

Klein, G., R. Calderwood, and A. Clinton-Cirocco. (2010). "Rapid Decision Making on the Fire Ground: The Original Study Plus a Postscript." *Journal of Cognitive Engineering and Decision Making* 4(3), 186–209. doi:10.1518/155534310x12844000801203.

Schwartz, B. (2004). *The Paradox of Choice: Why More Is Less.* New York: Ecco.

Fuzzy Trace

Reyna, V., and C. Brainerd. (1995). Fuzzy-Trace Theory: An Interim Synthesis." *Learning and Individual Differences* 7(1), 1–75. doi:10.1016/1041-6080(95)90031-4.

———. (2011). "Dual Processes in Decision Making and Developmental Neuroscience: A Fuzzy-Trace Model." *Developmental Review.* doi:10.1016/j.dr.2011.07.004.

The Teen Species. (n.d.). Retrieved February 8, 2017, from http://pages .vassar.edu/abigailbaird/additional-research-2/.

Developmental Reversals

Simon, H. A. (1992). "What Is an 'Explanation' of Behavior?" *Psychological Science* 3(3), 150–161. doi:10.1111/j.1467-9280.1992.tb00017.x.

The Tween Brain | Brain Games. (2016, March 1). Retrieved February 8, 2017, from https://www.youtube.com/watch?v=_sx1Ue415UQ.

Paradigms Lost

Teslovich, T., M. Mulder, N. T. Franklin, et al. (2013). "Adolescents Let Sufficient Evidence Accumulate Before Making a Decision When Large Incentives Are at Stake." *Developmental Science* 17(1), 59–70. doi:10.1111/desc.12092.

CHAPTER 8

Bloland, S. E. (2005). *In the Shadow of Fame: A Memoir by the Daughter of Erik H. Erikson.* New York: Viking.

Steinberg, L. (2001). "We Know Some Things: Parent-Adolescent Relationships in Retrospect and Prospect." *Journal of Research on Adolescence* 11(1), 1–19. doi:10.1111/1532-7795.00001.

"Just Right" Parenting

Baumrind, D. (1966). "Effects of Authoritative Parental Control on Child Behavior." *Child Development* 37(4), 887. doi:10.2307/1126611.

Steinberg, L., J. D. Elmen, and N. S. Mounts. (1989). "Authoritative Parenting, Psychosocial Maturity, and Academic Success among Adolescents." *Child Development* 60(6), 1424. doi:10.2307/1130932.

Steinberg, L., S. Lamborn, N. Mounts, and S. Dornbusch. (1991).
"Authoritative Parenting and Adolescent Adjustment Across Varied
Ecological Niches." *Journal of Research on Adolescence,* 1(1), 19–36.

Parenting 101

Kazdin, A. E. (2005). *Parent Management Training: Treatment for Oppositional,
Aggressive, and Antisocial Behavior in Children and Adolescents.* New York:
Oxford University Press.

Lochman, J. E., and A. van den Steenhoven. (2002). *Journal of Primary
Prevention* 23, 49. doi:10.1023/A:1016591216363.

Patterson, G. R., B. D. Debaryshe, and E. Ramsey. (1989). "A Developmental
Perspective on Antisocial Behavior." *American Psychologist* 44(2),
329–335. doi:10.1037//0003-066x.44.2.329.

Wang, M., and S. Kenny. (2013). "Longitudinal Links Between Fathers' and
Mothers' Harsh Verbal Discipline and Adolescents' Conduct Problems
and Depressive Symptoms." *Child Development* 85(3), 908–923.
doi:10.1111/cdev.12143.

Being There

Guilamo-Ramos, V., J. Jaccard, P. Dittus, and A. M. Bouris. (2006). Parental
Expertise, Trustworthiness, and Accessibility: Parent-Adolescent
Communication and Adolescent Risk Behavior." *Journal of Marriage
and Family* 68(5), 1229–1246. doi:10.1111/j.1741-3737.2006.00325.x.

Laird, R. D., G. S. Pettit, J. E. Bates, and K. A. Dodge. (2003). "Parents'
Monitoring-Relevant Knowledge and Adolescents' Delinquent
Behavior: Evidence of Correlated Developmental Changes and
Reciprocal Influences." *Child Development* 74(3), 752–768. doi:10.1111
/1467-8624.00566.

Marta, E. (1997). "Parent–Adolescent Interactions and Psychosocial Risk in
Adolescents: An Analysis of Communication, Support and Gender."
Journal of Adolescence 20(5), 473–487. doi:10.1006/jado.1997.0103.

Qu, Y., A. J. Fuligni, A. Galvan, and E. H. Telzer. (2015). "Buffering Effect of Positive Parent–Child Relationships on Adolescent Risk Taking: A Longitudinal Neuroimaging Investigation." *Developmental Cognitive Neuroscience* 15, 26–34. doi:10.1016/j.dcn.2015.08.005.

Reed, M. B., and L. G. Aspinwall. (1998). *Motivation and Emotion* 22, 99. doi:10.1023/A:1021463221281.

Supplemental Material for Perceived Family Social Support Buffers Against the Effects of Exposure to Rocket Attacks on Adolescent Depression, Aggression, and Severe Violence. (2015). *Journal of Family Psychology.* doi:10.1037/fam0000179.supp.

Whitaker, D. J., and K. S. Miller. (2000). "Parent-Adolescent Discussions about Sex and Condoms." *Journal of Adolescent Research* 15(2), 251–273. doi:10.1177/0743558400152004.

Whittle, S., J. G. Simmons, M. Dennison, et al. (2014). "Positive Parenting Predicts the Development of Adolescent Brain Structure: A Longitudinal Study." *Developmental Cognitive Neuroscience* 8, 7–17. doi:10.1016/j.dcn.2013.10.006.

Why God Created the Fruit Bowl

Bushman, B. J., and L. R. Huesmann. (2006). "Short-term and Long-term Effects of Violent Media on Aggression in Children and Adults" *Archives of Pediatrics & Adolescent Medicine* 160(4), 348. doi:10.1001/archpedi.160.4.348.

Council on Communications and Media. (2013). "Children, Adolescents, and the Media." *Pediatrics* 132(5), 958–961. doi:10.1542/peds.2013-2656.

Council on Communications and Media. (2016). "Virtual Violence." *Pediatrics.* 138(1):e20161298. doi:10.1542/peds.2016-2399.

Deputy UN Chief Calls for Urgent Action to Tackle Global Sanitation Crisis. (2013, March 21). Retrieved February 9, 2017, from http://www.un.org/apps/news/story.asp?NewsID=44452#.WJyVtxiZO-t.

Dong, G., Y. Hu, and X. Lin. (2013). "Reward/Punishment Sensitivities among Internet Addicts: Implications for Their Addictive Behaviors." *Progress in Neuro-Psychopharmacology and Biological Psychiatry* 46, 139–145. doi:10.1016/j.pnpbp.2013.07.007.

Hong, S., J. Kim, E. Choi, et al. (2013). "Reduced Orbitofrontal Cortical Thickness in Male Adolescents with Internet Addiction." *Behavioral and Brain Functions* 9(1), 11. doi:10.1186/1744-9081-9-11.

Lin, F., Y. Zhou, Y. Du, L. Qin, Z. Zhao, J. Xu, and H. Lei. (2012). "Abnormal White Matter Integrity in Adolescents with Internet Addiction Disorder: A Tract-Based Spatial Statistics Study." *PLoS ONE* 7(1). doi:10.1371/journal.pone.0030253.

Robinson, T. N. (1999). "Reducing Children's Television Viewing to Prevent Obesity." *Journal of the American Medical Association* 282(16), 1561. doi:10.1001/jama.282.16.1561.

Uhls, Y. T., M. Michikyan, J. Morris, D. Garcia, G. W. Small, E. Zgourou, and P. M. Greenfield. (2014). "Five Days at Outdoor Education Camp Without Screens Improves Preteen Skills with Nonverbal Emotion Cues." *Computers in Human Behavior* 39, 387–392. doi:10.1016/j.chb.2014.05.036.

Weng, C., R. Qian, X. Fu, et al. (2013). "Gray Matter and White Matter Abnormalities in Online Game Addiction." *European Journal of Radiology* 82(8), 1308–1312. doi:10.1016/j.ejrad.2013.01.031.

Zero to Eight: Children's Media Use in America 2013. (n.d.). Retrieved February 9, 2017, from https://www.commonsensemedia.org/research/zero-to-eight-childrens-media-use-in-america-2013.

Reframing Reward

Tamaroff, M. H., R. S. Festa, A. R., Adesman, and G. A. Walco. (1992). "Therapeutic Adherence to Oral Medication Regimens by Adolescents with Cancer: II. Clinical and Psychologic Correlates." *Journal of Pediatrics* 120(5), 812–817. doi:10.1016/s0022-3476(05)80257-4.

Getting Back to Gist

Reyna, V. F., and F. Farley. (2006). "Risk and Rationality in Adolescent Decision Making." *Psychological Science in the Public Interest* 7(1), 1–44. doi:10.1111/j.1529-1006.2006.00026.x.

CHAPTER 9

Lowell, R. C., and A. M. Gallup. (n.d.). The 31st Annual Phi Delta Kappa/ Gallup Poll of the Public's Attitudes Toward the Public Schools. *Phi Delta Kappan* 81, 41–56.

Wolfson, A. R., and M. A. Carksadon. (2005). "A Survey of Factors Influencing High School Start Times." *NASSP Bulletin* 89(642), 47–66. doi:10.1177/019263650508964205.

The Triumvirate of Good Health

A Conversation with Dr. Alison Gopnik. (2009). *Teaching Young Children* 3(2), 26.

Adolescent Sleep Working Group, Committee on Adolescence, Council on School Health. (2014). "School Start Times for Adolescents." *Pediatrics* 134(3), 642–649.

Assessing Recess: Growing Concerns about Shrinking Play Time in Schools. (n.d.). Retrieved February 9, 2017, from http://www.policyarchive .org/handle/10207/21362.

Copeland, K., S. Sherman, C., Kendeigh, H., Kalkwarf, and B. Saelens. (2012). "Societal Values and Policies May Curtail Preschool Children's Physical Activity in Child Care Centers." *Pediatrics* 129(2). doi:10.1542/ peds.2011-2102d.

GBD 2015 Risk Factors Collaborators. (2016, October 8). "Global, Regional, and National Comparative Risk Assessment of 79 Behavioral, Environmental and Occupational, and Metabolic Risks or Clusters of Risks, 1990–2015: A Systematic Analysis for the Global Burden of Disease Study 2015." *The Lancet.* 2016 Oct 7; 388, 1659–1724.

McKnight-Eily, L. R., D. K. Eaton, R. Lowry, J. B. Croft, L. Presley-Cantrell, and G. S. Perry. (2011). "Relationships Between Hours of Sleep and Health-Risk Behaviors in US Adolescent Students." *Preventive Medicine* 53(4–5), 271–273. doi:10.1016/j.ypmed.2011.06.020.

Murray, R., and C. Ramstetter. (2013). "The Crucial Role of Recess in School." *Pediatrics* 131(1), 183–188. doi:10.1542/peds.2012-2993.

National School Lunch Program. (n.d.). Retrieved February 9, 2017, from https://www.ers.usda.gov/topics/food-nutrition-assistance/child -nutrition-programs/national-school-lunch-program.aspx.

Ortega, F. B., J. R. Ruiz, M. J. Castillo, and M. Sjöström. (2007). "Physical Fitness in Childhood and Adolescence: A Powerful Marker of Health." *International Journal of Obesity* 32(1), 1–11. doi:10.1038/sj.ijo.0803774.

Owens, J. (2014). "Insufficient Sleep in Adolescents and Young Adults: An Update on Causes and Consequences." *Pediatrics* 134(3). doi:10.1542/peds.2014-1696.

School Lunch Initiative. (n.d.). Retrieved February 9, 2017, from http:// www.schoollunchinitiative.org/.

Simons-Morton, B. G., G. S. Parcel, T. Baranowski, R. Forthofer, and N. M. O'Hara. (1991). "Promoting Physical Activity and a Healthful Diet among Children: Results of a School-Based Intervention Study." *American Journal of Public Health* 81(8), 986–991. doi:10.2105/ ajph.81.8.986.

Teaching Resilience

Dale, E. (1969). *Audio-Visual Methods in Teaching*, 3rd ed. New York: Holt, Rinehart and Winston.

Jones, D. E., M. Greenberg, and M. Crowley. (2015). "Early Social-Emotional Functioning and Public Health: The Relationship Between Kindergarten Social Competence and Future Wellness." *American Journal of Public Health* 105(11) 2283–2290. doi:10.2105/AJPH.2015.302630.

Shatkin, J. P., U. Diamond, Y. Zhao, J. DiMeglio, M. Chodaczek, and J. Bruzzese. (2016). "Effects of a Risk and Resilience Course on Stress,

Coping Skills, and Cognitive Strategies in College Students." *Teaching of Psychology* 43(3), 204–210. doi:10.1177/0098628316649457.

The Science of Happiness

Beier, S. R., W. D. Rosenfeld, K. C. Spitalny, S. M. Zansky, and A. N. Bontempo. (2000). "The Potential Role of an Adult Mentor in Influencing High-Risk Behaviors in Adolescents." *Archives of Pediatrics & Adolescent Medicine* 154(4), 327. doi:10.1001/archpedi.154.4.327.

Larson, R., M. Csikszentmihalyi, and R. Graef. (1980). "Mood Variability and the Psychosocial Adjustment of Adolescents." *Journal of Youth and Adolescence* 9(6), 469–490. doi:10.1007/bf02089885.

Masten, A., J. Herbers, J. Cutuli, and T. Lafavor. (2008). "Promoting Competence and Resilience in the School Context." *Professional School Counseling* 12(2), 76–84. doi:10.5330/psc.n.2010-12.76.

McEwen, B. S. (2016). "In Pursuit of Resilience: Stress, Epigenetics, and Brain Plasticity." *Annals of the New York Academy of Sciences* 1373(1), 56–64. doi:10.1111/nyas.13020.

O'Leary-Barrett, M., L. Topper, N. Al-Khudhairy, R. O. Pihl, N. Castellanos-Ryan, C. J. Mackie, and P. J. Conrod. (2013). "Two-Year Impact of Personality-Targeted, Teacher-Delivered Interventions on Youth Internalizing and Externalizing Problems: A Cluster-Randomized Trial." *Journal of the American Academy of Child & Adolescent Psychiatry* 52(9), 911–920. doi:10.1016/j.jaac.2013.05.020.

Barely Breathing

Hjeltnes, A., P. Binder, C. Moltu, and I. Dundas. (2015). "Facing the Fear of Failure: An Explorative Qualitative Study of Client Experiences in a Mindfulness-Based Stress Reduction Program for University Students with Academic Evaluation Anxiety." *International Journal of Qualitative Studies on Health and Well-Being* 10. doi:http://dx.doi.org/10.3402/qhw.v10.27990.

Kabat-Zinn, J. (1990). *Full Catastrophe Living: Using the Wisdom of Your Body and Mind to Face Stress, Pain, and Illness.* New York: Delacorte Press.

Leary, K. O., and S. Dockray. (2015). "The Effects of Two Novel Gratitude and Mindfulness Interventions on Well-Being." *Journal of Alternative and Complementary Medicine* 21(4), 243–245. doi:10.1089/acm.2014.0119.

Marchand, W. R. (2014). "Neural Mechanisms of Mindfulness and Meditation: Evidence from Neuroimaging Studies." *World Journal of Radiology* 6(7), 471. doi:10.4329/wjr.v6.i7.471.

McFadden, C., T. Sandler, and E. Fieldstadt. (2015, January 1). "San Francisco Schools Transformed by the Power of Meditation." Retrieved February 9, 2017, from http://www.nbcnews.com/nightly-news/san-francisco-schools-transformed-power-meditation-n276301.

Nelson, K. S., and S. Lyubomirsky. (2016). "Gratitude." In Howard S. Friedman (ed.), *Encyclopedia of Mental Health*, 2nd ed., Vol. 2, 277–280. Waltham, MA: Academic Press.

Robins, C. J., S. Keng, A. G. Ekblad, and J. G. Brantley. (2011). "Effects of Mindfulness-Based Stress Reduction on Emotional Experience and Expression: A Randomized Controlled Trial." *Journal of Clinical Psychology* 68(1), 117–131. doi:10.1002/jclp.20857.

The Failure of Health Class

Breuner, C. C., and G. Mattson. (2016). "Sexuality Education for Children and Adolescents." *Pediatrics.* 2016 138(2). doi: 10.1542/peds.2016-1348.

Castellanos-Ryan, N., M. O'Leary-Barrett, L. Sully, and P. Conrod. (2013). "Sensitivity and Specificity of a Brief Personality Screening Instrument in Predicting Future Substance Use, Emotional, and Behavioral Problems: 18-Month Predictive Validity of the Substance Use Risk Profile Scale." *Alcoholism: Clinical and Experimental Research* 37(1). doi:10.1111/j.1530-0277.2012.01931.x.

Conrod, P. J., M. O'Leary-Barrett, N. Newton, L. Topper, N. Castellanos-Ryan, C. Mackie, and A. Girard. (2013). "Effectiveness of a Selective,

Personality-Targeted Prevention Program for Adolescent Alcohol Use and Misuse." *JAMA Psychiatry* 70(3), 334. doi:10.1001/jamapsychiatry.2013.651.

Kohler, P. K., L. E. Manhart, and W. E. Lafferty. (2008). "Abstinence-Only and Comprehensive Sex Education and the Initiation of Sexual Activity and Teen Pregnancy." *Journal of Adolescent Health* 42(4), 344–351. doi:10.1016/j.jadohealth.2007.08.026.

Sipe, T. A., H. B. Chin, R. Elder, S. L. Mercer, S. K. Chattopadhyay, and V. Jacob. (2012). "Methods for Conducting Community Guide Systematic Reviews of Evidence on Effectiveness and Economic Efficiency of Group-Based Behavioral Interventions to Prevent Adolescent Pregnancy, Human Immunodeficiency Virus, and Other Sexually Transmitted Infections." *American Journal of Preventive Medicine* 42(3), 295–303. doi:10.1016/j.amepre.2011.11.002.

Smoak, N. D., L. A. Scott-Sheldon, B. T. Johnson, and M. P. Carey. (2006). "Sexual Risk Reduction Interventions Do Not Inadvertently Increase the Overall Frequency of Sexual Behavior." *Journal of Acquired Immune Deficiency Syndromes* 41(3), 374–384. doi:10.1097/01.qai.0000185575.36591.fc.

How Do You Get to Carnegie Hall?

Adolph, K. E., W. G. Cole, M. Komati, et al. (2012). "How Do You Learn to Walk? Thousands of Steps and Dozens of Falls per Day." *Psychological Science* 23(11), 1387–1394. doi:10.1177/0956797612446346.

Marzano, R. J., and D. J. Pickering. (2007). "The Case for and Against Homework. *Educational Leadership* 64(6), 74–79.

Young, E. "How Iceland Got Teens to Say No to Drugs. *The Atlantic*. (2017). Retrieved March 19, 2017, from https://www.theatlantic.com/health/archive/2017/01/teens-drugs-iceland/513668.

CHAPTER 10

Toxic Stress

Bethell, C. D., P. Newacheck, E. Hawes, and N. Halfon. (2014). "Adverse Childhood Experiences: Assessing The Impact On Health And School Engagement And The Mitigating Role Of Resilience." *Health Affairs* 33(12), 2106–2115. doi:10.1377/hlthaff.2014.0914.

Felitti, V. J., R. F. Anda, D. Nordenberg, et al. (1998). "Relationship of Childhood Abuse and Household Dysfunction to Many of the Leading Causes of Death in Adults" *American Journal of Preventive Medicine* 14(4), 245–258. doi:10.1016/s0749-3797(98)00017-8.

Noble, K. G., S. M. Houston, E. Kan, and E. R. Sowell. (2012). "Neural Correlates of Socioeconomic Status in the Developing Human Brain." *Developmental Science* 15(4), 516–527. doi:10.1111/j.1467-7687.2012.01147.x.

Early and Often

Egger, H. L., and A. Angold. (2006). "Common Emotional and Behavioral Disorders in Preschool Children: Presentation, Nosology, and Epidemiology." *Journal of Child Psychology and Psychiatry* 47(3–4), 313–337. doi:10.1111/j.1469-7610.2006.01618.x.

Lavigne, J. V., S. A. Lebailly, J. Hopkins, K. R. Gouze, and H. J. Binns. (2009). "The Prevalence of ADHD, ODD, Depression, and Anxiety in a Community Sample of 4-Year-Olds." *Journal of Clinical Child & Adolescent Psychology* 38(3), 315–328.

Merikangas, K. R., J. He, M. Burstein, et al. (2010). "Lifetime Prevalence of Mental Disorders in US Adolescents: Results from the National Comorbidity Study-Adolescent Supplement (NCS-A)." *Journal of the American Academy of Child and Adolescent Psychiatry* 49(10), 980–989. http://doi.org/10.1016/j.jaac.2010.05.017.

Shatkin, J. P. (2015). *Child and Adolescent Mental Health, A Practical All-in-One Guide.* New York: W. W. Norton.

Wichstrøm, L., T. S. Berg-Nielsen, A. Angold, H. L. Egger, E. Solheim, and T. H. Sveen. (2011). "Prevalence of Psychiatric Disorders in Preschoolers." *Journal of Child Psychology and Psychiatry* 53(6), 695–705. doi:10.1111/j.1469-7610.2011.02514.x.

Changing Mindset

Aronson, J., C. B. Fried, and C. Good. (2002). "Reducing the Effects of Stereotype Threat on African American College Students by Shaping Theories of Intelligence." *Journal of Experimental Social Psychology* 38(2), 113–125. doi:10.1006/jesp.2001.1491.

Blackwell, L. S., K. H. Trzesniewski, and C. S. Dweck. (2007). "Implicit Theories of Intelligence Predict Achievement Across an Adolescent Transition: A Longitudinal Study and an Intervention." *Child Development* 78(1), 246–263. doi:10.1111/j.1467-8624.2007.00995.x.

Yeager, D. S., and C. S. Dweck. (2012). "Mindsets That Promote Resilience: When Students Believe That Personal Characteristics Can Be Developed." *Educational Psychologist* 47(4), 302–314. doi:10.1080/00461520.2012.722805.

Yeager, D. S., and G. M. Walton. (2011). "Social-Psychological Interventions in Education: They're Not Magic." *Review of Educational Research* 81(2), 267–301. doi:10.3102/0034654311405999.

Mentorship Matters

DuBois, D. L., N. Portillo, J. E. Rhodes, N. Silverthorn, and J. C. Valentine. (2011). "How Effective Are Mentoring Programs for Youth? A Systematic Assessment of the Evidence." *Psychological Science in the Public Interest* 12(2), 57–91. doi:10.1177/1529100611414806.

DuBois, D. L., and N. Silverthorn. (2005). "Natural Mentoring Relationships and Adolescent Health: Evidence from a National Study." *American Journal of Public Health* 95(3), 518–524. http://doi.org/10.2105/AJPH.2003.031476.

Garringer, M., J. Kupersmidt, J. Rhodes, R. Stelter, and T. Tai. (2015). *Elements of Effective Practice for Mentoring*, 4th ed. Boston: MENTOR, The National Mentoring Partnership.

Don't Mess with Texas

Don't Mess with Texas. (n.d.). Retrieved February 12, 2017, from http://www.dontmesswithtexas.org.

Policy Statement—Children, Adolescents, Substance Abuse, and the Media. (2010). *Pediatrics* 126(4), 791–799. doi: 10.1542/peds.2010-1635.

Media Literacy

Henriksen, L. (2006). "Industry Sponsored Anti-Smoking Ads and Adolescent Reactance: Test of a Boomerang Effect." *Tobacco Control* 15(1), 13–18. doi:10.1136/tc.2003.006361.

Can We Teach Our Kids to Drink Responsibly?

Friese, B., and J. Grube. (2005). "Youth Drinking Rates and Problems: A Comparison of European Countries and the United States." Pacific Institute for Research and Evaluation.

Kaynak, Ö., K. C. Winters, J. Cacciola, K. C. Kirby, and A. M. Arria. (2014). "Providing Alcohol for Underage Youth: What Messages Should We Be Sending Parents?" *Journal of Studies on Alcohol and Drugs* 75(4), 590–605.

The Surgeon General's Call to Action to Prevent and Reduce Underage Drinking. U.S. Department of Health and Human Services, Office of the Surgeon General, 2007.

Social Norms Marketing

American College Health Association–National College Health Assessment II: Reference Group Executive Summary. (Spring 2015). Hanover, MD: American College Health Association.

Moreira, M. T., and D. Foxcroft. (2007). "Social Norms Interventions to Reduce Alcohol Misuse in University or College Students." *Cochrane Database of Systematic Reviews.* doi:10.1002/14651858.cd006748.

Perkins, H. W., J. W. Linkenbach, M. A. Lewis, and C. Neighbors. (2010). "Effectiveness of Social Norms Media Marketing in Reducing Drinking and Driving: A Statewide Campaign." *Addictive Behaviors* 35(10), 866–874. doi:10.1016/j.addbeh.2010.05.004.

Backseat Parenting

Chen, L. (2000). "Carrying Passengers as a Risk Factor for Crashes Fatal to 16- and 17-Year-Old Drivers." *Journal of the American Medical Association* 283(12), 1578. doi:10.1001/jama.283.12.1578.

Hartos, J. L., P. Eitel, D. L. Haynie, and B. G. Simons-Morton. (2000). "Can I Take the Car?: Relations Among Parenting Practices and Adolescent Problem-Driving Practices." *Journal of Adolescent Research* 15(3), 352–367. doi:10.1177/0743558400153003.

Shope, J., and C. Bingham. (2008). "Teen Driving: Motor-Vehicle Crashes and Factors That Contribute." *American Journal of Preventive Medicine* 35(3). doi:10.1016/j.amepre.2008.06.022.

Steinberg, L. (2015). "How to Improve the Health of American Adolescents." *Perspectives on Psychological Science* 10(6), 711–715. doi:10.1177/1745691615598510.

Williams, A. F. (2005). "Commentary: Next Steps for Graduated Licensing. *Traffic Injury Prevention* 6(3), 199–201. doi:10.1080/15389580590969076.

ACKNOWLEDGMENTS

WHILE WRITING A BOOK IS typically a solitary activity, in this case it was hardly a solitary endeavor. I wish to thank first the magnificent Bonnie Solow, my literary agent and new friend, for recognizing the potential in this story from the very beginning and guiding me through the entire process. I also wish to give heartfelt thanks to my editor, Marian Lizzi, and her staff at TarcherPerigee, who believe in this book, its message, and the approach I've taken in writing it; and whose insight and skill supported me in producing the most cogent and applicable version of my thinking on the subject. I was fortunate to have a number of readers who kept pace with me throughout the writing process and provided expert advice at every turn: My colleagues and friends Charles J. Mayer and Ursula Diamond helped me clarify my thinking on the subject, while F. Xavier Castellanos deftly guided me through much of the wonder and often puzzling intricacies of the neuroscience.

After listening to me speak for many years with great excitement about adolescent risk-taking behavior, my wife, Alice Jankell, finally insisted that I write it all down. In addition to her loving support and kindness, Alice acted as dramaturge and repeatedly drew my attention back to the "story" of this book. Alice helped me identify the key elements in translating the masses of scientific data into usable wisdom and always took the time to help me out of a jam. She's simply a superb partner and editor.

There are a number of other individuals to thank and without whom this book would never have been possible. Louise Braverman, Sarah Lieff, Sara Haberman, and Brittany Elias all served invaluable roles in helping me bring this book into the light of day.

The spark for this book emanated from my personal experiences, but the material herein is based upon my clinical work and research, reinforced by hundreds of research studies, scores of books, and dozens of interviews with scientists and others whose work and/or personal lives regularly involve making risky decisions. Scientists are understandably often hesitant to overstate the bounds of their knowledge; they typically explore a specific subject area in great depth and make observations and recommendations within a prescribed domain in which they have extensive knowledge. The job of an academic clinician and educator like me is to take that scientific understanding and translate it into practical recommendations for patients, their parents and teachers, and the public at large in a wide variety of domains, from managing risk-taking behavior to dealing with learning problems to treating mood and anxiety disorders to managing sleepovers to enforcing punishments, and so on. We all do the best we can with the knowledge and tools that we have at any given time. I have been diligent in trying to present accurately the research and thoughts of the many esteemed scientists and professionals I interviewed throughout the writing of this book, although I alone bear the fault of any shortcomings or misinterpretations of their work. I wish to thank the following individuals for sharing their time and thoughts with me: Jeremy Affeldt, Larry Brown, Bill Carroll, B. J. Casey, Ron Dahl, David Diaz, Naomi Eisenberger, Susan Ennett, Michael Frank, Daniel Kahneman, Joe LeDoux, Leonard Marcus, Bruce McEwen, Alberto Molina, Anthony Petrosino, Karl Pohl, Daniel Rysak, Barry Schwartz, Laurence Steinberg, Elizabeth Streb, Regina Sullivan, and Fabio Tavares Da Silva.

A very special thanks is due to Valerie Reyna, whose incredibly comprehensive research review from 2006 (along with Frank Farley), "Risk and Rationality in Adolescent Decision Making: Implications for Theory, Practice, and Public Policy," became a touchstone for much of my exploration into the science of adolescent risk taking and decision making. Valerie was exceptionally generous in speaking with me on numerous occasions, spending hours answering my questions, and clarifying massive amounts of often difficult-to-translate research. Valerie Reyna is an extremely generative and altruistic scientist, for whom all of us interested in the health and well-being of adolescents must be extraordinarily thankful.

I also wish to thank my psychiatry and psychology colleagues all over the world who continue to teach me, challenge me, and sharpen my thinking in all areas related to child and adolescent development. Equal thanks are due to the many patients who have shared their victories and challenges with me over the years and allowed me a privileged glimpse into their lives. I have told some of their stories in this book, but all details and identifiers have been changed so as to protect their privacy. To my childhood friends as well I owe a great debt of gratitude. Without you, I wouldn't have survived or thrived.

My family, of course, also deserves special acknowledgment. I thank my parents, brothers, and sisters, with whom I faced the adolescent years. Five kids, an endless number of pets, the '60s and '70s . . . there were a lot of shenanigans going on, yet somehow we all made it out alive. Here's to Eugene and Joyce, and their other four offspring—Karen, Greg, Marc, and Stacie—thanks for all of the support, guidance, listening, and teaching you have done over the years. I love you all.

Finally, I wish to thank my children, Parker and Julian, who demonstrated a remarkable understanding of my desire to write this book, which resulted in me taking far more time away from them than I would have liked. Alice and I have had the great privilege of participating in our kids' dynamic changes and been dumbfounded by the growth of their intellect, skills, and emotions. Through conversations, celebrations, homework, travels, sick relatives and pets, SAT prep, soccer, gymnastics, college applications, leaving home, and wounded knees and egos, we've learned all over again what it means to be an adolescent, make decisions, and take risks. It's been a tempestuous and joyful time, and your mother and I *still* love you more than you will ever know.

INDEX

fear, 69–71, 84, 87
Felitti, Vincent J., 227
Fey, Tina, 217
fights, physical, 4
filtering, 95, 209, 210
Finckenauer, James, 31
firefighters, 138, 140, 143–44, 146–48
first meetings, 135–37
fixed mindset, 234, 235
Florida Agricultural and Mechanical
    University, 97–98
FOMO (fear of missing out), 105
food, 196–201, 219
    eating disorders, 4, 53–54
    mindful eating, 215
    nutrition, 196–201, 211
    school meals, 199–201, 221
football players, 86
framing, 131
"free" parties, 191
Freud, Anna, xi, 158–59
Freud, Sigmund, 91, 93, 128, 212
friends, *see* peers and peer pressure
frowns, 124
fruit bowl, 178
Fugelsang, Jonathan, 149
Fuller, Buckminster, 2
functional magnetic resonance imaging
    (fMRI), 39, 101, 103–5, 107, 111, 150, 151
Future Doctors of America, 16
fuzzy-trace theory, 146–47

Gage, Phineas, 38–39
Gallup Polls, 194
gambling, 47, 48
gay adolescents, 5–6
Gaza Strip, 176
ghrelin, 73, 200
gist, 147–48, 154–57, 185–86, 220
    analogies and, 186–87
    statistical, 187–88
Goldman, Lee, 143
Gopnik, Alison, 198

gratitude, 215–17
Gretzky, Wayne, 225, 247
growth mindset, 208, 234–35
Gun-Free Schools Act, 32

habits, 122
happiness, 206–12
Harlow, John, 38–39
Harris Interactive, 51
Harry Potter and the Sorcerer's Stone
    (Rowling), 89, 155
hazing, 97–98
health:
    decisions about, 120–22, 133
    insurance, 51
    public, 18, 120–22
    good, triumvirate of, 196–201
Health Belief Model, 120–23
heart disease, 143, 145, 201
helmets, bicycle and motorcycle, xii, 3, 4,
    21, 26–27, 35–36, 122, 237–38
herd effect, 218
heuristics, 129–32
HIV/AIDS, 6, 17, 83, 156
    risk of contracting, 11–12, 15, 22
Hochbaum, Godfrey, 120–21
Hollis, Keon, 98
Homer, 23, 27
homework, 222–23
homicide, 6, 20, 24, 36
    brain development and, 44
hormones, 72–77, 80–81, 87, 90, 127, 139,
    220–21
    endocrine disrupters and, 81, 199
    sex, 72–77
    stress, 75–76, 228
hunger, 73, 80, 104, 200
    decision making and, 98, 124–25
hypertension, 84, 201

Iceland, 221–22, 243
identity crisis, 158–59

ABOUT THE AUTHOR

Jess P. Shatkin, MD, MPH, is vice chair for education at the Child Study Center at Hassenfeld Children's Hospital of New York at NYU Langone and professor of child and adolescent psychiatry and pediatrics at NYU School of Medicine. He is founder and director of the nation's largest child and adolescent mental health undergraduate studies program at NYU, and hosts *About Our Kids*, a weekly call-in radio program on SiriusXM. He lives in New York City with his wife and two adolescent children. You can learn more about his work at: drjesspshatkin.com.